Helen Weber
Seattle, Wa.
Aug - 1996

*Destiny's Journey*

# EUROPEAN SOURCES

SERIES EDITORS

Russell Epprecht and Sylvère Lotringer

# Destiny's Journey

*by*
## ALFRED DÖBLIN

*Edited by Edgar Pässler*

*Translated by Edna McCown*

*Introduction by Peter Demetz*

PARAGON HOUSE
*New York*

First American edition, 1992

Published in the United States by

Paragon House
90 Fifth Avenue
New York, NY 10011

Manufactured in the United States of America

This American edition is based on Walter-Verlag's edition of
*Schicksalsreise* which is part of *The Collected Works of Alfred Döblin*
edited by Walter Muschg in collaboration with the author's sons and
Anthony W. Riley.


Library of Congress Cataloging-in-Publication Data

Döblin, Alfred, 1878–1957.
   [Schicksalsreise. English]
   Destiny's journey / by Alfred Döblin : translated by Edna McCown.
—1st American ed.
     p.  cm.
   Translation of: Schicksalsreise.
   ISBN 1–55778–265–2 : $18.95
   1. Döblin, Alfred, 1878–1957—Biography—Exile.   2. Authors,
German—20th century—Biography.   I. Title.
PT2607.035Z4685   1992
833'.912—dc20
[B]                                           91–21024
                                                   CIP

# Contents

[ *v* ]

# Contents

## PART 3
## Rescue

## BOOK II
## America

## BOOK III
## Back Again

## Departure and Return

# Introduction

*I*n the last years of the Weimar Republic, Alfred Döblin was known as an important Berlin writer, but it is clear today that his many and rich achievements—as novelist, critic of literature and the arts, and author of philosophical essays—have made him into one of the most influential figures of German literature in the twentieth century. He was like ancient Proteus, a restless man of many ideas, loyalties, and engagements, and his unwillingness to identify completely with any political party of his time made him as many adversaries as did the metaphysical, if not mystical, strain of his sensibilities. He was, by birth, a Prussian Jew who had strong doubts about the cohesion of the Jewish people. By profession a psychiatrist who admired Freud more than psychoanalysis, for many years, he was a radical socialist who wanted his socialism free of Marx and, if possible, class warfare. He went into exile once, in February of 1933, because the Nazis wanted to arrest him, and for a second time in 1953, when he (after having returned to Germany as one of the first emigrés) again left because he believed that although Hitler was gone nothing else had changed. In the late 40s and in the 50s, he was thought to be totally *passé* in the West and in the east of his homeland, and only in the late 60s did younger writers in search of new literary ideas and narrative methods rediscover Döblin, an early prose expressionist and ally of the avant-garde, as their forerunner and teacher. Günter Grass publicly confessed that it was unimaginable to him to think about his own development without thinking of Döblin. In one of the essays of his early exile, Döblin had counted Thomas Mann, with condescending irony, among the traditional *bourgeois* humanists, while seeing himself, together with Kafka and Brecht, among the true "revolutionaries of the mind." He would have enjoyed the fact that a new generation of writers shared his ideas about literature.

Döblin later remarked that he felt newly born when he moved, as a ten-year-old boy, from Stettin, his Pomeranian birthplace (1878), to Berlin. The family facts were less resplendent; his father, talented in many ways but frustrated in a tailor's job, ran away to America with a girl twenty years his junior, and Alfred's mother, together with her five children, had to move to the big city where her brother supported them. Alfred had a chance to attend proper schools and later to study philosophy and medicine in Berlin and Freiburg. He worked as an intern in Regensburg, specialized in nervous diseases, returned to a Berlin hospital ward, and opened his own practice (1911) in a less than fashionable district, in East Berlin, among the poor. He married Erna Reiss, a medical colleague, who stayed with him through all his vicissitudes and bore him four sons (she knew that, earlier, he had fathered a son with a doe-eyed nurse whose name was Kunke). As a young doctor, Döblin published his research, but also joined the avant-garde gatherings at the *Café des Westens* and at the restaurant *Dalbelli*, printed provocative art criticisms in the aggressive periodical *Der Sturm* (he was the first who welcomed futurist art in Germany), and published his first novel to considerable acclaim in 1916, *Die Drei Sprünge des Wang-Lun* (*The Three Leaps of Wang-Lun*), a massive story about religious longings and the brutalities of war in old China. When World War I broke out, he shared the enthusiasm for the German cause with many, worked as a physician in army hospitals near the western front, wrote his *Wallenstein* (published in 1920), an expansive novel about the Thirty Years War, and returned to Berlin to join the socialists in support of the revolution. The 20s were among his most productive years; he wrote about daily events from the viewpoint of an independent socialist, was active in writer's organizations, traveled to Poland to explore his Jewish heritage, and published *Berge Meere und Giganten* in 1924 (*Mountains Oceans and Giants*), a melancholy and vast novel about the dubious technological future of mankind. In

1929, his *Berlin Alexanderplatz* appeared, which cast, or rather mis-cast, Döblin for a long time in the role of social novelist. By studying the sad life of the Berlin plebeian Franz Biberkopf, Döblin had brought to life the immense panorama of Berlin, the masses, the media, technology and all. He was compared with James Joyce and John Dos Passos, yet few noticed the rich biblical allusions and his metaphysical views of human suffering.

In late February of 1933, the German *Reichtag* (parliament) burned and the National Socialists accused the communists of arson. Nazi troopers roamed throughout the city and Döblin, with his family, had to escape to Switzerland and later to Paris, where so many German-Jewish refugees, among them Hannah Arendt and Walter Benjamin, had gathered. In the first years of exile, Döblin returned to studying Jewish history and energetically participated in the activities of Jewish organizations, including ORT (providing technical training to young people) and the *Ligue Juive pour Colonisations*, exploring the possibilities of Jewish mass emigration to South America and Angola. He published a number of controversial essays about Jewish renascence, arguing against Talmudic scholarship and the ossification of Jewish traditions. Paradoxically, he continued his work as a novelist, writing an epic narrative about the wide open spaces of the Amazon River and the sixteenth and seventeenth century social experiments of the Jesuit fathers who organized Indian communities, subservient to the Spanish king only in name. In 1939, Döblin (by now a naturalized French citizen) was asked to join the newly established French Ministry of Information (charged with countering Nazi propaganda), but the German military advance forced him and his family to seek refuge in the south of France, and later in the United States. The present volume describes and interprets the troubles of these voyages. In Hollywood, Döblin was hired by MGM for a stable of exiled writers (some scenes of the famous movie *Mrs. Minniver* are possibly his), but after some time he was let go; and when he turned to Catholicism, he was, among the exiles, lonelier than ever before. He was living on the dole when he decided, immediately after the war, to join the cultural offices of the French army headquarters in Baden-Baden, to work as a literary advisor for the military government. German intellectuals were, on the whole, unwilling to welcome the returning emigré who was an employee of the occupying powers and who had declared, in a

speech in a divided Berlin, that intellectuals should humbly return to
the metaphysical sources of creation. In ill health he returned to
Paris, continued to write in great pain, and died (1957), half blind
and nearly paralyzed, in a German hospital in the Black Forest. His
wife Erna committed suicide a few months later.

Döblin insisted that *Destiny's Journey* constituted both a report
and a confession, and clearly suggested that it was a text that profoundly differed from his other narratives. He had always, almost
aggressively, defended an impersonal epic stance from which the ego
of the narrator totally disappeared and intimate confessions were
rare. Only *Journey to Poland* (1926) and *Destiny's Journey* reveal what
he feels and thinks, without mediation, and it is characteristic of
both these voyages, however different in geographical terms, that
they are spiritual guests for more daily certainties—the earlier text
exploring the Jewish tradition of Eastern Europe, unchanged (then)
through the ages, the latter in search of the *Urgrund* (primal cause)
in its Christian shape. Usually, Döblin wrote fast and furiously,
oblivious to his surroundings, yet the manuscript of *Destiny's Journey*
was more than eight years in the making, and on two continents. As
soon as Döblin arrived at his Hollywood exile, he told the story of
his escape and his reunion with the family in a manuscript which he
called *Robinson in France* (written November 1940 to January
1941), possibly more a report than a confession, and returned to the
manuscript (which he had offered in vain to American and other
publishers) eight years later when he arrived in Baden-Baden; it was
originally published as *Schicksalreise* (*Destiny's Journey*) in Germany
in November 1949. But the years between beginning and finishing
the manuscript were decisive in almost ontological terms; Döblin
and his family converted to Catholicism on November 30, 1941, in
Hollywood, and the writer who finished the manuscript was not the
man who began to write about his terrestrial vicissitudes. It was not
that he added mechanically to the manuscript; he revised *Robinson in
France* in light of his more recent experiences and revealed that his
movements across France and the Atlantic were a metaphysical
voyage of illumination, ultimately directed by the hands of transcendental powers.

In *Destiny's Journey*, two texts were conflated, one about the
erratic movements of the refugee and his family, along the "classical"
itinerary of German-Jewish refugees (Paris-Marseilles-Lisbon-New

York), another about a pilgrim's progress between earth and heaven. At first, Döblin travels with his colleagues of the French Ministry of Information, hoping, as they do, that the offices will merely be shifted to another location further south; but traveling in trains and trucks from Paris to Tours, via Moulins, Clermont-Ferrand, Arvan, Capdenac, and Cahors to Mende, the team quickly dissolves. Trying to find out where his family went, Döblin moves obsessively in a desperate circle, and after a curious time of reflection and stillness at Mende, father, mother, and son are almost miraculously reunited at the Toulouse railway station, as if they had been on a vacation trip, to go on from there. In spite of all the misfortunes, the Döblins are possibly luckier than many other refugees, especially in the later part of the voyage. He carries impressive identification papers confirming that he is a French citizen working for the Information Ministry (directed by the famous playwright Jean Giraudoux), and *gensdarms* and police let him proceed (other German-Jewish refugees were sent to camps and handed over to the Gestapo). When it came to the exit crunch in Marseilles and Lisbon, fortunately everything worked well. Passports are prolonged, exit and transit visas granted, and an unknown French civil servant even provides cash when it is needed most. There is a wait in hot and noisy Lisbon, and the entire Portugal chapter shows the epic grasp of the true novelist.

Yet there were, even in Döblin's confessions, a few hesitations and gaps, either because he could not or would not speak about some personal experiences to a wider circle of readers. He dedicated the book to his wife Erna, yet there was not the slightest hint in the entire text about what a "Strindbergian" marriage (as a friend remarked) the union of Erna and Alfred had been from the very beginning, and what storms and passions raged behind the calm appearances of seemingly untroubled loyalty. Döblin lived for a long time with two women, his wife, and from the early 20s, young Yolla Niclas, daughter of a Berlin banker, and "sister of his soul." He did not leave his family because he did not want to repeat what his father had done, but Yolla followed him into exile, to Paris and to New York (Erna prevented regular correspondence) and later died in East Hartford, Connecticut. It may be equally important to know that Döblin's loneliness among his fellow exiles in Hollywood had more than private reasons: He kept aloof from Thomas Mann and his circle, and the Stalinists and their sympathizers kept him at arm's length because he never hesitated to disparage recent developments in the Soviet Union (his closest friends were Leopold Jessner, once the expressionist director of the Prussian State Theater, and the talented actor Alexander Granach, one of the three commissars in *Ninochka*, who died early). Döblin said very little about his talented son Wolfgang who fought in the French army. There were some later references to Red Cross inquiries concerning his fate, yet only until the summer of 1945 did Döblin note that his son, who had been decorated for valor, died a soldier's death near a small Vosges village—the tragic truth was that Wolfgang, after he had lost contact with his battalion, had committed suicide rather than fall into the hands of the Germans.

Döblin himself rightly believed that many of his friends and fellow exiles would be angered by his turn to Catholicism, and he tried, as best he could in a small refugee community, to keep it a family affair. He had always been aware of his Jewish origins and fondly remembered his mother who wrote her letters in Hebrew and Yiddish. But he did not feel a lasting loyalty to family traditions and counted himself among the assimilationists; in 1912 he left the Jewish community officially, and his sons were baptized, as Protestants, at birth. His relationship to Judaism and its traditions remained paradoxical, iridescent, and for many, a provocation. As early as 1921, he published an article in which he talked about "offended" (Zionist) and "unoffended" (assimilate) Jews, yet after anti-Semitic unrest in his Berlin home district, he went to Poland (1924) and admired the intensity of Jewish life there. In the first years of exile (1933–1937), he returned to the Jewish question, and worked for Jewish organizations and articulated his personal thoughts in a number of essays, among them *Jüdische Erneuerung* (*Jewish Restoration*), in which he defined his own idiosyncratic ideas. There were a number of diffuse motifs which recurred when Döblin spoke about Jewish problems; he had no doubts about his assimilation and yet deeply respected Jewish life in the *shtetl*; he preferred Yiddish, the language of the people, to Hebrew, the language of the learned elite; he believed that Palestine was too small for the new masses of Jewish refugees; he felt an aversion to any close identification of Jewish religion, nation, and state, and ultimately declared that religion should not be for one nation only, but for all humanity. It is not unthinkable that Döblin wanted to escape the fierce pressures of Jewish history and, by embracing Catholicism, forced his way into a transcendental sphere in which history and the burdens of having been born into it were of little relevance. He substituted Catholicism for the Jewish Kabbala of which he knew little.

Döblin's turn to a new faith did not result from weighing argument against argument, pro and con, or a sudden illumination flashing through the mind of an exhausted refugee in the church of Mende, near his refugee camp. Philosophical and biographical reasons, at least in the narrow sense, were insufficient to explain what happened, and it would be more illuminating to think of Döblin's life-long, stubborn, and contradictory thirst for a metaphysical view of the world and himself. This was always strongly present in the sensibilities of an intellectual whom most of his contemporaries considered to be an atheist, a radical, and with some justification, a neurologist who looked to physiological causes for psychological change. The signs were all there, yet they were ignored or explained away as the quirks of an anarchic mind: his interest in the humble religion of Wang-Lun in his first novel, and in his second, with the mystical demise of the Austrian Emperor; his philosophy of nature which recognized that all matter was imbued with a soul streaming from the primal fundament of all existence; his reference to the Book of Revelations in *Berlin Alexanderplatz*; his sympathy for the Jesuit fathers in South America. His own metaphor of a "crystallization" of elements that was long present in his perceptions seemed to be far more appropriate in defining the tortuous process of spiritual change than the usual references to the tired man who looked for irrational consolations. These were arguments which he never hesitated to formulate by and against himself, and the passages in *Destiny's Journey* in which he rehearsed a new view of life were part of his moving and unsparing self-scrutiny.

It was also true, as his confessions revealed, that the crystallization of new religious feelings quickened when Döblin found himself in the French maelstrom of 1940 to 1941, deprived of his human dignity, uncertain about the fate of his sons, far from Yolla and Erna, carrying his heavy luggage, a pair of shoes, and a manuscript along the dusty roads of France (I shudder at the thought of Thomas Mann in a similar situation). He had confronted Christ as a symbol of human suffering before, but in a different context. On his voyage to Poland, he had entered Saint Mary's in Krakow as a tourist, and he was surprised and strongly moved by the many worshippers praying to Christ, a "man" whose image "emanated horror." Nevertheless, he returned the next day, incapable of freeing himself from this strange fascination. In the church at Mende, he confronted the *Crucifixus* again, after nearly twenty years, yet during a journey full of "signals" and "portents" he did not feel horror anymore but rather "radiating warmth"; the thought of God, the primal cause, and Christ, incarnation of the suffering in the world, fell into their Christian place. Of course, these passages were written or revised long after he had been accepted into the Church. One of the few people among his contemporaries who tried to understand the old man was the Berlin writer Elisabeth Langgässer, a Catholic engagée who had barely survived the Nazis because of her Jewish origins. Berlin intellectuals will never forgive Döblin, she wrote in a letter of February 1947, not because of his new faith (possibly even chic for one coming from France), but because, and this was the really unpardonable sin, Döblin did not play an aesthetic game but had really gone on his knees, "like an old peasant, heavy and stiff." It was not fiction anymore but "the intimately personal and imperfect truth" of life itself.

—Peter Demetz

# BOOK I

# Europe,
# I Must
# Leave You

# PART 1

# JOURNEY INTO THE UNKNOWN

# 1

# Paris, Awaiting the Catastrophe

## The Radio Reports

On May 16, 1940, a Thursday, I concluded a work that had occupied me for months. The radio droned in the next room. The announcer reported that the French army had been unable to close the "pocket" on the northern front. The report mentioned nothing of a breakthrough, of a hole in the front, but anyone who had ears could hear. My pen dropped from my hand.

I was not unprepared. For days strange figures had been moving through our neighborhood, St. Germain, near Paris. The magnificent park was in full summer bloom, its paths crowded with people taking a hike or a stroll. Children played on the commons. But on the wide avenues that cut through the park and the small town were eerie, bizarre-looking vehicles—not tanks, not cannons, but cars, oddly packed, with beds and mattresses lashed onto the roofs, hung with household belongings. With entire families crowded together inside.

They were refugees from Belgium and northern France and they brought fear with them into our peaceful surroundings. Farmers' wagons, pulled by teams of horses or oxen, moved slowly

[ 5 ]

among the mattresses-on-wheels. Old people and children were lying or sitting in the hay, with sturdy-looking men and women marching in long strides in front of or behind the wagons. Obviously entire villages were on the move. Men and women, farmers in top boots, pushed carts in front of them loaded with small children and tools. The whole line of them stopped to be fed in the square in front of the train station.

One evening, late, it was military trucks that stopped on the square. Young soldiers crouched atop them, smoking. They didn't speak and they didn't sing. They looked down at us silently, dully. It was said they were on leave from the front. They were not, it appeared, returning from victorious battle. And when the news of the terrible breakthrough at the front was announced in a hushed voice on that 16th of May, and the fateful word "Sedan" appeared in the military bulletin, I went to Paris and contacted a friend who worked for a government agency I was loosely connected with. We discussed what we should do. A relative of his was a highly placed officer, so he was always well-informed. His own situation was simple. In case of emergency, he would be evacuated with the agency.

This serious and intelligent man advised me to prepare for the worst, and not to put off my departure from Paris for long. From one day to the next Paris could become a war zone, and be evacuated. And after the experiences of the last years, I could imagine what an exodus of hundreds of thousands of people would be like.

When I didn't seem inclined to follow my friend's urgent advice to take my family and leave immediately, we came to the following agreement: he would notify me the minute he heard bad news. My wife and child would then leave, no matter what the circumstances. He suggested that I remain behind and be evacuated with the agency at the last minute. The authorities had been told to abandon their posts only in extreme emergency, and even then only by government order.

And so I waited, uneasy and with growing anxiety, in St. Germain until the evening of the 25th, when his call came. We were about to go to bed. My friend, in an agitated voice, urged me to take the last train into the city. Enemy tanks were moving at such alarming speed that it was possible we could be cut off from Paris by the next day. But we didn't leave that night. We set off early the next morning, the three of us, refugees from our place of refuge. We sent one large piece of baggage ahead, hoping it would arrive. Each of us traveled with one piece of hand luggage; our boy with a knapsack and a blanket for the night.

Our belongings consisted of one large and two small suitcases and one knapsack. Since the war had begun, we had been shedding things like an animal sheds its skin: first all our furniture and our library—it was all stored somewhere—then our linen and clothing and the last of our books; they remained behind in St. Germain. We were shrinking down to what we could carry. But it was still too much.

We arrived in Paris before noon—the old, cheerful Paris. This wonderful city received us with the same smile as always. It appeared not to have noticed what was happening—and what was to come. From the café terraces, people looked in amazement at the handful of heavily loaded mattresses-on-wheels merging with the other traffic.

But not two weeks would pass before that marvelous, glittering city would be touched by an aura of death. From countless garages similarly laden cars would set off. And after three weeks, an immense wave of human beings would emerge from the city and hurl itself onto the same highways the Belgians were now traveling.

That day we stayed in a flat in the center of the city, where my friend was storing furniture. Then, late that evening, I accompanied my wife and son to the train station.

The huge station appeared ghostly by night. The wartime blackout made it seem deserted. But on entering, we were pulled into a clamorous, milling crowd consisting almost entirely of families. It looked as if they were all hurrying off on holiday. But there was no trace of pleasurable anticipation here. In the inner city one could have gotten the impression that it really wasn't so bad, that the newspapers were exaggerating the situation, that the war was still far away. Here it appeared otherwise. Every train to the south was coupled with extra cars in front and at the rear. People rushed into the cars, sitting or standing with their children in the corridors. Families who usually traveled third class spent their money on first- and second-class tickets in order to ensure that they could leave.

The conductors ran up and down the platforms. "All aboard!" they cried. I bid my wife a tender goodbye. My son wept against my cheek. He held me tightly and said, "We'll be back in a week." He didn't want to leave at all; he missed his friends in St. Germain and his beloved dog, Zita. We two adults were thinking, this trip is only a precautionary measure. We're doing it for the child . . . perhaps we're being overly cautious. . . .

But a dark premonition, a portent, swept over me as I left the station alone and walked down the desolate street. "This is wartime—you never know what will happen in war—we shouldn't separate in times like these."

But they were already on their way south.

## Last Days in Paris

I remained for more than two weeks in the flat my friend used for storing furniture. He had put up another friend there, a teacher who was fulfilling some duty or other as a soldier in Paris. I sat in the dusty room without a carpet or curtains, read a little, wrote a little, and visited this or that library.

One morning as I opened the window to listen to the concierge's loudspeaker in the courtyard, I heard the voice of Paul Reynaud, the president. I couldn't hear his words too well from the third floor. But Reynaud's voice, usually so youthfully sharp and ironic and aggressive, now sounded muted and agitated.

I run down the stairs as fast as I can. The concierge's booth is surrounded by people. I arrive just in time to hear what happened yesterday, what has happened to us in Belgium. The young king, son of the brave "Chevalier-King" Albert I, ordered his army of 900,000 men to lay down their weapons. He did this, we hear, without having conferred with his ministers. He hadn't even informed his allies, the French and the English, whom he had only recently appealed to for support. He had put those who, the day before, had been his allies in an appalling, a desperate, situation. The word "betrayal" wasn't mentioned, but you could sense it in Reynaud's address.

Those of us standing around the speaker understand. It is a matter of life and death. The women near me begin to cry. One young woman is sobbing: her husband is in Belgium. The concierge sits with her head in her hands: a young relative of hers is in the army.

Alfred Döblin

I slowly trot back across the courtyard. It's a bright, sunny day. I climb up to my dusty flat, to the junk room, and sit before my manuscript, spreading a sheet of newspaper over it. What good is a manuscript, what good is any of the work from the past?

It descends on us. We can offer no resistance. The Germans have the superior strength. Their methods are cruel, unnatural. First the Austrians, then the Czechs, the Poles, the Danes and Norwegians, then the Dutch and Belgians, they are all being effortlessly defeated. They fall before the enemy like a bird paralyzed in fear falls before the snake. As if offering themselves as sacrifice. No, this is no mere material, military victory. There is something behind this that instills horror. But perhaps war is not merely a material, military matter.

Days follow on which the newspapers tie themselves in knots to do everything possible not to report anything on their two small pages. But you can piece together events from the brief reports, until you understand what is really happening in Flanders: the German general staff wants to take the French coast in order to cut off France from England, it wants to conquer each country individually, in the same way it did Poland and Norway. Now it's our turn. They want to crush the part of the French army that has been isolated. We follow the race to the sea in Dunkirk breathlessly. The ill-fated army is making for the harbor. We hear of the tragic battles being fought in Flanders between an army that is scattered and without supplies, and the enormously strong, well-led, organized enemy. The enemy is closing off the roads to the harbors. Groups of isolated troops must break through on their own. Brave men are being sacrificed everywhere to hold back the enemy.

But what is happening at Dunkirk is clearly not a military incident at all, rather, a human one; a primal, human one. All available ships of the Allies are assembling in the port at Dunkirk to collect what is left of the wretched army. At the request of the English government thousands of fishing boats have set out from their coast. They are making for this other coast to save what can be saved, their allies' men and their own. And the heavens, which can distinguish between what is human and what is not, have favored them, have done everything during these days of horror to rescue the vanquished, to save them for other things. For on these days the sea,

[ 9 ]

the channel, otherwise so violent, was totally calm. The small English boats and steamers could travel back and forth between the two coasts as if crossing a river. And to deliver those rescued from the enemy bombers, the heavens covered the water with an unusually thick, constant fog. Warships covered their retreat. They suffered heavy losses. But they were built to fight.

The soldiers of the great army arrived exhausted and in tatters. They were embittered. But behold: they showed not a trace of discouragement.

I remained in Paris. From the newspapers we learned that the Germans were now turning their fury on us. Paris became quieter and quieter. In the north, preparations were being made for the decisive battles of the Somme and the Aisne. There was a procession in front of Notre Dame Cathedral. Thousands took part. Priests and believers prayed in the open air, entreating St. Genevieve, who once before had saved the city.

Every day I went down to the street, bought the paper and took it to the nearby Tuileries gardens to read. There I saw a strange sight. A steam shovel was at work, it was digging—constantly digging—bomb shelters. There were frequent air raid alerts; I had to run into some house or other; the shelters were never ready. They still weren't finished when we finally left Paris.

The day came when Paris was bombed. Sirens were wailing as usual, it was midday, police cars raced through the streets. Fifty of us were sitting in the basement of our building, there was antiaircraft fire, but it soon receded, then was followed by a few heavy explosions. Three-quarters of an hour later, the alarm was over. Paris looked as if nothing at all had happened. People strolled about, the cars whizzed by as usual. To the west, in the direction of the Eiffel Tower, a white cloud of smoke could be seen. It was said that large factories had been hit, as well as the Ministry of Aviation. I saw worse when I traveled to our former residence in St. Germain a few days later. There were army manufacturing plants along the way. There, I saw houses with roofs blown off, houses without windows. One long, new plant had suffered a direct hit: it looked as if a knife had cut away the middle section of the white box. And when the elderly, hunchbacked housekeeper received me in our former residence in St. Germain, she laughingly showed me a handful of shell fragments that had landed in our street.

Alfred Döblin

The number of shops that closed because their proprietors were fleeing was on the increase. A growing number of cars laden with mattresses traversed the city. The train stations never emptied. On the streets, people began standing in lines in front of the food stores, and we, too, had the good fortune to experience this. Everyone wanted cooking fat, coffee, and sugar, particularly sugar. The papers reported an alarming order issued by General Weygand, who warned troops fighting to the north of Paris that it was the final quarter-hour before the decisive battle.

And the decision came quickly, as did everything in these frightful days. Actually, there was no decision to wait for, it had already been made, and a cynical German propaganda sheet basically had been correct when it printed that winter, under the title "Why We Will Win": "The decision concerning the resolution of the coming battle was made on the day when France and England allowed the introduction of compulsory military service in Germany, and the occupation of the Rhineland."

## Leaving Paris

It was a hot Sunday, June 9. My friend arrived at the empty, quiet flat that morning to tell me we would leave the next day. I was to pack the necessary items and take my suitcase to his office that very evening around ten o'clock. He wouldn't say anything more.

I see myself on that Sunday evening, crossing the silent, moonlit court with my suitcase. The concierge and two nurses were sitting in the concierge booth. They looked at me as I approached with my luggage. The concierge anxiously asked if my friend the official was leaving also. I said yes, and gave her the key to the flat. She asked again if my friend were also going, that is, if the authorities were leaving Paris. Then she and the nurses stood at the front entrance, looking upset, and watched me leave.

There was no car available. I slowly dragged my suitcase down the totally empty Rue de la Paix. The Place Vendôme is dead. A few camouflaged streetlamps are burning. The Ritz, to the right, is dark; a few days ago doormen with braids on their uniforms were hurrying down the steps to help the elegant clientele out of their cars. A column rises up in the center of the plaza. It offers a sorry sight. In securing itself against bombs, it has dressed its lower third section with boards and packed it with sandbags. But it had rained in the last few days, the sand had gotten soaked, and the bags had burst, the whole thing had fallen apart and spilled out onto the square. Now the refuse lies around the Vendôme, in this elegant neighborhood. The area has been roped off. No one deems it necessary to clear away the rubbish.

I drag my bag along in the darkness to the Rue Rivoli. The Tuileries are dark. I come to the quarter where the ministries are located. The spotlights are blinding. I hear voices. Soldiers move along in the same direction as I.

And then I stand, perspiring, before the main gate of the building my friend has summoned me to. I look around me. The quiet, affluent street has been transformed into a field camp, trucks and automobiles are being loaded with crates and sacks. Soldiers and civilians are lugging things around, running back and forth. The air is filled with the sounds of orders issued by officers standing on the sidewalk, and with yelling and the sound of horns blowing.

Trucks are being loaded in the semidarkness of the building's courtyard. Boxes, whole cabinets, are continually carried down the steps and placed there.

The huge building is being emptied. The courtyard is swarming. Suddenly someone turns on a light in the third story of a private house across the street. Two huge windows throw broad swaths of light over the street and reveal what is going on. There is the immediate cry of "Light!" The packing stops, threats are directed upward, but nothing is moving up there. Finally two soldiers run into the house, yelling; we wait to see what will happen; then a relieved "Ah": a soldier appears at one of the windows and closes it, pulls the curtains, and then the second window is dark also, the street lies in darkness, everyone calms down and goes back to work.

Now private automobiles, directed by the military, rush up to be loaded. This work is overseen by officers, the officers themselves sit in the cars amid bundles of paper and cartons.

Finally my friend arrives. He hands my suitcase to an orderly. Then we walk up and down the street. He has heard the ten o'clock news and other broadcasts from farther away. He thinks the situation has improved somewhat; there is a possibility that Paris can be held. We agree to meet at ten the next morning.

I sleep in my storage room for the last time. It is Monday, Paris awakes to life. Yesterday's uproar has vanished from the elegant streets of officialdom. Double sentries, in the black uniforms of the *garde mobile*, with their steel helmets and bayonets, are still stationed before the imposing buildings. But there is nothing left to guard.

The administrative office I now enter offers an eerie impression. Overnight, it has been ravaged, emptied, gutted. Only the grand façade has been spared. I can see vestiges of the night's activity: scraps of newspaper and straw cover the steps and carpet, here are empty crates; books stacked high against a wall, there, will be forgotten. The doors stand open. How difficult it usually was to get through them. Now we can look in anywhere, even walk in. Who is in there? In most rooms, no one. People stand in the corridors, discussing, whispering. Yesterday many of the doors bore name plates—they have been removed.

I come to the rooms where my friend worked with others. Women are standing there in hat and coat, ready to depart, and at one table they are dashing off letters—letters to relatives and friends, telling them about the big move. They will announce that the old address is no longer valid, and that they hope to be back soon, but they will have difficulty giving their new address. Hurried, private conversations and frantic telephoning are taking place in these splendid rooms.

I know a few of these men and women. Many of the women are stenographers, secretaries, the wives of officials. But others have taken a further step and have dragged along close and distant relatives, mothers, mothers-in-law. And my friend, looking over the numerous members of our party, is worried that the total number will swell dangerously, we have only a limited number of cars.

A typed slip of paper is pressed into our hands: rendezvous at two at the Porte d'Ivry train station. We've never heard of this station. The driver who takes us there around noon isn't familiar with it, either, but the address is correct and proves to be the entrance to a freight depot.

We enter a small restaurant where rail and transport workers are eating. The mood is cheerful, the radio is turned off. We ourselves discuss how the world will look when we return—we are now *so*, and the world looked *so* then: *we* decide that we'll celebrate here on our return. Our entrance to Paris will be made through the freight depot at Porte d'Ivry, not along the Champs-Élysées. We decide this more flippantly than seriously. We act as if we don't know what's going on.

It's one-thirty. We go over to the tracks and meet the first advance party of my friend's administrative department, husband and wife. A young *abbé*, a colleague, is there also, he shakes everyone's hand goodbye. He has not gotten permission from his spiritual superiors to go with us. Paris, he says earnestly, will need help in the coming weeks. (In the coming weeks, in the coming months, in the coming years . . .)

I stand in the crowd and am racked with a horrible feeling: how unfair, how shabby and pitiful it is to leave here for my own safety. That it has come to this, that we have to flee, flee and flee again. What a sorry, undignified fate. Who has driven me to this?

I am not the only one to experience this bitterness. In the first half hour of standing around I hear in the comments others are making that they, too, feel revolted, anguished—and the disquiet and tension. The question of provisions arises; everyone lists the quantity and type of food they have brought along. This livens things up, and for a few minutes it seems as if we are taking an ordinary, spur-of-the-moment trip.

To the trains. But where are they? And this is no train station, in any case. It is a jumble of tracks and switches stretching out into infinity. We stumble and stagger about aimlessly until someone calls out from a train rolling in and points us to a row of sheds before which ancient passenger cars are stopping. These railroad cars are pathetic. They're empty and wait with their doors open, apparently for passengers. But who wants to travel in them? We stand next to them. Our hearts whisper in foreboding: this indeed seems to be the train.

The cars are marked in chalk with letters and numbers. The Captain, our transportation leader, runs frantically along the train, his sky-blue cap in his hand, looking for our department's address. But nothing is to be seen. Other people, unknown to us, are already taking seats on the train, which suddenly looks better to us. The Captain disappears, horrified, and charges back after a few minutes, fanning himself with his cap: this is the right train, this is our train, only our mark—or our cars—one of the two is missing!

A decision has to be made, time is short, and this riddle cannot be solved rationally. In a quarter hour this dismal train will start off and we have already melted in the sun and dissolved into sweat, if we don't leave soon, we'll wash away.

The little Captain screams for chalk. Now we know the meaning of action: he wipes the strange, hostile-looking marks off several cars and writes ours on! And we immediately take our seats in the dark train, and no one will succeed in evicting us.

We're still laughing, "Well done," as we start off. We glide out of Paris without even noticing, without a song, without a sound, without a thought. . . .

Not long ago, in a Paris newspaper, an executioner from a famous line of French executioners told how he got those entrusted to him to the bench and under the ax so quickly. He would deal his victim, who had been led to the bench with great ceremony and who at that moment was inclined toward sentimentality, a severe blow, first to the stomach and then to the back. Before the condemned could recover from the audacity of this attack, he was prostrate, then no longer there, having missed the crucial moment in a minor rage at the executioner—a substitute for narcosis. There, at Porte d'Ivry, fate treated us in a similar manner. It relieved us of taking our leave, it allowed us to stand back from our anguish, our anger, our bitterness and sorrow. It gave us our missing railroad cars and our small pleasure at the heroic deed of our Captain.

And now came the endless maneuvering to get us past the kilometer of freight sheds. The last thing Paris revealed to us was these warehouses, filled with provisions destined for the "belly of Paris."

They also filled the bellies of others.

# 2

# Flight
# Through France

## *To Tours*

Now, in America, on the other side of the great ocean, on the Pacific coast—when I think of the days and the weeks that followed, of the flight and confusion, of the endless anxiety, the waiting and desperation that were to come, that entire part of my life seems unreal to me. I don't remember any other period of my life when I was so little "I." I was neither "I" in my actions (mostly, I didn't have to act, I was either told what to do or I laid low), nor was my way of thinking and feeling the old way.

I had the dark feeling: something is wrong here, something has changed. Perhaps one day I will discover what.

And if I sketch the events of those coming weeks in the following pages, I do so not because of their special historical significance, but because I wish to preserve what was unique, strange, and unreal about that time.

During those weeks I was sure that I would experience major events—against my will—and acquire an unusual insight of some sort. I want to force my way back to this insight. I want to preserve it; keep it safe. That is why I am writing this down. I will not allow

Alfred Döblin

such extraordinary events to flit by me like a ray of light and to leave me once again in night and fog.

We traveled the entire day. The train moved slowly toward Tours. Actually, it was only at the outset that it was certain we were going to Tours. It was possible that another destination might be decided upon in the course of the journey. That depended on some reports that reached us along the way—us, that was the Captain and the conductor. The rest of us sat passively in the train. Some faraway thing had laid its hands on us. We left Paris knowing only that we would disembark "somewhere."

The countryside stretched out before us. The longer we traveled, the more we saw things we hadn't seen in Paris. The first part of our journey had begun. We were carried into the country, protected and looked after, still observers, still engrossed. But it was decreed that we would soon leave our places in the audience and climb down into the arena.

Black lines traversed the broad expanse of lovely country outside. As we neared the lines we saw that they were moving. When we got up close and could make out details, we saw a picture that became familiar to us: the highways transformed into a child's toy that wasn't working properly. It was a continuous belt on which cars and pedestrians moved in fits and starts. The belt jumped its track and everything stopped. We heard nearby a nervous tooting of horns. Did that help? The highways were horrendously blocked: flight.

Trains rolled by without end, loaded down with soldiers and war supplies, with searchlights and antiaircraft guns. When we pulled into stations simultaneously with soldiers, we saw that they were fresh troops, well outfitted. Soldiers who walked past our train, or who, like us, were fetching water, told us they were coming from Dunkirk! What had happened there? "We had no tanks and no planes."

More military trains, all carrying strong, fresh troops. They had not seen battle, for the most part.

Everything boded ill. But no one wanted to know the bad news. After all, it was just the beginning, they were strong, perhaps there weren't enough weapons to go around, but they were armed, they were the great army of a powerful nation.

Conversation in our train: perhaps there had been a defeat,

perhaps Paris would be temporarily occupied, but France was over-flowing with soldiers and there was no dearth of courage. The army hadn't even called up the reserves. What bothered everyone was lack of initiative. If only someone would give the country a push! During the months since the war had begun in September, I had not seen any enthusiasm for war in this country. But, like others, I believed you could fight a war even without enthusiasm, at precisely that moment when you are living in peace and forced against your will to defend your country. Then you would fight bitterly. That's what we thought as we traveled. France was caught in a terrible bind. The next step would have to be an all-out effort.

If you ask, however, why this effort never materialized, if I ask myself this question, the simple answer comes to me immediately: because it all happened so fast and because the attack was followed by near-fatal strangulation. Before people could even become con-scious of the situation, before the will to resist could follow their dismay, they were crippled, choking.

The war, the surprise attack, came so quickly that by the time you emerged from a state of stupor, you were already trapped in a different situation. We traveled on, it became dark, the cars re-mained darkened. The train stopped exactly at midnight. They said it was a station, and we were in Tours.

## *In Tours*

But we could see neither the station nor the city of Tours. We were enveloped in unimaginable darkness. We had to rouse ourselves and collect our things. My suitcase was with the other luggage; I didn't have to worry about it. I had only one special package to look after, it was lying in the overhead luggage net; a pair of shoes and a hand-written manuscript. I had not wanted to pack either of them in my suitcase in Paris because I foresaw an ill fate for this suitcase. I had almost forgotten the shoes in my storage room that morning in Paris and had pulled them out from under the bed at the last minute. I now held on tightly to both the shoes and my manuscript, and got out.

It was hard to get off the train. It was a dark night. Finally there was the flicker of flashlights. A platform. There were men, women, and children, standing and sitting around. They lay on their luggage.

The train station at midnight had been transformed into a caravansary.

The people made very little noise. I soon discovered the reason for this and also the reason for the total darkness of the train station: a bomber attack. A large airport lay close to Tours and it was continuously bombed. When we asked how long we should wait, we were told that waiting was useless, we had to find refuge. As we decided that a railway station was hardly the place to seek shelter during an air attack, we set off immediately. We had to wind our way through the crowd huddled on the floor. We accomplished this with difficulty; the hardest part being not getting lost. The Captain led the way, his sky blue cap could not be seen now. We called to him every few steps, his name echoed toward him in stages from the back of the line to the front, and he answered with a forceful "Here!"

Outside, masses of people lay silently on the street. Some of them were asleep, waiting for a morning train. You could hear shots in the distance.

Our Captain went into action when we reached the buses. "Ladies and married couples first, then the rest," he ordered. I took a later bus; we were delivered to a large hotel.

Upon our arrival, those who had already arrived broke the news that the hotel was full, others had gotten there first. After we crowded into a large hall, we found many others who had already forgotten their disappointment and were asleep on chairs or on the floor. We looked around for a place for ourselves. This was our Captain's great moment. He had found another hotel, which strangely enough still had vacancies. He added, in order to put this miracle in proportion, that there were not enough rooms for everyone, of course, only for women and married couples. The rest of us could sleep in chairs.

It seemed to me to affront the rules of eternal justice that couples, who already had the pleasure of traveling together and helping one another, now also enjoyed, *gratis* and *franco*, a free bed in the middle of the war, at the cost of the state, while we solitary men, destined to loneliness, were sentenced to hours of sitting on chairs. Already on the train the benches, though made of wood, had hardened under us to stone and granite. As mine was not the calloused skin of a monkey's behind, I could not accept my sentence without protest. So I protested, stating that it was not necessary to further reward someone who was traveling with his wife. The

Captain found this understandable, though he had the right to give orders and comprehend nothing. I then climbed into the bus with a few chosen others.

It turned out, however, that the second hotel did not have vacancies as reported, but was totally booked for the French Parliament, which had not yet arrived, but could at any moment. We placated the lady at the reception desk who informed us of this by saying, "The gentlemen will hardly arrive tonight, it is already one in the morning." On top of which, who knew if they would arrive at all? They might go directly to Bordeaux.

We rattled the poor woman so badly that she turned over all available rooms to us for better or worse. And so we spent our first night outside Paris sleeping until midmorning, alone and in pairs, praising the local custom of not announcing air raids. For there had of course been bombers.

We met in the city before noon and spread out in groups. The government agency that had taken me along had a lot of fancy ideas. High officials had arrived that morning in departmental or requisitioned cars, still possessed by the lofty attributes of their office. They wanted to set up the old agency straightaway. They were awaiting the department's mountains of belongings, a part of that unbelievable mass of paper I had seen hauled away on Sunday evening. On its arrival they seemed to wish to begin work again. To this end, they left the main party in Tours to look at a house they intended to occupy provisionally. It was a one-story villa, totally empty, and located on the wide access road to the north of the city. I accompanied my friend there. The house at that moment was equipped for nothing more than sleeping in overnight, and from the piles of straw in the basement rooms, it was clear that someone was staying overnight here already. The order came down to give the place a good airing and cleaning.

The next morning, the hotel manager appeared to tell us that she had to reclaim most of the rooms she had given us the day before, for the French Parliament now was truly on its way. We settled in the hotel's large, enclosed courtyard, full of skepticism, and awaited their arrival for hours. Instead of the Parliament, a number of women finally arrived, with heaps of baggage, hatboxes, bags, and suitcases. They were pointed out to us as the wives of the parliamentarians. Their husbands never appeared and the ladies soon disappeared.

\* \* \*

I stayed only one night at the hotel. We were ordered to vacate, but never knew for whom. And so in the company of others I walked out into the late-night darkness, into that absolute darkness that I associate with Tours. Bombers had once again appeared, and just as we approached the great bridge over the Loire, things began to flash and explode. We heard the droning and buzzing of engines. Where to? My companions, all of whom were familiar with Tours as tourists, said coolly, "Keep walking!" And so we set off. The bridge proved to be enormously long. In the black skies above was a dazzling display of fireworks. The action was taking place to our right.

We knocked and rang, people were fast asleep in the tiny house, the door opened and the house looked like a cozy stall. I, too, was given some straw. I took off my outer garments and slept just (as badly and well) as usual.

The city swallowed hordes of refugees. We had been the first. Now came the rest. Enormous numbers of people were scattered over the city. The streets were never empty, day or night. Once a strange group of motorized behemoths appeared, powerful, sparkling machines, resting on rails. What kind of machines they were and what their purpose was, we did not at first comprehend, until we realized that they were connected with factories that had been evacuated in order to rebuild them elsewhere. So they were anticipating a long war.... The machinery was attended to by male and female workers, and attracted a great deal of attention.

But then came the flow of refugees that threatened to breach all the dikes. We had no radio and only occasionally did a newspaper pass through our hands. But we could see what was happening with our own eyes: the enemy was not to be stopped. No one was stopping them. We were naked, defenseless. And people were arriving on wheels or on foot, without knowing where they were going; they found accommodations here and there and then continued on their way as before—and no voice was raised in explanation, in comfort or encouragement. Where were the leaders, what decisions were they coming to? The people had been abandoned, left to their own devices.

And they behaved nobly. Fewer crimes were committed during this time than ever before. The local laws were obeyed matter-of-factly. No one thought of obtaining private "rations," even as shortages were being endured. The French do not respect official disciplinary measures, but during these weeks they demonstrated their own splendid discipline and equipoise. They revealed themselves to be a mature, civilized people, an autonomous people. It is certain that no one remains immature for long here.

We strolled down the main street in Tours, walked along the Loire, and looked out over the great river, using it as our reference point. We dined formally and at great expense only at that first lunch at the hotel; then both men and women decided on a new kitchen regime. A group of ladies was designated to do the shopping and to rent a room for us in the vicinity where we could eat cheaply and comfortably. We also enjoyed a few good, full meals in a local restaurant. But before this wartime food cooperative could bloom, it wilted. Everything happened faster than we had thought possible.

Three days later it was finished. The stream of refugees grew and grew. Military traffic increased. The city, particularly the northern sections, reverberated with the noise of the cars and people. And then it got much worse, as the flow of civilians was directed away from the main streets, as the military roared onto them and over the huge Loire bridge. The rumbling and rattling went on all day and night. The entire army—they were definitely not being deactivated—appeared to be rolling by. Was it an army in retreat, or were they there to establish a new front on the other side of the Loire?

Rumors were spreading among us already. Unsuspecting soldiers were still cleaning the house where they were billeted and hanging up their duty roster. I had been lodged, in the end, in a little house, the gate to which was surrounded by shell splinters, which was hardly comforting. Then the order came to meet the next morning, with our belongings, at what was to have been a headquarters. We packed in haste what we had overhastily unpacked. Typewriters disappeared again into their cases. Sacks were retrieved from the cellar to be refilled with piles of paper. Once again, wrapping cord and hammers. The house, having just been cleaned, reassumed its previous condition of disorder, dirt, and straw.

Through the chaos I see a somber city official approach the acting head of the department. Electric lights had already been installed, tables had been brought in. "And you want to just abandon all this?" the magistrate asked. The head of the department shrugged his shoulders; this time it was merely light bulbs and tables.

The crates and sacks were dragged out again. I got the impression that the files lost value with each move. Now they were being tossed onto the trucks. I could foresee the day when the trucks stopped with their papers on some highway. I even thought it possible that someone would simply toss the papers off the trucks, scatter them over the ground, thereafter being responsible only for himself and the trucks.

We assembled in front of the house, thirty men and women, and contemplated the situation. What would become of our pleasant communal kitchen? The shelling at the airport hadn't really been all that bad, after all. . . .

We would head south. Would the army be able to resist at the Loire? Our vehicle drove up, it was a truck. Our suitcases were lifted onto it. A number of departmental crates followed, it wasn't bad, you could sit and lean back on them. But before we boarded we were told to say goodbye to some of the others, because several of the men, government officials, announced that they had to go to Bordeaux. Doubtlessly, they had to. They had orders to, surely. But as people are, we—those left behind—having bid a pleasant goodbye to them, were left with an uneasy feeling, and it was formulated discreetly: "They want to go to Bordeaux right away." This was said in a less than friendly manner. At such moments even habitually respectful people can change their attitude.

So rather than speed off in comfortable official cars, we took possession of the heavily loaded truck, our behemoth. We were helped on and we sat there, sat there and rode.

We were observers and travelers no longer. Now we were the masses. It was the first stage of the metamorphosis.

## Moulins

It took us a long time to leave the city behind us. Our driver finally disentangled our truck from the knot of other vehicles. Once again we looked down from the Loire bridge at the broad river and its islands of sand. The landscape now opened up. We drove along the edge of the stream of refugees. Close by we saw other drivers struggling to escape the whirlpool. Then we turned off the beaten track. We crossed main roads, all stuffed full with people and soldiers on the move. Once we stopped in a village for water. Vehicles full of soldiers, some wounded and bandaged, had stopped there, the soldiers wore the numbers of various regiments. An old soldier limped over to us, looking very solemn. He asked where we had come from and what news we had. He pointed to himself and his comrades: "Gentlemen, things have changed in this country."

It began to rain. Our truck had no cover. We did what we could against the downpour, pulled coats over our heads, huddled together, hid behind the crates. We crossed over a wide body of water.

It was still light as we approached a city, Moulins. Our truck snaked through the streets and drove up to a building where we recognized several members of our party who had left Tours before us.

Our truck was directed into a broad, square courtyard, obviously a schoolyard. It was the secondary school for boys. Other vehicles were parked in the yard, a row of rooms facing the yard carried the titles of several government bureaus that apparently had already set up office here. When I saw this, I sadly remembered our experience in Tours.

Our truck was unloaded and we inspected the school. It was a vast structure. There were steps leading up to the buildings, and down to the dining halls in the basements, and at the back of the school there was open terrain, bushes and trees. I got lost climbing these hills and all the steps.

They actually began unpacking here as they had in Tours, as though they planned to resume their old activities: "Persevere at all cost." Rooms were assigned, the soldiers dutifully dragged crates here and there. We went downstairs as a group to eat dinner. The dining rooms were pleasant and spacious. Men and women were sitting there, eating and drinking. It was said that they were refugees. We were taken to dormitory rooms on the second floor where we would sleep, men and women segregated. There were already people here, too, a boy among them who had first claim to the place, as we found ourselves in the school's dormitory. Along one of the long walls, separated from the rest of the room by a white curtain, stood the elevated bed of the teacher on duty. It actually looked as though the various agencies and departments intended to work here. My friend was summoned and stood in the yard in lengthy conference with the others. I took a walk with his wife and other ladies. We made our way to the city.

It wasn't as chaotic here as it had been in Tours. Only the post office was busy; everyone wanted to send a telegram. The few clerks were working frantically and were at their breaking point. Happily, they could unload half their customers, for telegrams had to be taken to police headquarters, approved and stamped, whereby many lost the desire to send one. I telegraphed my wife in central France. Others tried to send telegrams to places farther north and were immediately refused.

Moulins looked pleasantly sleepy. As I walked alone through the clean, narrow streets for a half hour (the ladies were shopping for groceries as a precautionary measure) I thought: Why continue on, why attach myself to officialdom, why not play the traditional loner and just slip away? A bit of desertion—but it wasn't really desertion. No one would care. But that was only a dream. These peaceful town-dwellers themselves probably would be fleeing by tomorrow or the day after. Tomorrow, this sleepy street, too, would awake. I could already imagine how. . . .

And so I returned to my group and, after some wandering around, we again located the school. And found—everything had changed.

For reasons I could not fathom, the men had seized upon an entirely different view of the world situation during our tranquil, sanguine walk.

I saw several elderly gentlemen, who an hour before had been happily making plans for beginning work, now standing side by side, pale and frozen, with their heads together. They then separated to confer with their wives. Interest turned quickly from the public sector to the personal. It all happened so quickly. Official business seemed to take on a life-threatening character. I saw how rapidly interest in the heavy, official baggage I had seen being loaded on Sunday evening in Paris weakened, faded entirely, then abruptly turned to one's own personal luggage. I heard terrible comments concerning that sacred official property: They intended to burn it— at least part of it!

That afternoon it became clear that I had not misheard the news. Soldiers seized a number of sacks by the neck and shook their contents onto the underbrush of the school's grounds. With brutal kicks and shoves, they piled up that officially stamped, sacred material into little heaps, as if they were dealing with logs, and set the piles on fire. Thus did we rid ourselves of much of our carefully protected baggage, doubtless in order not to have it fall into enemy hands.

The fires flickered happily. The flames seemed to cast light on the sad situation. We were in serious trouble indeed.

And it wasn't only the fires that indicated this. As I crossed the courtyard I saw men, still pale, distressed, and gloomy, pacing up and down with their wives. They were aloof, preoccupied. That evening we discovered the end result of their discussions: many of these ladies and gentlemen were no longer to be seen. They had gone home. They had bargained. They had bought cars in town at high prices and were up and gone. It was then openly proclaimed that we could no longer remain here. None of us. No one knew the actual location of the Germans, but that was not as important as the fact that we had to leave to make room for strictly military units. At the same time, a word was circulating in our group that originated with our sky-blue Captain, who wasn't my favorite. He used it often. The word was *dégonfler*. It meant: to reduce a swelling. Whose or which swelling did Sky-Blue wish to reduce? No one here looked swollen. But our group had swollen. There were too many of us. The Captain didn't know how to procure cars to transport us. He couldn't burn us like the baggage. He now discovered, to his horror, that we all wanted to go with him.

He went from one person to the other, commending those who had left—namely because they had homes in a part of France that had not yet been occupied or because they were blessed with a family. He praised familial feelings. He weighed each person's situation. Everyone listened with suspicion to what he had to say. At first no one said anything. We all promised to think it over, to search our hearts. But he demanded quick decisions. Everyone assumed an air of profound and stubborn contemplation.

He didn't get anywhere. Nor was it clear how we so suddenly had become so many. In Tours, we all crowded easily into a single vehicle. Now our number had increased considerably. Apparently we had been joined by other departments. But "departments" was too dignified a word. Looking around, we got the feeling we were loaded down with a lot of new hangers-on, wives, sisters-in-law, parents-in-law.

Sky-Blue turned to me. And behold: I was angry. He was making me angry. And that made him happy. While everyone else was veiled in a mulish contemplation that covered them like a magic cloak they used to postpone their decision until later, "after the war," the Captain's kind words disturbed me. He said: "Your family is in Le Puy, isn't that so? It is more fitting, more natural, believe me, to go to your family now, rather than hang around here to no purpose. Who knows how long we will remain together?" That pricked my conscience. For he was not entirely wrong. On the other hand, the future was quite uncertain. And I didn't want to be frightened off.

But I had been stung. Sky-Blue's suggestion had fallen on receptive ground. I had read daily dispatches of the French General Headquarters, and there was mention that the fighting might be nearing central France. What would my wife and child do? I could not abandon them to their fate.

I was in a quandary. I discussed it with my friend and his wife. They themselves intended to leave. But they hadn't made a final decision.

I went upstairs to the dormitory with my friend. It was pleasant and quiet there. Several people were resting in bed, reading. I packed my bag. We stuffed the manuscript inside, separating it from its twin, my shoes. I laid my heavy winter coat over my arm. I said goodbye to no one, least of all to the Captain. My absence alone would give him pleasure enough.

## My First Escape

I found a man who would carry my bag to the station for me. I went ahead to ask about the train schedule. When I had zigzagged my way to the main street leading to the station, I got a shock. What I saw there was astonishing. I was used to the hustle and bustle of crowds. But this put everything else in the shade. It was the limit.

They were all civilians, on foot or in wagons. They crowded, flooded, the streets, the vast squares, the buildings. The sun beat down on them. People swarmed in the bright light, in the heat, hundreds of them, thousands, up to the train station in the background. A movie theater to the right was being cleared out to house refugees.

I pushed my way through to the station and made it to a counter. The clerk wrote down the times of the next two trains to Le Puy, one in half an hour, my preference, the second in an hour and a half. Both trains stopped at Vichy. That sounded wonderful. I was determined to leave.

I walked back, thinking happily: I'll slip off on the first train. The chaos here frightened me badly. I took one wrong turn, then another. When I finally reached the school and was joined by my friend and the man who would carry my bag, I had just enough time to make the second train. We set off immediately. And soon my friend and I were standing with many, many others at the door leading to my platform. I had bought my ticket (I carry it in my briefcase to this day). We waited with the others, in the crush of people, sweating. Now and then someone up front was let through, God knows why he, and not someone else. The time of the scheduled departure had long since passed. Nothing was happening. We stood there and waited. We shoved and were shoved. Suitcases were pushed between our feet from behind, and we had to balance ourselves in order not to fall. A young fellow stood to my right. He stood there, talking and sweating. And when he had talked and sweated enough, he took out his handkerchief, wiped the back of his neck, then his forehead, and finally he tossed his hair out of his face with a great shake of his head. He had long blond hair that was parted, but that always fell back down over his face. This boy was not interested in the least that I was standing behind him. His head banged against my nose roughly every five minutes and his freshly soaked hair flailed my glasses. I sighed, I suffered.

Once again I got angry at the sky-blue Captain. It was he, it seemed, who had placed me in this situation, behind this young man. I alone was supposed to reduce the swelling of our party. My anger led me to a decision, as it had once before. This time I decided to have a coffee, just that, to drink coffee to spite all captains. My friend, waiting loyally with me, agreed. It was his opinion that one needed his wife's nerves to fight for a place on the train. I was unfamiliar with his wife's nerves, but he should know. He would also drink a cup.

So I was liberated and absolved. And so I maneuvered my bag out of the throng and left the unhappy crowd—this rising dough— to itself. I could still see the boy from far off, jerking his head. We drank the coffee we wanted. I smoked two cigarettes to top it off. I

Alfred Döblin

checked my bag at the counter. We'd had enough of all this travel. We departed in relief.

We were received by our friends at the school. They shook their heads, not at my unsuccessful action, but that I had undertaken it at all. Sky-Blue had badgered them, too, to contribute to the *dégonflement* of the group, but they had ignored him. Why should we make his work any easier? they said cold-heartedly. He'd like it if we'd all get lost, they said.

I moved back into the dormitory and ate and drank with the others, who had not noticed my escape attempt. I went up to the ill-humored Captain and gave him my report. It had been too much for me, I said. He said nothing. He hadn't succeeded with anyone. In the courtyard, the fire was still burning cheerfully.

## The Cattle Cars

The next day brought a turnabout, my reward, a surprise, a birthday present for me. We were told to make preparations to leave that afternoon. We were going to—Le Puy! Exactly where I wanted to go. It wasn't a dream, I hadn't heard wrong, it wasn't a misunderstanding. I still had my ticket in my pocket. I couldn't believe my eyes and ears. But it was true. It was repeated. So I could have made it easier for myself. And we needn't have rushed around so the previous afternoon.

But what was done was done, and I was a lucky fellow, everyone who knew of my undertaking the day before told me so. But only until noon. Then we were told we were going to—Clermont-Ferrand. Later, much later, I comprehended that it was a cosmic joke, this news that we were going to Le Puy. It was a mockery, a trick that I was to be exposed to many times, a whole series of them.

And as we climbed into the car that was to take us to the station, it changed again. We were going neither to Le Puy nor to Clermont-Ferrand, but "somehow, to the southwest."

At the station, or next to it, stood a train, the sight of which made us all grow pensive. As it did others who were slowly approaching it. The train consisted, namely, of cattle cars.

[ *29* ]

This can't be right, we thought defiantly, knowingly. Until a high official appeared and said "yes" and asked us to take our places.

We did so in resignation. The cars didn't smell good. But worse was the lack of straw. Some cars had a moderate amount of straw, others a less than moderate, but none had an abundance. It was not easy to board. In the course of the long journey that followed, the ladies and gentlemen of the agencies and departments and their entourages learned to climb in and out with difficulty. It was an adventure every time.

We were now a large group, 120 to 150 people. Only a few of us knew each other. All were from Paris. Some had been in Moulins. There were civilians and military, officials and hangers-on. Men and women and now children, too. I saw a boy of twelve, and a baby. We constituted a collective transport. The leader was no longer our Captain but an erect, elderly commandant. I had seen him already, in the school courtyard.

We patrolled the neighboring cars to report back where the most straw was. We reported back and at the same time reported that these cars were already occupied, by soldiers. We formed groups of forty in the cars that we were forced to accept, lining the sides and filling the centers.

At first I thought a corner would be best. I put my suitcase in the angle, covered myself with my coat and, with my legs stretched out, now believed that I was splendidly situated. A half hour later it turned out that my legs were sticking out too far and that other legs from the wall were crossing mine. I had to draw them in until I was crouching. I had room overhead, but was pressed against the wall from the right and the left, and couldn't do anything about it.

It was the same for the others, but for other reasons. They started out first by sitting on their bags, then on the floor, and then they didn't know what to do with their legs. My fellow travelers were constantly changing their seats, their positions, now sitting, now crouching, now half lying down—until all of them had discovered (which took some time) that there was no correct way to sit, and no correct position. It was a matter of sitting now this way, now that.

And when our posteriors tired of the lengthy crouching, we had to stand up and walk around. And when we tired of that we were once again in the position of trying to sit on a suitcase, then of balling ourselves up and lying on one side. We also changed places in the car whenever possible, even changed cars in the assumption that it would be different somewhere else. But it was only difficult in a new way (and whoever was smart and had some experience knew this already). For in the end, a cattle car is a cattle car and wood is wood.

We boarded this cozy abode around noon. And as I climbed up and looked back at the train station, from which trains were no longer departing, I thought that we had done well with this, after all. Many had grumbled at seeing what we were offered. They didn't understand what was happening in the world. But in the course of the journey everyone had it pounded into their heads and, in the end, everyone understood.

## It's Good to Sit in a Train

It's good to sit in a train. It would be even better if the train would move. There was something lacking here in this last respect. We couldn't determine why our train was stalled. At the moment it seemed to suffice that it was taking pride in being a train.

We had been instructed to assemble at the station at noon and to take a place on the train. But this was only to say (which took us a long time to figure out) that they simply wanted to give the train the opportunity to get used to our presence—only then to move. But it didn't take the opportunity. It only demonstrated, in a nerve-racking way, its ability to stand still. We thought we would be leaving Moulins at noon, but we were still there that afternoon. We were there that evening and into the night.

From time to time we sent someone up front where the locomotive was, or should be, or to the rear, where it also could be. But it was neither in the front nor the rear. In the evening, a jerk ran through the train, reverberated happily through the cars and our hearts. The locomotive had arrived. But it was a hoax. Nothing happened. It wasn't the locomotive, but another car. But then the locomotive did appear. It arrived, after all. It was there. And it was joined to the other cars. The train stood there stalwartly, like a statue.

We now sent messengers to those close to the engine to find out what it was doing, how it was, what was happening in its vicinity, whether it was stoked, not stoked, how the engineer was doing, whether or not there was a stoker. The messengers went out and came back with their tidings, the entire car gathered at the sliding door to hear: the engine is there, the engineer is there, too, and both are doing well. The engineer is sitting in the baggage car with the stoker and another man, they're fixing their dinner.

A half hour later the messengers returned: The three have just sat down to dinner in the baggage car.

Then: They've begun to eat. They're having their hors d'oeuvres. Then: The stoker's getting another bottle of wine. Then: The stoker's gone again, no one knows what he's up to. The others are still at table. Then: We know what the stoker's doing. He's getting coffee. The whole thing was reassuring and suggested long duration. And so it was. Late in the evening we were walking up and down the platform (still in Moulins), we sat in the car and tested our limbs' compressive strength and resistance to shock. When it got very dark we were told to stay in the car and prepare for the night. The train, this hay ox, this rhinoceros, neither jerked nor budged. It was something we had to live with.

The stoker and engineer had now disappeared. The table with the leftovers of their meal was still visible in the baggage car. They were spending the night in the city, we were told. Had we retained any trace of our original jitters about the journey, we would have now hit the ceiling. But we accepted it.

We thrashed about in the car. First we sat, then lay down, then were pushed together. A few heartless souls slept till morning and didn't awaken even when we bumped against them. When they finally got up, they stretched and were well rested.

The rest of us couldn't get to sleep. Mostly because of our legs. No matter how short they were, there was no room for them in the car. So we were relieved when it was dawn and were happy to get up and onto our feet. It was almost five in the morning.

We looked around, looked outside, and behold: we were in Moulins!

We greeted our trusty platform through the open sliding door. Several people were walking around with towels, going to wash. Our incredible train had managed to sit here the whole night. We considered what that could mean—we walked across the tracks to a small café to figure it out. Someone waved from the train. We hurried back. Woe if this cursed train should leave without us! And sure enough, it moved, but only two hours later. It needed two hours to get started.

## In the Cattle Car

It was done. We had left Moulins.

People everywhere get involved in predicaments and try to make the most of them. They are shortsighted, wrapped up in the moment. They take what the present offers them. They make themselves fairly invulnerable in this way. They tend to joke about the most awful predicaments. If at all possible they forget the awful predicament, adapting to it as if they were comfortable with it. I am certain that if most of the men I am traveling with landed in hell, they would reach into their coat pockets after a few days, pull out a cigar, and ask the devil himself for a light. It is not inconceivable that some of them would propose a compromise with the devil, coming up with some efficient ideas about how to heat hell.

A child deserves a bed, a clean, smooth bed with pillows and sheets. But a small child just learning to walk slept in the straw near me in the cattle car. Without question he felt as comfortable there as in a cradle, and during the day he was delighted by the rattling of the car and the people pacing back and forth.

Many of the adults went around looking glum, and many tears were shed during the long journey. But we laughed a lot, too. All in all, we proved to be unworthy but tenacious weeds of the species "human."

We were in the cattle car for three days and three nights. I do not say "we traveled for three days and three nights" for an understandable reason. The train moved on occasion; on occasion it didn't; no one could crack its code.

We were forty people in one car, slightly more females than males. At some point along the way, when a new car was coupled on, I, too, changed residences and boarded the new one; it was half-empty. It filled quickly, however.

My friend's wife appeared after a while on the other side of the car, also in search of a better spot. She managed to spread out her sleeping bag along one side. She was a vital young woman who wasn't bothered by hardship (see my friend's earlier reference to her nerves). Actually, she could have done without the sleeping bag more easily than others. But precisely because she often hiked and bicycled, she knew what travel comfort was. She was the only one in our car who had come well equipped for our important journey. She had several blankets, which she shared with her husband and me, she had her sleeping bag, and furthermore, plenty of provisions and canned foods. The existence of such persons was of great significance to the whole car. Most of us were mere pedestrians from the past era of peace. We lived on her as parasites, as hangers-on.

My friend joined her occasionally from the neighboring car, always bleary-eyed, always serious. He slept badly and would ask what there was to eat. He used the occasion to stock up on food.

The young woman settled in splendidly during the next few days. She mastered the situation. When the train stopped she visited the other cars, sat down with acquaintances, new and old, and played cards. Or she stayed to herself and read a book. She'd also brought a supply of books! Or she leaned back against the wall of the car, drew up her legs, and wrote, copiously and quite fast. She lost not a moment in thought. She was amazingly talented and up to the situation. She wrote in a great rush, and with her pen flying so quickly that it was certainly not letters. Nor could she be describing her surroundings, for she never glanced up while she was writing to look around, to make comparisons or check things. Doubtlessly she was recording her impressions, her thoughts and reflections. She was reporting her opinions. These opinions were of a piece, as she herself was. Afterward she would shut her notebook and put it back in its place. Things could continue, she would have her opinions about them.

To the right of me in my corner of the car, a small family had secured a nice place for itself. The child was positioned on the inside, then the mother and the father. He was an officer assigned to one of the many government agencies now in retreat. The mother was an Englishwoman. They spoke only English.

Then there was a group that quickly caught my attention: German emigrants. The parents were in their forties, the two sons were sixteen and eighteen. I had met this group in Tours and had seen them again in Moulins. The man must have had connections

Alfred Döblin

with some department or other, for at this time all emigrants, unless they were naturalized, were in camps, even the famous and important hadn't escaped this fate. This Family X, who had appeared in Tours, was on our train and sat in our car. The four of them sat quietly, as their circumstances dictated. But they were noticeable nevertheless, without themselves noticing why. It was not their accent. But in contrast to the others, they traveled with a great deal of baggage, with the most, actually. It was modern, and this luggage, like that of world travelers, bore stickers from elegant hotels and the names of great ship lines. This luggage attracted attention and mistrust. I heard remarks from many sides about this odd group being carried along with us. They kept their provisions primarily for themselves, but sometimes they invited others to share them.

There were also several learned men, professors with their wives and relatives. We all got along well, watched each other, and took up for each other. But we remained in small, discrete groups.

A "boss" was appointed in each car. He was responsible for keeping order and for seeing about food. Order was present from the beginning, the food, unfortunately, was not. The situation quickly worsened, food became more and more scarce and neared depletion. We now saw that we were unprepared for such a journey. Which explained our sky-blue Captain's fear. First there were no train cars, then our destination was unknown, and how was such a large group to be provided for under the circumstances? But I will speak of hunger only when it appears.

Despite our superficial cheerfulness, we had been in the grip of severe anxiety during our long wait at the Moulins train station. And the fact that we were now under way and knew that our destination was uncertain did not lessen our concern.

What a strange mix of emotions, what a confusion of clear and clouded thoughts we traveled with, stretched out and tried to sleep with, with which we awoke and found ourselves in our car amid our companions, our fellow sufferers. There was sorrow, grief over the fate of the country that was our fate, also. And once again I was overwhelmed by a feeling of distress that was more than psychological, that had not loosened its hold on me since the 16th of May, and that was entangling me ever more in its grip.

Like a bee drains the flower of honey, my distressed state took sustenance from all of the bad things that had happened to us. There was a dark quivering in me that called itself train fever, then fear, then simply grief. And I saw that I was not alone in it. It could also be read in the faces and gestures of the others. It was rarely articulated. I noted: this is what the vanquished look like in retreat—even when they're laughing.

We stopped often. And wherever we stopped we found ourselves in a crowd of people waiting, people who wanted to continue their journey and who could not be taken along. The train, our pathetic cattle cars, appeared to the fearful crowd as a major miracle, as salvation—and then it steamed away. It was terrible to look down at them from our open barn doors. They begged us to take them along. The boss shook his head and called "No!" Which was according to the regulations, for we were forty people and constituted a special transport that was to be issued rations. But after all, it was wartime, we thought, a time of need. Why not take a few people along? But then the commandant would come running along the train and order us to close all the doors. He screamed at a few of us who wanted to debate the issue.

The train traveled on and on. The train halted and halted. We were supposed to move southwest. At night the cold was very bad. With forty people in a cramped space, we could not keep the doors completely closed. I lay near the door and tried in vain to protect myself from the cold drafts. But one was safe from it only in the crowded corners. Lying at the crack in the door, which everyone avoided, was—my friend's wife. She climbed into her comfortable sleeping bag. She drew it up to her chin, only her head peeked out. She slept warmly thus and awoke full of energy.

There was no morning drink. But there were natural needs. What a bother that was. It disturbed the males of the species less than the females. It is true that we stopped often, but the question was always where to go to relieve oneself. Later, when we were again in a town and houses demonstrated their wonderful versatility, the women spoke with particular revulsion of this part of the trip. At any rate, they solved the problem splendidly each time. They sent scouts into the vicinity and posted guards.

Outside our train, France surged by in flight. Troops were still heading north. Once, a lone middle-aged soldier appeared at a small station. He was unarmed and he was ragged. He was sunburned and unshaven, and carried bread and fruit under each arm. He sat down with it at the station, near the water spigot, and began to eat and drink. Gradually, people joined him. A circle formed around him. He told of the Battle of the Somme, from which he had escaped on foot. His unit had been thrown into confusion, been wiped out; he had broken through the German lines. Then he made sweeping generalizations about the German and French armies that ended in a frightful glorification of the Germans. We gave the poor wanderer, who, as he put it, was making the pilgrimage back to his hometown, provisions to add to his existing supply (to buy ourselves out of it, so to speak, and to ease his difficulties). He piled up everything on the ground next to him. Many of us looked upon it with envy. He immediately sampled a few of the donations. They appeared to taste quite good to him. His appetite hadn't suffered.

He was still sitting at the station as we moved off. Business was going well. No doubt he tramped through the entire region with his story and fed himself well from it. He exploited the situation. As he wore a uniform, the only thing that was certain (we later deduced) was that he had bolted. But we quasi-identified with him and were glad that he had been spared. Only later did it occur to us that he was in great shape and good humor for someone who had straggled away from the Battle of the Somme.

Once, we stumbled on crates of oranges. The moment we saw them we (and they) were done for. They were at a station, near the tracks, bound for Paris. The top crate had already been cracked by an earlier group of treasure hunters and was half empty. The station-masters were not going to protect the defenseless fruit. And so followed its systematic distribution. We stuffed our pockets: an easy victory.

On the second day, military trains rolled by. They were huge, with long-barreled cannons, and spotlights—antiaircraft regiments. It rained and rained. These enormous trains rolled alongside us in the rain, accompanying us. It was as if they wanted to mirror us, but they provided us with an inexpressibly sad and horrible, and oh, so pitiful sight. The immense cannons and powerful lights glided by us under a veil of rain. But riding on top of these cars, mixed in with the soldiers, were civilians: women and children and a few lone men. They rode partially covered by the canvas that was stretched over the cannons, but partly in the open, unprotected and lying on the platforms. In the pouring rain. They traveled this way day and night, glad to escape. Those of us who witnessed this image at this ominous moment, an image imbued with apathy and dread, witnessed the absolute misery of the time, the general misery and our own as well.

When we talked with each other, when in our whispered conversations the pessimistic word "capitulation" fell, we were only articulating what, it appeared to us, had already in fact occurred. Capitulation was visible.

Our dismal journey continued. When we stop, again across from military trains, we find out (it nevertheless comes as a cruel blow) that the government has requested a cease-fire.

We have no proof of this rumor. But it is accepted anyway. A young woman climbs into our car and lies face down in her place. She sobs loudly. No one in the car speaks.

We try to look at each other. We try to divine what the other person is thinking. We want clarification . . . actually we want diversion. We don't want to face the horror of the situation. We feel we are personally involved and don't yet know how. We cling to the crowd.

We talk quasi-objectively about the effect of a cease-fire. England will not agree to it, of course. But how can England wage a war alone? What will become of the blockade? France itself will be in the territory under blockade. At this, conversation dies.

Each of us has his or her own personal reaction. We cling to the group, and at the same time the whole societal net is unraveling. There is something primal about this situation. . . .

This is not a new feeling to me. I experienced it once before, seven years ago when I left Germany. But it wasn't so bad then. Was it because at that time I had found immediate asylum in another country, had hidden, and today didn't know where to turn? I am, in fact, not thinking about escape or asylum at all. My thoughts don't extend that far. Like the others, I feel only a heavy, dull blow. I see how those sitting here with me in the car are silent, or talk, or act as if they are asleep: we have been shaken and left to our own devices. We have been led and protected by a nation—and no longer are. A primal condition, defeat.

I am profoundly affected by this. Why? The answer, the full answer, came to me only slowly in the following weeks.

Once, when we stop somewhere, they say we are going to Riom. But when we move in the other direction it changes to:

Clermont-Ferrand has been bombed, that stretch isn't open. We stop again. The wheat is high. We're traveling through a fertile land, it will soon be harvest time.

Our diet leaves something to be desired. At noon we eat a thin half-slice of bread with goose liver pâté and half an orange. In the evening a half-slice of bread once again, a piece of Dutch cheese, and a few cookies from someone's private pantry. The second night we unexpectedly get something warm to drink. I wake up at one-thirty in the morning, the train is stopping somewhere, someone has already opened the door to our car. The beam of a flashlight passes over me. I look into a big white cup that someone is holding in front of me. The cup is filled with a yellowish liquid. And as I sit up, someone holds the cup to my lips. She is a nurse with the civilian auxiliary service. What I swallow is a weak bouillon, but the warm liquid is pleasant. I am warmed by it and go for a walk with others from our car. Look, we've stopped at a large station. It's Clermont-Ferrand after all! It's amazing what our miserable train can do! Red signal lights shine eerily.

When I hear the name Clermont-Ferrand I think to myself, it would be easy to get to Le Puy from here. I think it's possible. I imagine everyone's surprise when I suddenly show up there.

But when we stop the next morning, the place is called Arvan. And with that everything is decided. We have turned to the south-west and Le Puy is behind us. In Arvan the locomotive takes pity on us and gives us warm water to bathe in and shave with. We even find a newspaper stand. Someone runs over to get an issue of the *Populaire,* the socialist paper. In it we read an announcement made by Marshal Pétain. It informs the French people of the gravity of the situation and establishes the necessity of a cease-fire. The expression *d'un coeur serré* stays in my memory: with a heavy heart, oppressed with grief. We stand together there and read. No one speaks.

The Germans are said to have gotten beyond Nevers and occupied Avallon. Their fighter planes are disturbing the wildlife.

We no longer see trains with soldiers. The landscape gets more wooded and hilly. We are moving up into a mountainous region, and if we felt freer, this trip would be a joy. But our eyes merely skim over the beauty in shock, morosely. At one point we see an ancient castle, as if we were in the Loire Valley. There's a summer freshness, it's June.

Once again a station. What's the news? Russia is getting involved? A likely story. This evening the radio will broadcast the German response to the French request for a cease-fire. This evening? Why should Germany be in such a hurry to answer? If it answers at all in the positive there will first be—I remember 1918—long formalities, the naming of negotiators, the determining of the setting, and only then the announcement of the conditions that will probably have to be swallowed whole. At any rate, a new element of tension has been introduced, a new source of bitterness: when will the Germans deign to respond? And what will it please them to demand?

At noon we experienced a minor hunger revolt in our car. It was carried out civilly. There was so pitifully little to eat. The half-slice of bread went down so quickly. But there were those who had supplies of canned goods and cookies, etc. There were those who knew how to locate things at the stations more quickly and ingeniously than the others. But they didn't share it with the others. They devoured it in front of everyone.

There was discussion about the unequal distribution of food. Some, even women, openly stated they were hungry. That was something. I can still see the bitter, taciturn face of one woman sitting across from me who had swallowed her small piece of bread in one gulp. Then she had nothing to eat until evening, and she had eaten nothing that morning. But in other corners of the car sat groups who ate uninhibitedly; they were playing a provocative game of private life.

Words were exchanged. It had an immediate effect. The boss was summoned and there was more gruyère—and the well-off kept their supplies better concealed.

The landscape flattened. We had been in the cattle car for two days and two nights now. That night I joined the group of German emigrants, who proved to be kind people. Everyone was struggling to find a place for the night. They arranged it so I could join them. During the day I could sometimes sit on a bench they had constructed from their luggage. And there were crumb cakes and cheese for me. I had gotten used to lying at night on a blanket that belonged to my friend's wife. I was astonished when she asked for the blanket for a sick old lady in the car. I'm a sick old lady, too, I thought—but I wisely swallowed my words.

It rains outside without stopping and we try to find the best

Alfred Döblin

way to kill time. Those with books, read. Some play cards. Our space, which up to now has been living room, bedroom, and dining room, has a new function: it's a drying room. The ladies have decided to use one corner for drying small articles of linen, wet coats, and other clothing.

On the evening of the third day we arrive in Capdenac, a large station. Many trains stop here, including military transports, and life as a rule is happier here. The air is warmer, Midi air.

Whether it's the many smiling people, men and women, soldiers and civilians, or the fact that we have escaped the prison of our train, or the strangely sweet air—whatever—everyone feels much different here, elated, awake. We seem to be reclaiming ourselves. The gloom, the disquiet let up for a while.

What a scene! No one here seems to have heard of the war— and nothing at all of anything terrible, unimaginable; of catastrophe or defeat.

Strangely enough it is here, at the eleventh hour, that another rebellion takes place owing to the situation in the cattle car. An elderly man from our train is standing on a platform. We call him the League of Nations official. He's in indignant conversation with the commandant. It has occurred to the gentleman, as it has to us all, that not everyone in France views travel in a cattle car as the last word in luxury, so to speak. There are passenger cars in our train, even! It's enough to make anyone rant and rave.

A close circle forms around the two men arguing on the platform. In the end, the commandant marches off with martial gait to the office of the stationmaster. And when he returns he gives the interpellator a terse reply: there's a war on, monsieur, and there simply are no more passenger cars available.

A shrugging of shoulders, resentment and—we disperse.

I walk along beside the train thinking that the worst part of the trip is over. We'll get off in Cahors tomorrow, we hear, sometime during the day. It seems like an "arrival." There is animated conversation. The Midi landscape is also having its effect on us.

We don't complain as we now board the cattle car for the last time. It has gotten us through the country. We pat our horse on the neck in satisfaction. It wasn't all that bad. We'll trust ourselves to the old nag for one night more.

[ 41 ]

Nothing happens until the moment (at three in the morning) when the train stops and the doors are pulled open. Harsh lights flood the car. "Get down. The trip is over."

We are in Cahors.

I had carried a gas mask with me since Paris. In Tours someone had switched his mask with mine. I now purposefully left it behind in our cattle car as a memento, and to say that I considered the war up to this point, no, this part of the war, to be finished.

The war had only just begun.

## Cahors—Every Man for Himself

We had been dragged through the countryside with great difficulty. We had been saved. The end of all this was near. The roof over our heads would be torn off by the storm, the floor under our feet would collapse beneath us. We would be scattered to the ends of the earth.

We were taken to a long building not far from the train station. We immediately became suspicious when we saw its large, square courtyard; yes, it was another school, this time a girls' secondary school.

The dormitory was already occupied. We were given mattresses and blankets. Then we stretched out luxuriously on the floor and slept off the three days and three nights of the cattle car. But first we were offered warm bouillon, something obviously associated with war.

We were awakened early, however, by the sound of retreat, the droning of heavy, then heavier vehicles. At this we got up. We washed and shaved in the courtyard and sat down at tables set up in the refectory. We were Europeans again. We sat on chairs. We drank from cups. We enjoyed hot coffee and had milk, sweet condensed milk. We breakfasted as our great-grandfathers had.

The terror was over. We surmised that we had escaped the storm, and rejoiced. We had survived an adventure that we would later extol as miraculous.

The commandant positioned himself in the courtyard and summoned us together, a roll call. He announced to the group when meals would be served. (Many of us would not be here for breakfast the next morning.) We were allowed to leave the school, but only between two and three o'clock in the afternoon, the rest of the time was to be "for work." A puzzling remark. It caused a stir. But it was a military command and no questions were permitted. The commandant noted in passing that it would be undesirable for even more people to be in the streets with nothing to do. (The following week we read something that threw light on our commandant's order: there was a report from Bordeaux on the behavior of the newly arrived groups, on how they were conducting themselves in these hours of adversity, on how they were comporting themselves badly on the café terraces, to put it mildly, considering the gravity of the times.)

A loudspeaker sounded from the concierge's booth at the entrance to the courtyard. We gathered around it. Never before had we gathered around a loudspeaker the way we did during those days. We surrounded the thing, we crowded around it, we awaited its verdict.

It began to speak of a cease-fire. Everything was still in the initial stages. The formalities had not yet been decided upon. We understood—the victor wanted to hunt down its prey for a few days more. It was reported that Germany had received the French request for a cease-fire through the Spanish ambassador.

We get a better and better idea of what defeat means. Mighty France, with its powerful army, its colonies, its wealth, is capitulating. After one month of war. Just like in 1870. But what kind of light does this cast on the France of the recent past, on the France of 1918–1940? How could a world power of 1918 waste itself so!

The loudspeaker imparts another message, this time (finally) to us. The government will permit no further exodus of civilians. It forbids any further evacuation. Rail travel will be permitted only under special authorization. As automobiles are already out of the question owing to the gasoline shortage, this signifies an end to all nonmilitary travel. We have to stay where we are. At last a definitive word from above.

We loiter about the building and the courtyard. The heavy luggage arrives. Cars pull up on the street below. Soldiers and anyone else who wants to work form a chain up the steps and toss the sacks up to one another. We try to find out from the authorities what they know. But they don't know anything either.

Some high-ranking official has apparently gone to Bordeaux to find out what is going on.

A small private drama takes place before our eyes. It concerns the German family. What an effort this man must have gone to, to arrange things so skillfully that they had not yet been locked up, but taken along. But that was over now. Early that morning he had already appeared unsure, doubtful, and upset, pacing up and down the courtyard, listening. His two sons were also on patrol. That morning the commandant had had to turn over to the local authorities a list of persons traveling in our group. In this way the police stumbled on the four Germans' passports and nationality.

The man was soon summoned to the office. When he returned he acted distracted, but was optimistic, as was his habit. The police had taken exception to his presence, he said. But the Captain and commandant would surely protect him and his family. We weren't so sure. He would telephone Bordeaux soon, he said. An hour later he was summoned again. He staggered out of the office crestfallen. As he passed by me he whispered, "Now it's all over." He had been ordered to collect his things and be interned with his family. The police did not want to make an exception for him. And the leaders of our refugee train allowed it to happen.

The father and his two sons glumly dragged their extensive luggage into the yard. It had only just arrived. His wife didn't appear. They left accompanied by the police. The Captain, our sky-blue friend, shrugged his shoulders. The story could no longer be kept under cover. Orders were orders, the police here took things seriously.

But soon after dinner the man reappears in the company of one son and a soldier. He is subdued, he has only come for the rest of his luggage. Yes, they have a lot of luggage, that had caused bad blood already. He laments the fate of his wife. She has been housed in a monastery somewhere together with Nazis. Now, after they had supposedly gotten through the worst of it, she had been put into a camp.

But what are we to think an hour later, when the man again appears in the courtyard, smiling and this time alone! He is free. He joyfully informs everyone of this. The police have released him. They have told him they can't detain him. He doesn't want to stay in

Cahors at all, he says. He wants to go abroad with his family, to Mexico, he can furnish proof of this. And the police have allowed him to find lodgings somewhere in the city, and to arrange for his departure. The man is happy because he has been proven right. "Right," he says. We're astounded. Even our Captain is surprised. At this, the man says goodbye to us and goes in search of an apartment. I had known right off that he wasn't cast for a tragic role.

We saunter into town, the weather is pleasant, sunny. The streets are teeming with soldiers. Groups of civilians go from house to house asking for lodging. In several of the side streets long, empty tables and benches are set up, where refugees are being fed. We walk across a lovely plaza to sit in a café, as if this were peacetime. The terrace is closed. We chat for an hour, we think we'll be here for a while. We returned to our girls' school quite content, carefree. And as it was in Moulins: the wind has changed.

While we were contentedly strolling along, others were making trouble. My friend's wife started it. She was suffering from travel fever. She doesn't trust the peace. So she ran around the city and found out that one could pick up the special authorization the loudspeakers had mentioned that morning from the local prefect. It would take a day or two. She had applied for one immediately.

My friend, as distrustful as she, advises me to do the same. You can never tell how things are going to go. It is known that the soldiers who accompanied us here are leaving tomorrow.

By that afternoon, travel fever has seized the entire group. There is panic. We had just been sitting in a café, content to let things take their course. Now everyone is caught in the maelstrom. In addition, the official who was to go to Bordeaux has returned. He wasn't permitted to enter Bordeaux; the city has been closed to civilians. What will become of us?

Now, everyone begins making his own arrangements.

I deliberate. There are several possibilities. I can simply stay here and let come what may. I can find private quarters. I can search for my family in Le Puy. Staying here and waiting was something I immediately ruled out. Everyone was taking action, believed they must take action, and I behaved like a herd animal and believed that I, too, must "act."

I had assumed at first that we would remain here, and that my family would join me, but this morning the radio had said that no one is permitted to travel. So I must go to them. On top of which the radio announces that the fighting is approaching this region, Clermont-Ferrand and St. Étienne are mentioned.

It becomes clearer to me every minute: I must go and get them. By the time I go to the train station around four to inquire about trains, I have made my decision. However, I am not leaving here as I did in Moulins, because someone is forcing me to, but rather because I want to. I am alone and must act. That is required of me now.

Why was this desire in me so suddenly urgent, almost compulsive? External influences and considerations played a part. But there was something else that I knew nothing of at the time, a dark, secret telepathy. For I later found out that the situation in Le Puy had also become critical at precisely this moment. At this moment my wife decided to leave, decided to look for me.

I . . . perceived this. And it made my plan urgent—this and something else.

A train was leaving the next morning at six, going toward Le Puy, but only for those under official orders, of course. When I got back to the girls' school and sought out our infernal Captain concerning these official orders, he was busy with the German emigrant, to be sure, who had been released! He, too, wanted an official order. He mentioned overseas, Mexico, the United States, which he had already visited. His suitcases proved it. The Captain was sweating in the face of this demand. And the man was requesting an official order not only for himself, but for his entire family.

It took awhile. I don't know what happened. I only heard that the clever Captain passed the difficult matter on to the commandant. I am sure it went well for our unsinkable fellow sufferer.

Then it was my turn. But what official order was I to be obeying? The Captain chewed on his pen. Then he said quietly, "You received official permission to travel with the group. For that reason you are now returning to your family. I cannot write anything else. The main thing is that 'official order' be at the top of the page." And so I received authorization that "ordered" me to return to my family.

I found this piece of paper comical as, apparently, did he. But I had to have something in hand. The commandant signed it without any fuss. The thing was now there for all the world to see.

And as if I were a machine I took my newly won piece of paper and marched, with a speed that did not suit my usual languor, to the prefect together, as it turned out, with the irrepressible German emigrant, who already knew the way. The German had grandiose ideas. He talked about America and Mexico and whether he should take me with him to Mexico. (What a strange suggestion, I thought. But how would it appear three months from now?) The man said he had connections. It sounded unlikely. I am certain he carried out all of his plans, with wife and children.

I soon had a *sauf-conduit* in my pocket. It went amazingly smoothly. I had triumphed, it was going to work.

That evening, at my first and last meal in the dining room, I was overcome with regret and sadness—because we were all sitting here so peacefully, eating, and I heard no one say they were leaving the next day but my friend and his wife. They had gotten hold of a car in the city and would drive to Toulouse. There they would be picked up and taken to the wife's parents' house, where they would stay. With my friend's departure an essential reason for my remaining with the group was lost. But my journey remained a dark chapter. My friend talked openly to me about it at table and afterward. Once again everything was analyzed in excruciating detail. Leaving is a good idea—but would I arrive? Totally unequipped as I was? Before we went to bed he brought me canned goods, bread, and fruit for the trip.

My black briefcase, split at the seams, was lying by my suitcase. It held my thick manuscript. I had packed the shoes. Because I had to carry everything myself the next day, I put my manuscript aside; it represented only weight to me, and what meaning did its contents now hold? (I became aware not long after just how uncanny its subject was, how it continued to live on in me.) My friend took the manuscript. Before we said goodbye he repeated, "Think this over one more time. You can come with us."

But that wasn't my intention.

# 3

# In Search of My Family

## *The First Interludes*

I awakened very early. At five-thirty I was ready. When I crossed the courtyard and reached the sentry box, the soldiers were astounded that I wanted to go to the train station: "The trains aren't running." "Yes, they are. I have an official order." They continued to doubt me but wished me luck.

As in Paris, I dragged my heavy suitcase along myself, very slowly. I was alone in the train. It was a freight train with a few passenger cars attached. I sat down. My suitcase was overhead in the luggage net. The train left. It was finished. Adieu, Cahors. Adieu, the train from Paris.

I now set pen to paper and begin to describe this part of my journey—a journey out of a France defeated in mid-June 1940, shortly before the signing of the cease-fire agreement. I ask myself, after a brief overview: What is it all about? Is it worth writing it down, my journey from here to there, the difficulties that arose, the other events? Is that really of interest to anyone?

If I were to say it precisely, bluntly: it was not a trip from one French town to some other place, but a journey between heaven and earth.

From beginning to end this journey had a—I almost said a dreamlike, fantastic quality—but what I mean is a quality that was not only real.

It was "I" who made this trip from beginning to end (did it end?) But the traveler was not your usual passenger with his ticket.

The journey happened to me, with me, and over me, all at the same time. Only because it happened in this way do I undertake to describe the trip and its circumstances.

At first I simply traveled, sat in the train, and observed, as did Adam before Eve was created, that I was alone. I didn't speak. No one spoke to me. But that would not last for long because I was going "home" after all. I was filled with a sense of urgency.

I acted as if I were under official orders. The orders were not only on the paper I carried, but had been put there as an order at my wish.

At "my" wish? I always stumble over the words "I" and "my." On the one hand I certainly was part of the wish, and wanted to go. On the other hand I felt like my plan wasn't well thought out, I had gone over its weak points with my friend; it was not at all certain that, despite my papers, I would find trains to take me, automobiles were out of the question. And what would I do if things broke down in some totally unknown landscape, among people who didn't know me and might take me for a foreigner despite my passport, maybe even for a spy. And I planned to move north, in the opposite direction of the general escape route, toward the Germans?

I was aware of all of this, I felt I was doing the right and feasible thing. But one fact made it difficult: I had received no news from Le Puy for eight days, and when the Captain asked me, "Is your family in Le Puy?" it is true that I had answered "Yes," but I actually didn't know for sure, nor could I.

But all of these obstacles that troubled me had no influence on the "urge," on my urge to go and get my family. It is possible that I was rushing into the jaws of the enemy. I was prepared for it, as were others I spoke to in Paris and during the trip. This one or that one carried a revolver, to put an end to himself if he fell into the hands of the *Boches*. I was also prepared, but in a different way. Death towered above me and behind me, too, I looked into its jaws. But I refused to think about it logically and objectively. I felt bound hand and foot.

My will had been taken captive in a way that often infuriated me, had thwarted my conscious "I," forced it into a corner. It wasn't crippled. I was totally involved. But behind my urge to travel there was a dull defiance, an unfathomable seriousness, sorrow.

Defeat had arrived. Defeat, a major defeat, pushed its way into me. I went to meet it.

No, I didn't want to hide in Cahors.

By noon I was in Capdenac, at the station that two nights before had received us so pleasantly after our arduous journey.

The station had returned to its normal activity. I had to wait here for an undetermined number of hours in order to change trains. So I checked my bag at the counter and smoked a cigarette. I played tourist and sat down to watch what was going on.

Others were watching me. If you are alone for long on a platform peopled with a mix of military and civilians, a platform that itself is being watched, then you are being watched. There were tables set up in front of the restaurant, it was lunchtime. What should I do? I got up from my chair—who knew when I would get the chance to eat again?

Some train workers arrive. They sit down noisily at the tables. I, the loner—during the entire trip I carry the burden of being alone, which is already a mark against me, a suspicious sign—sit down on a vacant chair, it's a public place. Those sitting next to me tell me the seat is taken. I stand up. So it's not a public place after all. I can't protest, for I know I am alone and already dangerous as such, and would quickly be exposed as a "foreigner" in any altercation. So for a while I stand there in front of the restaurant, not saying anything; others are doing the same. They soon disappear. I must remain, for my train will be along at any time.

A while later, as tables are being reset and the swarm of train workers has subsided, I bravely sit down again at a table. The seats to my right and my left are free. Someone soon sits down across from me and asks for a menu. He begins talking to me. I answer in monosyllables so as not to betray myself. The first course passes without incident.

Suddenly, without warning, a young man who is sitting next to the first man addresses me, he is apparently a train worker. He sticks out his neck and fixes me with an unembarrassed stare. Only when I

[ *50* ]

return his stare and then turn my attention to my bread, does he say in German, with a French accent: "You speak German, no?" I am taken by surprise and don't answer. When he repeats his question, attracting the attention of those nearby, I shrug my shoulders, laugh, and say in French, "But you speak French. Why don't you talk to me in French?" He replies, "So you do speak German." I answer in French, "You hear that I am speaking French. What is it that you want?" He glares at me and doesn't reply.

My second course arrives. From my left, two gendarmes in khaki uniforms are weaving their way among the tables toward mine, heading straight for me with everyone looking on. They position themselves behind me. One gendarme bends down to me, taps me on the shoulder, and gives me a sign to follow him.

At the door of the restaurant he asks for my papers. My table is watching us intently, but we are quickly lost in the crowd moving back and forth in the station. I have several valid pieces of identification. I have my French passport and my orders. The two study the papers, question me, I answer. They keep my papers, one of them disappears with them somewhere, the other stays with me, not letting me out of his sight. I am allowed to finish my lunch. My fellow diners turn their backs to me. The young man who wanted to sound me out as well, he too turns aside ostentatiously. I am then summoned by the gendarme who is guarding me and led into the building. There, the first gendarme and a civilian are still examining my papers. The gendarme finally marches up to me, my papers in hand, gives them to me, and says briefly, gruffly and contemptuously: "In order." He waves me on my way.

I take my papers compliantly and again walk to the platform, close to where my bag is. All the tables are empty now. They are being carried away. It's a bad thing that has happened to me. It's nothing surprising in itself. The train stations are being watched, of course, and I'm conspicuous, alone and loitering about. Perhaps without even speaking there is something foreign about me in my dress, my posture, or expression. But when they discovered their mistake, they didn't apologize. The gendarme said: "In order. You can go."

At this station—it was, after all, the station at Capdenac that had seemed so sunny to us on our arrival—I bought a timetable. I kept this timetable for years. There was a train map on its cover. I used it day after day to locate where I was and where I wanted to go.

Where I was, I wasn't. I always wanted to be "elsewhere." My entire nature had changed.

I arrived in the small town of Rodez around evening. At first I was afraid of evening arrivals, for there were no hotel rooms free and I didn't know where to spend the night. But as time went on I learned there was always someplace I could spend the night, I had my coat and could always lie down on it. It is in the nature of night that it passes.

In Rodez I crowded to the exit with the others, and outside I noticed that the group split up: the smaller part set off somewhere on foot, the others gathered in front of a huge bus. Still hesitating, I was pushed over to the bus and had to climb on board. It was difficult to explain to the ticket taker where I wanted to go. When I said I wanted to go into town, to the center of the city to find a hotel, he became impatient. There were hotels everywhere, he said. Finally he pressed a piece of paper into my hand and turned to the next passenger. I got out somewhere, when the buildings got larger and others got out.

I found myself on an inviting square. People were walking about peacefully, even happily. It was a summer evening, a pleasant, somewhat cool summer evening. I was elated at the sight of several terrace cafés and decided that wherever I spent the night, I would return to a terrace table, with a cigarette in my mouth, a cup of coffee before me.

I lugged my suitcase into the first hotel. Nothing available. Into the second. The lobby swarmed with people. I couldn't even get to the reception desk. People there were arguing with the owner and the head receptionist. I did not plan to compete with them, my chances in such an argument were nil.

At another hotel the lady shook her head and said sympathetically that the best thing for me would be to try the "barracks." She told me how to get there. At that I left my bag at her hotel and sat down as planned on a café terrace.

A curious world. This small town was playing "peaceful summer evening." People on terraces drank their aperitifs, strolled up and down the streets. It got dark and the traffic increased. I liked the weak coffee. I stood up and left.

Yes, it was a happy crowd that passed by on the broad street to the left of the square. Lanterns burned, though they were dimmed. I was now on a lovely avenue. There were many young people, young men and young girls, neatly dressed, many walked arm in arm. I let myself be carried along by the crowd. It got brighter and louder ahead.

I reached a place in the avenue where it widened like a square. Incredibly, there was a country fair with booths, a carousel, sweet things to eat, and music. It fit this forgotten little town. I saw cars, they probably towed the booths, and behind them more booths. Or were they perhaps the barracks? Some people, including soldiers, were walking toward them. I followed.

Two young fellows in motorcycle outfits were standing in front of the barracks (yes, they were barracks). I saw beds inside, so these were refugee barracks. When I inquired about staying for the night, I was directed to a refined-looking man with a full beard. He led me to a barrack and showed me a bed. I could occupy it immediately. This was settled promptly, no papers were required and no questions asked. The room had a wide central aisle, there were compartments or cubicles to the right and left, open wooden partitions, each with four beds—two bunk beds—each bed equipped with a straw mattress and blanket.

I lay down. During the night one other person entered my "compartment," undressed silently, and fell onto a bed across from me. For a while I could hear the cheerful noise from outside, could hear women and children whispering as they moved along the aisle and stopped somewhere near me. My neighbor, a soldier, got up around five in the morning, dressed, and disappeared without a word. We could wash behind the barracks. I got up around seven.

Outside were the fairground and the street. Today it looked more like there was a war on. People were milling about, alone and in groups, with and without luggage. Normally it didn't look like this here, normally there wouldn't be so many heavily loaded cars. What should I do now? How should I proceed?

I sat down in a café, brought my suitcase over, observed the square. The bus had stopped there last night; I wanted to go to the train station.

A man with a suitcase sits down at the next table and asks where I want to go. He says I can try inquiring about train schedules, but not even the stationmaster knew when the trains would leave. Anyway, if I wanted to take the bus to the station, I had to cross the square and walk up the other side of the street. I would see the buses there.

The man did not trust any form of public transportation. He stood at the curb, his suitcase on his shoulder. He succeeded in getting a car to stop; he climbed in after a short discussion. He knew where he was going—it wasn't far. I walked up the street he had pointed out. Buses were standing there. Mine was to leave in half an hour. As I am standing there a group of people with a great deal of luggage gather near me. A bus drives up. The driver and his assistant climb onto the roof. The luggage is tossed up to them. I am surprised that they are in such a hurry, and ask when it is leaving for the station. The fat driver, standing bent over on the roof, his face red from exertion, looks down at me in disbelief. Then he stands up and turns to his assistant behind him, who is stacking the bags. "He wants to know when we are going to the station." And they both laugh. I am given to understand, as he bends down again and lifts up a heavy bag: "No, monsieur, we are driving directly to Toulouse."

I wasn't prepared for this. I hadn't known, of course, that there was a bus connection between Rodez and Toulouse. But even so— why should I go to Toulouse?

I become confused and push my way out of the crowd. I envy these people. They're traveling straight to their destination. I stand to one side for a while and watch the bus fill up. Then the aisle fills up. But why should I go to Toulouse?

I turn to a man who is cleaning another bus. "When will the bus to the train station finally come?" And then add: "I want to take any train going in the direction of Le Puy." The man thinks it over. I get out my schedule with the red map. We stumble on the name Severac. In that direction, he says. And I could get there on a bus leaving here in fifteen minutes. I didn't think it over for long. Ten minutes later the bus appears and I get on.

It begins to rain along the way. I get out at a small station. The station is dead. No one knows if and when a train will depart. I should wait around to see.

I look around outside. A man comes out of the station and walks energetically across the square. He looks as if he knows the place. I follow him, ask him about a car or a bus. He is of the opinion that both are creatures of the imagination. If I don't believe him I can ask someone nearby who owns a car, he says. He'll take me there himself.

The man isn't home. His wife answers the door, cheerful and very polite when I say that I will be able to come to an agreement with her husband on the price. She asks me to take a seat in the living room. The man appears and sizes me up. I can already envision him calling a gendarme, who will ask me for my papers. Once again I've made a stupid mistake. But the man is interested only in the price. He begins to calculate the distance in kilometers, the cost of the gasoline. His wife looks at the notebook he's toting up figures in, and he notices that she's pushing him to make a deal. But he doesn't. He gets to a point where he pauses, and even his wife can't help him. It would be possible, he says, to get to Le Puy, if not today, then tomorrow. But first: he could get stuck on the way, owing to the congestion on the highways, and, second: the Germans. He could be captured by the Germans. They are no longer so far away, he says.

So that's how it stood, and his wife agreed.

I thank them and return to the station. There is nothing to eat. The lunch hour is long past. I divide my chocolate and eat two cookies and one of the confiscated oranges. I'm not hungry.

## I Want to Force It

As I'm sullenly sitting around with the rain coming down, more and more people appear and I have the feeling a train is expected. And I'm right—a train going in the other direction. I cannot find one person on the platform who has any real information about the departure schedule. I am finally informed that if I were to take the train now coming in, and go to this or that station, I might then be able to find a car, maybe even a train, going in the right direction—before I would find one here, at any rate, where nothing at all is happening.

As I am fed up with waiting around, and it seems to me that things have already fallen apart, which is what my friend had warned me about in Cahors, I join the others on the platform and a half hour later am sitting in the train. It is indeed a train, a moving train, though moving in the wrong direction, it's true. It gets dark quickly in the rain. And it is night when we get off, a gloomy night. I watched it coming in horror. I'm afraid of the night, for where am I to stay? And I am right, my fears are justified.

I am standing on a small, dark platform. The people near me slip away. The ones who had advised me to take this train rather than wait have all gotten off along the way. My question: "Is there a train going in the direction of Le Puy?" is answered with a shrugging of shoulders and a shaking of heads. I'm so meek that I say "in the direction of." A car or a bus is out of the question. Who told me something like that? they ask.

And when I've finished with my questions I have to leave the tiny station, they are locking the doors. I attract neither attention nor interest here.

I stand outside the door with my suitcase and consider what I should do. I've been taken for a ride, but I've been reckless, irresponsible about travel. Then I realize that it is not the time to be making observations, I must do something. I'm already caught up in a miserable little game. The last people from the train are disappearing before my eyes into town. It is best to get up and follow them.

I collect my suitcase and set off. I see in front of me a dark place, or better said, a nocturnal, tree-lined path that apparently leads to the town to which I have been enticed. After a few minutes of stumbling along in the mud, in the rain, with my intolerably heavy bag, there is a fork in the path, and from that point on I can see nothing at all.

There are no automobiles, I hear no voices, the people have disappeared like ghosts. I walk on for five minutes more in total darkness. It continues to rain. Then I set my bag down under a tree. I do this so that I can throw the heavy winter coat I carry on my arm (I have my summer coat on) over me to protect me from the rain. This doesn't work because of my sodden hat, I can't find a place for it. So I drape the coat over my shoulders and stand there for a while, indecisive.

I could perhaps just continue marching briskly along, walking in the muck between the two rows of trees. But my suitcase has become very heavy, I can't carry it for long. And it is the middle of the night. I have trouble enough maneuvering dimly lit city streets owing to my weak vision. Whether I take one more step or not depends on my resolve.

As I stand there soaked by the pouring rain I think: What would I feel under normal circumstances, in a forest, at night? But I'm unable to escape the present. The trees, the rain, the night won't allow it. These are not, after all, normal circumstances. I have only the pragmatic desire to get out of the wet and to go somewhere with my suitcase. If only someone would see me here, I think. My situation is already comical, silly. I'm behaving like a total fool. But what have I done that was foolish? I couldn't stand around forever at the train station, waiting for a train. I had to do something and now I've done it. It's not the worst thing I could have done. I've gotten lost. I'll turn around.

I am quite alert, wary and overwrought. I'm very worried. It seems cruel to me how I get lost, how everyone sends me first here, then there. But that's the way life is. The word is: every man for himself.

I've had it with trees and pouring rain. I pick up my suitcase again and walk back. I'll find my way back to the train station. It promises me shelter.

I walked back to the closed station and settled down there for the night. There was adequate protection from the rain. The next day I would take the first train I could find back to the station that my impatience had driven me from.

This night passed slowly, slowly. I doze through the hours, leaning back on a step. An inn lay perhaps fifteen minutes away, I was sure of it. But I couldn't make it there.

I re entered this not very attractive existence at dawn, as a group of men, one of them in uniform, materialized before me I got up. They nodded to each other casually in greeting. They sat down next to me and ate. They were waiting for the first train and weren't surprised that I was already there. Anyway: who was surprised by anything anymore? There were too many trials and tribulations. Each person dealt with his share. We all looked on sympathetically when one of our fellow human beings was knocked down and got up again.

Our train arrived in semidarkness. That it arrived at all, and so early, seemed to me an omen of a better day to come. I took it back to the station I had left the day before.

Yes, it was a better day. I was wet and freezing—and found hot coffee. I was given a piece of dry bread. All of this was unbelievably good. The little room was lit by a lamp. People talked. I was among people again.

A train going in my direction would depart only that afternoon. This time I located a rail worker. He confirmed it. This time I would not experiment. The hours refused to pass. I wanted to, had to, continue my journey, and I wasn't being allowed to.

The hours won't go by, it is only eleven in the morning, I again left my bag at the station and went in search of a car. There were garages, but either the owners weren't there or there wasn't enough gas. In the end I ran into the woman whose home I had visited the day before. She recognized me immediately and was surprised that I was still there. She wasn't as friendly as she had been yesterday. She quickly disappeared and I decided it was better to go back to the train station.

It's noon, I haven't gotten any farther. I am sitting alone at the station. I can scarcely believe that yesterday morning I was in Cahors. That was yesterday! Maybe they're all still sitting at the girls' school. I want to go on, but I'm not allowed to. I feel ever more strongly and fearfully that this is not about the trip to Le Puy, but about me, myself. But I don't want to believe this. It's as if I've been lassoed; I struggle against the snake that entangles me. I study the train schedule ceaselessly, so that it will give me a sign. It's an obsession.

Then a man wearing a strange outfit appears on the platform. He has a rope across his shoulders and each end is tied to a heavy suitcase. He's in his early fifties. He seems intelligent. He looks pale and worn out. He's wearing a yellow summer overcoat with a wrinkled, dirty collar. His boots and pants are spattered with mud. He unharnesses his burden on the bench next to me. Then he sits silently for a while, bent forward with his arms on his knees, recovering. A trackman is crossing the tracks, the man calls out something to him. He asks about the trains. I hear that he wants to go in my direction.

We've already exchanged glances and recognized each other as men belonging to the same circle. I start the conversation. No, he doesn't want to go to Le Puy, but to Mende. We'll get a train there if we're lucky. I've lowered my expectations. I'll be happy with the least progress. We knock at the stationmaster's door. He proves to be an affable man. He asks us for our authorization to travel by train. He is satisfied with our papers. My companion is an industrialist from Paris whose firm was evacuated. He is coming from Toulouse, where he has left his wife, and wishes to visit his mother in Mende. He is hoping she is still there. There is no doubt that she is still there. He doesn't know where she lives, it's true. But he will find out. So he too is searching for someone. The stationmaster gives us the good news that there will be an extra train to Mende scheduled for that afternoon. It will arrive toward evening. How I proceed from there is another story. A matter of luck, he says.

We remain together for the rest of the journey. The train fills up. The people riding with us are refugees. An elderly couple relate the experience of how they walked from Paris to Orleans with many others, how they lost their belongings—or left them behind—one after the other along the way. Now, they said with gallows humor, they had only paper on them, paper money. They are looking for close relatives. They hope to stay with them. But are they still there? They will try it. It is getting dark. My companion tells about the barrack he stayed in overnight in Rodez. I know them. He points at the barracks we are passing in the train and laughs. I would like to spend the night there, he says.

We are in Mende.

## Fighting the Demons

The train empties. A swarm of people move down a hill toward town. We form into a tight, closed column. There is no reason for me to drag my suitcase along. I don't want to repeat the mistake of yesterday. I do as the others do: we put our bags in the open anteroom of the station, building a kind of suitcase fortress. There is no one to guard them. But we trust that the station will be closed at night.

As we turn right onto a large street and cross a bridge, we see a sign hanging from a pole that reads *Centre d'acceuil* (tourist information), with a hand that points toward town. But the sign has been turned around and we can't tell which direction is the correct one. A soldier who is directing traffic on the bridge—there are many soldiers here—says the *Centre* is located down the river. But he becomes unsure when others contradict him, saying it's located in town. So we proceed to town, up the main street. In the darkness we can glimpse only a few gardens and houses. My traveling companion, in search of his mother, goes off to the left where he discovers a large hotel. I am standing on a square that several streets feed into. It is obviously one of the town's hubs of activity. The *Centre* should be in the dark street to my right. I follow a group of bicyclists and end up in front of a building, the lower floors of which are lit up. People are crowding at the door. Two men on scooters are directing traffic.

I get in line. As I enter—everyone is admitted without questions—I find myself in a long, low dining hall with benches and tables where men, women, and children are eating. Two rows of people stand behind the benches, waiting. No one calls attention to himself or looks at the others. These are, for the most part, common people, young and old, with a conspicuous number of youth between sixteen and eighteen. (I later find out they have arrived, most of them on bicycles, from occupied territories because they fear being captured by the Germans and forced into labor in factories and elsewhere.) There are also several well-dressed men and women.

The food is served on tin plates. It goes very quickly. There are noodles with gravy and potatoes, and a small slice of bread. Several requested a double helping and got it. The servings were small.

Then I had finished eating and once again stood on the dark street. It was no longer raining. The night problem began.

I moved toward the central square. A group of bicyclists had gathered there; some were going to the *Centre d'acceuil*, others in the direction of the train station. A policeman had told us there was a refugee shelter in that direction. I took the way back with the others. This place wasn't bad. Not as bad as yesterday.

At the bridge everyone turned right onto a wide highway that ran along the river. I could see nothing to the right or to the left. But there was a crowd walking that way. Finally we went through a dark portal and entered a garden or a park. Then we went up steps and it turned out that we had entered a large stone building, an official building, maybe a school. It was ten o'clock at night.

As we start up the steps, others are coming down them, angry and disappointed, and call out: "It's no use. It's filled up!" We go up nevertheless and find the stairwell full of people. There are doors to the left and right: the one to the left is open, but is just being closed, and two soldiers stand guard before it. When I see some people continuing up the stairs, I join them and end up in a large, very long, wide corridor that is being explored by others like myself. It really is a school, all the doors are locked, but there are benches in the hall and people are sitting there, putting away their things. They are making preparations for the night. Not a bad idea. We have a roof over our heads. I found a bench farther on and, spreading out my coat, lie down on it. People moved back and forth. I began to doze off. Suddenly I see the men in front of me get up, hurriedly collect their belongings, and run down the steps. Then others rush off without my being able to tell what's going on. So I, too, get up, take my coat and reach the second floor just as the door to a large room is being unlocked, many men are running toward it. The door didn't open. Different keys were tried. Finally the door was given a shove, it flew open and lights were turned on inside. It was a large dormitory with four rows of beds. People ran wildly through the room to find a bed. In two minutes the room was filled. I felt relieved when I sat down on a bed. I took off my cold, wet clothes, finally removed my soaking shoes and socks. We had wool blankets. I was warm again.

Around five in the morning the room gets noisy. Instead of rejoicing in having a bed, these fools set off once again. Around seven, I thought, I will do the same.

It was no longer raining. I went downstairs and read the announcements, which confirmed that this was indeed a school I had spent the night in. I passed through a garden and found myself on the highway that ran along the river. I wanted to inquire about my bag. It was in the anteroom at the station.

Throngs of troops were moving toward the station, infantry, heavily loaded down. The square in front of the railroad station was filled with military vehicles. People blocked the entrance to the station. I was the only civilian.

I forced my way through. My suitcase stood there with two others; the suitcase fortress of yesterday had been torn down. Now I had to find out today's train situation. I had no illusions. I listened to the soldiers. Where they were coming from, where they were going.

To my horror the name Le Puy came up again and again in their conversation. They were coming "over from Le Puy." The town itself was still open.

It will be difficult to find a train or a car going north, I thought, if they are coming from there.

Where were they going? Some said to Tarbes, others to Perpignan. Is this flight, retreat, or do they intend to stand and fight at the Pyrénées? Will troops be sent to Africa? The soldiers are happy, they are under orders.

I remain at the station for an hour. The troop trains are being made ready. Then the station shuts down. The ticket counters are closed. Lone civilians appear in the anteroom, look around, ask a few questions and leave.

I must find a car. I wearily begin walking the town's few streets. I inquire at all the garages. I have known the answer since yesterday: we don't have any *essence*; if you get the gas, we'll take you. I offer money to no avail. I spend the morning making inquiries. Military vehicles are rolling by the entire time, truck after truck, car after car, transports, spotlights, ambulances, racing along the main street, one after the other. They take the street down to the bridge and then turn right along the river. Now the soldiers are also directing traffic, soldiers and traffic police.

The town I am pushing my way through is filled with fleeing civilians who, like myself, are searching. They knock and ring at every house. They are looking for a place to stay. I do not intend to remain here. The sight of the soldiers, the droning of the vehicles (which has followed me since Moulins) frighten me. I want to go to Le Puy.

And I cannot. I cannot get there. At every street crossing I find a sign with an arrow to Le Puy. Sometimes the arrow points right, sometimes left. It is 110 kilometers away, that isn't far. But how am I to get there?

At the prefect's office is the notice: gasoline coupons are being turned in. As I make my way back from the center of town to the train station, I encounter the man who yesterday had been my traveling companion. He is now an elegant gentleman, is wearing new clothes, is taking a walk, contentedly smoking his cigar. He has located his mother, at the finest hotel in town. He's doing fine. He doesn't have much hope concerning my intention to leave here. But there is always a chance. Perhaps a car can be found after all. Where will I spend the night? I don't yet know, I say. Last night, in a school. Yes, everything is taken.

After this I stand on the bridge, my heart full of bitter resentment, resentment at the soldiers who are racing around, for whom

I have to make room, and because of whom I cannot leave this place.

But I am not yet ready to lay down my arms. I have been forced onto this path, I will prevail.

Ever since my encounter with the gendarmes at the station in Capdenac I have had the dark, even desolate feeling that I am being led into misfortune, into bad luck.

And then I remember that on the evening before I left Cahors my friend advised me (his wife is the daughter of a former prefect): if I encountered difficulty anywhere along the way, I should turn to a prefect. They are educated, polite people, he said, not just clerks. What can it hurt? I think. Perhaps he's right.

At the prefecture I am received politely and taken to the office of a young man who is apparently the underprefect—an echo of my former existence, to be so received. He listens to my lament, nodding sympathetically. I must be familiar with the gas situation, he says, it's a problem everywhere. And as for the train: he wishes to assist me in as far as he can, given the schedule. But when I ask him if he could perhaps telephone Le Puy and ask to speak to my wife, or leave her a message, he politely refuses my request. The telephone cannot be used for private calls; the lines are already overloaded.

As he sits there in his chair, looking peacefully out the window as he talks to me—the man is living in his own world, little has changed for him, the chaos has remained remote—I think over what I should ask of him. For in all probability I will not see him again soon. I say (I say it, but don't believe it): in the event that I cannot get farther north, could I ask for permission to return to the south? He nods and finds that understandable and calls his secretary. The conference is ended. He wishes me luck with the greatest of civility.

In the secretary's office a woman takes a sheet of paper and asks me where I wish to go. It was all impromptu, senseless, I hadn't wanted this. It was an absurd situation. I named Cahors, from which I had come—and Toulouse. Whatever name occurred to me. The paper was stamped, signed, and I put it in my pocket—and was once again on the street. It was ridiculous, I had gotten permission to return from where I had come! In my wildest dreams I had no intention of going back. What would I do now?

And as I am standing there by the river, already tired—it is almost noon, I've been on my feet for five hours and cannot remember when I last ate—with the current swirling around the bridge supports, I feel a confusion, a dizziness, a strange fear in myself. The lasso, the rope. . . .

What is it, what's happening with me? I am confused and the confusion fills me up and carries me along. Everything in me shuts down. I have been trapped in a magic circle.

It again occurs to me (accompanied by a deep-seated fear): this has nothing to do with your family, but—with yourself. Why? This isn't about me. I was comfortable in Cahors. I was not destined to just calmly remain there. I was destined to be thrown onto the highway, out of my safe asylum, to stand here on this bridge.

Why? Why are you still standing around here thinking you will do this or that? That isn't what it's about. You won't get away from here. . . .

Then I detach myself from the bridge and think, I want to sit down by the water. As soon as I see a rock or a bench, I will sit down. The military vehicles are still rolling by without end. This infernal chase will not end. I pass by the school where I spent the night.

And then a few meters farther along—are barracks, some of stone, most of wood. Men and women are moving among them. There is a sign on one of the barracks: "No entrance." I had heard in town that there was a refugee camp here. I feel sluggish and think: I'd just like to sit down somewhere—to lie down.

## The Refugee Camp

A path leads up to the barracks. The rain has turned the ground to sludge. Women are standing by the trees, filling bottles with water at a fountain and washing cups. I ask where the office is. It is to the right, in a barrack. Two civilians, a man and woman, take my papers. Then they whisper to each other and point to something in my passport. I know: it is my birthplace, Stettin—Germany. They question me. I confirm what they ask. I have once again been trans-formed into a beggar. But finally I hear the words "In order," and am handed my papers, my criminal file. A stout young man, a Belgian, takes me to a barrack.

Boards have been laid down in front of each door because of the mud. We balance ourselves, tottering across them to my destination. The glass doorpanes are broken. Inside, a long wooden table stretches the entire length of the room; it is accompanied by backless benches. Everything is constructed of unfinished wood. To the right and left are cubicles, closed off by dark blankets. The man with me pulls back one of the curtains and asks if there is room for one more person. Finally, a bunk is found for me in a cubicle. It has, as do all the others, four beds—two bunk beds, a window, a rustic table in the middle, and a small bench. The lower bunk on the left, I am told, is occupied by an old woman.

She soon appears. I have already seen the old woman at the table in the barrack, dressed in a black dress, sitting alone with a bitter, even evil face. She was sitting by herself on one side of the long table, staring straight ahead. I am assigned the other lower bunk. The old woman looks at me. We exchange a few words. I appear to have found favor with her. She shows me where I can hang up my things. Though it was better, she said, not to hang them up at all, but to spread them out over the upper bunk. We didn't need anyone else in here. And sure enough, she had also claimed her upper bunk. Didn't I have a suitcase? Yes, it was at the station. Where at the station? In some corner or other, I said. She looks at me, shaking her head. I'll probably never see it again, someone has long since taken it, she says. What was in the suitcase? I say: underwear, clothes, books. She continues shaking her head. She marvels at me. She possesses only what she is wearing. She doesn't even have an extra blouse. She has been here for weeks. Where am I coming from? I think to say: I am a naturalized Swiss. She is satisfied with this, goes out and sits down again at the long, empty table, alone.

I look around the cubicle. The window doesn't close. I fear there will be a draft at night. The space smells of turpentine and eucalyptus, the old woman coughs, she has asthma, obviously emphysema, takes medicine. The bed—a straw mattress covered by a linen blanket and two wool blankets. The upper bunk is so close to the lower that I can sit on the lower only if I bend over. And it is difficult to sit on the wobbly, narrow little bench. So I stretch out on the bed for fifteen minutes. I don't know what will happen next. It looks as if I'm stranded.

I go to get my suitcase. It's right where I left it, undisturbed. And early that afternoon, as I slowly leave the camp again to go into town—I see a large sign on the other side of the highway, with a big poster reading MAY 16TH. I go over to it.

May 16. That catastrophic, fateful day—that's when it all started. Strange, that I encounter this date. What's with May 16, what's it about? A "Circus Bureau" is announcing a performance. It is The Only Circus Without Illusion.

I stand there for a long time, amazed at the poster. "Amazed" is a weak word. Where did the poster come from? Why has it been put up here, right in front of my nose?

It knows something about me. The poster looks innocuous, but isn't. The poster wants to give me a sign. It's the warning bell: *Open your eyes*.

Strange. Should I believe it? It really says "May 16." The circus played in town, of course, the poster was left behind, but—that the poster should be hanging here and catch my eye.

"Circus Bureau." On May 16 I ended my work in my "bureau." My "bureau" is being called—a circus. A bitter verdict, but—not a false one, really. The Only Circus Without Illusion. Mockery. A strange poster hanging here that no one pays attention to.

I cross the bridge and move up the long street. Direction signs point to Le Puy. I consider how long it would take me to walk the 110 kilometers without a suitcase. I figure it would take thirty hours on level ground. If I walk six hours a day I will be there in five days. In five days. I picture myself walking, sleeping outdoors.

It occurs to me to telegraph Le Puy. I could at least do that. My hands are not totally tied, after all.

I stand in line for over half an hour at the post office, for the post office is a public locale, well frequented, a place that many people have in common. The mischievous demon that is toying with me has limited power here. I spend a long time here because the telegram has to be formulated correctly, it must pass through the hands of the police and be stamped. I write on the form: *I am in Mende, cannot get any farther, my wife should telegraph*. There was nothing else to say. Perhaps my wife would find a car and would be here tomorrow or the day after. She knows Le Puy; it won't be as hard for her as it is for me. I spend the rest of the day wandering aimlessly about town, until six when dinner is served at the camp.

The old woman makes room for me beside her on the bench. She tells me that after each meal I must wash my own cup and put it in the box on my table. I must also put into the box bread I don't eat, wrapped in paper so it won't dry out. She mothers me.

We ate on tin plates, got a spoon and fork but no knife. I used my old pocket knife to cut with. The food was carried out in vats and bowls. A joyful sight, steaming food. We are served hard beans, but they were hot, and I swallowed them down gratefully. One or two potatoes were tossed onto the empty plate and a small piece of cooked beef, more often fat than meat.

That evening as I walked up and down in front of the camp I debated with myself: What now? What's my destination? Have I come all this way for this?

## Last Efforts

And then morning comes, the day has arrived when perhaps I will get word from Le Puy. At noon I go to the post office. The woman at the counter tells me that telegrams have arrived, but there was no clerk to process them.

By the time I leave the post office, the wild chase of the military trucks, of retreat, has taken on a frightening aspect. Civilians are banned from the main street. The rolling and rumbling of the powerful vehicles is something awful. I couldn't sleep all night because of it. They thunder by the camp. There is no end to them.

We've been deserted.

And then, as I cross the street toward the square where the town hall stands, to the other side of the river of retreat, I stumble upon a strange scene. Soldiers are gathered on an unpaved section of the square. They are shoveling. A noncommissioned officer watches over them. They are digging a shelter. The soldiers are answering the civilians' questions. They don't know why the shelter is being built. I have seen such dugouts along the way here, not far from town in the open, in the underbrush. They are probably there for retreating soldiers to take cover in and fight. Civilians gather around the soldiers, they are upset. No one understands why trenches are being dug when a cease-fire is being negotiated.

I turn into the street with the sign, LE PUY, 110 KM. And there—stands a bus! I walk over to it, ask the man who is cleaning it where it is going, and to my astonishment find it is going to a station between Le Puy and Mende. I could get a connection to Le Puy there.

And I've run all over town questioning every Tom, Dick, and Harry, and no one has mentioned the bus!

When would it leave? Around three in the afternoon. Today? Of course.

At this news I run back past the soldiers to the camp. I'm confused. This is wonderful. I could even be there today. I will be there. It occurs to me that I should reserve a seat. I go back, the man is still at the bus. He says it is not necessary to reserve a place, I need only to be there a half hour beforehand. Then I see two soldiers standing idle in front of a restaurant across the way, go up to them and ask if they will get my suitcase from the camp for a few francs. They set off immediately. They should be back in half an hour.

But I can't get across the bridge.

A fortress of cars has piled up here. It's a traffic jam. I hear screams. I see a big car lying right across the walkway, resting against the railing of the bridge it has hit. They say someone has been hurt or killed. I don't want to know anything about it. I don't want to know anything about this town. What am I doing here? It frightens me that an accident has occurred here. It is a bad omen.

In the camp, they are sitting down to eat. My neighbor, the old woman, is sorry I am leaving. Whom will they room her with now?

And then, as I dash from the table back into town, traffic is moving again and the miserable military transports are rattling along, rattling and thundering.

But the walkway on one side of the bridge has been closed, and a dead man is lying there, a civilian, an elderly man. His face, turned to the left, is yellowish-white, covered with blood and dirt. Dirt and blood cover his brown, torn jacket. Only his right leg is stretched out. His left—has been thrown onto his body, in its trouser leg. His thigh must have been crushed and broken. His left foot lies on his stomach, still in its shoe. A car must have sped onto the walkway, crashed through the railing, and crushed him. He has been tossed onto the bridge in the midday sun.

An incredible sight. A sight that turns everything dark, that illuminates the bright day with its darkness.

Alfred Döblin

# The Gorgon's Head

This man would no longer be going anywhere. His day's work is done; he would not go about it again. The military trucks continue with their war. The man is swept aside with the mud in the street. This is how we are. But I must get by somehow. There is nothing for me at the post office. I meet the two soldiers at the camp. I notify the office of my departure. The three of us set off.

The soldiers make a major detour. I realize that this has to do with their tip. They take turns carrying my bag. My bus is already on the street. The soldiers accept their pay. I get my ticket and pace up and down in front of the bus. My heart is pounding, my mind is not clear, I am torn with doubt. The last few days and this town have taken their toll on me.

Two civilians emerge from the restaurant the bus is parked in front of and come directly over to me. At five paces, I know they are policemen.

One tall one and one short one. The tall one has draped his light gabardine coat over his shoulders. The short one has no coat, his hands are in his pants pockets. Both are smoking cigarettes. They stop in front of me. Not a word, just a nod of their heads and a glint in their eyes—"You already know what it's about, don't you"—the tall one lifts the left lapel of his jacket a bit, then lets the lapel fall. I have nothing to say.

I could admit right away that I am a naturalized Frenchman born in Stettin, in Pomerania, in Prussia—in Germany They can't accuse me of anything, which makes me even more suspect. To the authorities the admission "I am a native Pomeranian. From Stettin, I lived in Berlin," says it all.

But it irritates them that I can present a French passport, that I am even in possession of a special authorization.

While the tall one gives my papers a superficial going-over— how nice that nature has provided the criminologist, in addition to his keen perception, with the ability to read—the short one engages me in conversation. He has pushed up close to me. He is bullying me. Where have I lived, where have I come from, where do I want to go, why have I come here, why was I born in this place and not that one? I tell the truth. My yes means yes, my no means no. He gives me

[ *69* ]

a look designed to penetrate my treachery. If the little criminologist would only tell me what my crime is. . . .

People have gathered around the bus, they are watching us, they know what's going on here—a spy? He's been caught. I wanted to take the bus, but the criminologists have caught me.

The tall criminologist with the coat around his shoulders has disappeared into the restaurant. I can imagine what he is doing; he's studying my papers, telephoning the camp, checking with his head-quarters whether I should be detained or not.

Just as the short one is about to knock me over—but I bounce back like rubber—the one in the coat rushes out of the restaurant. His face is expressionless. He can find nothing against me. I come from Stettin but am not a criminal. He gives me back my papers and says, "In order." And actually tips his hat. And the other one, the short one, exchanges a glance with him, and does the same. They point to the bus. "You can go to Le Puy." At which they disappear into the restaurant.

## Le Puy

We are passing through a mountainous, wooded, uneven landscape. Mende and its horrors are behind me.

The bus is full of civilians. But in the back sits a young soldier, a steel helmet on his head, his belongings piled up in front of him. This young man is obviously happy to be nearing his hometown. At one stop a gendarme looks into the bus. My bad conscience cringes. But this time it concerns the young soldier. An angry discussion develops between soldier and gendarme. The soldier refuses to get off the bus. But he doesn't have the proper discharge papers. The military officials want to put a stop to the intolerable abuse of "self-appointed leave." When others get involved, the soldier gets off after all. A nasty scene develops outside. The man, in a fury, throws his things at the gendarme's feet. He remonstrates, yelling that he, a soldier from the front, has been thrown off the bus. He wants to go home. He has that right. What was he supposed to do, take the two days to walk there?

Finally he sits down on a bench outside an inn and calms down. He disappears into the restaurant at the invitation of the proprietor.

It starts to rain. We travel on. There is thunder and lightning. Is this the weather that I will arrive in? I ask myself faintheartedly. The windows are curtained by, are covered with, water. Then the storm lets up—and suddenly a magnificent rainbow appears. I look at it with joy, with skepticism, I don't trust it. I can't believe in it. Toward evening we stop at a small train station. The connection to Le Puy? No. I'm not surprised by this; I would have been astonished to find it waiting. It had left a few hours before. The next one would depart early the next morning. I'm no longer impressed by jokes of this sort; I'm beginning to be bored by them. I find out there is a hotel here that still has available rooms. When I get there, there are no vacancies, but I am offered the bellboy's room in the attic.

It is raining, storming again. When I inspect the garret I think: It may be a garret, but it's a room, nevertheless. Can it be locked? In principle, but the lock isn't working. There is also something wrong with the dormer window over the bed: first, it's broken and second, it doesn't fit its iron frame. A single slim line of icy rain falls on the bed, but I can move the bed.

How strange the hotel appeared later that evening, when I left the attic room on my way to the front door. In June 1940, it was a peacetime hotel with summer guests relaxing there. Elegant ladies descended the stairs, powdering their faces as they did so. Downstairs, they made telephone calls here and there, laughing into the receiver. I found a large room with well-dressed families dining at tables with place settings and floral arrangements. Peacetime. The rumor of what had happened had not yet reached here. But I carried with me the journey from Tours, Moulins, Mende, the camp, the dead man on the bridge. . . .

The cold, stormy night passed. Crates were stacked around the room, equipment for a locksmith's shop. I added my shoes to the pile. They were thick with mud, both soles had worked themselves loose. I left them with the other junk and put on my other pair, the pair I had carried under my arm so carefully with my manuscript. I thought I would attempt a symbolic gesture, an invocation: I will now walk on new soles.

Many people were gathered in the dining room the next morning. It was pouring down rain, everyone drank coffee. Then we stormed the bus. I bravely joined the storm. It gave me courage, for I had the feeling the devil had his claws in me.

And now it was done and I was on my way to Le Puy. I had made it, by hook or by crook.

When we arrived at eight o'clock in the morning, it was storming and raining. We stopped on a large square, a pleasant place, with gardens, villas, modern buildings, not to be compared with where I had come from. I left my suitcase, my fellow sufferer, behind in the café we stopped at. I treated it worse than a dog, really. But it was a loyal animal and suffered its master's moods.

I then hurried to the boardinghouse where my wife and child were staying, across the square to the right, up a long street. It was supposed to be next to a rail overpass. I was once again wearing my winter coat over my summer one, as protection against the dreadful rain. Water streamed down from my hat.

There is no one on the street in this terrible weather. I walk and walk. Some houses have numbers, others don't. I am already on the far side of the overpass. A woman coming out of a door is familiar with the boardinghouse. I have to go back in the other direction. They will be astounded to see me like this. I haven't shaved for days. The mud of the camp still clings to my pants. My thick winter coat acts as a sponge, soaking up the wet.

Near the square I run into a postman; he tells me the house is set back a bit. I see the garden and the plain-looking house behind it.

Up the steps. The front door is unlocked. I knock. Someone opens the door. I introduce myself and ask to see my family.

A friendly woman looks at me, perplexed.

She says, "Oh, God, you are Mr. D." She shakes my hand and invites me in. An elderly man comes out of the next room and she introduces me: "This is Mr. D, the husband of Mrs. D, who lived here."

And then, as we sit down—my dripping coat is taken away, they apologize for the fact that I have arrived in such weather—I find out that my wife and child left three days ago. Yes, they've left. . . .

It had been peaceful in the town up to that time. But three or four days ago panic broke out. Soldier after soldier passed through the town. Seeing this, my wife and child left.

The woman raised her hands, gesturing: "And the gentleman has made a special trip to come and get the lady." I tell her where I have come from. The woman is amazed; she had read in the papers that the government officials had gone to Bordeaux. My wife had located a car and had gone there herself. She must have arrived already.

The woman advises me to get the details from a woman in town

my wife and I know. The man has listened to all of this sympathetically and offers to take me there.

As we are standing at the door, a bicyclist arrives, a postal
messenger. He delivers a telegram. It is—my telegram, the one I had
sent the day before yesterday from Mende.

## Crusoe, Stranded

The man led me through leafy streets. Our friend, who is from Paris,
isn't at home. Her landlady takes me to the kitchen and sits down
with me, stunned. What would my wife, Mrs. D, do now?

She tells me things about the town, about the day my wife left.
Finally our friend arrives. She is amazed. She takes me to her room. I
tell her what I have to tell. We sit down in her spacious room and she
gives me a coherent description of events. Essentially I know it all
already. New to me is how my family was provided for during those
critical days, and with what hospitality they were received.

I couldn't talk to the woman about my predicament for long.
Her face clearly expressed worry. And she talked about herself, her
concern for her relatives in the war zone; she has had no news for
some time. Tears.

To ease the tension a bit, we talked about the general situation.
She wants me to explain it to her. I tell her what I have seen. The lady
becomes bitter. She suggests I go to the authorities and get information from them. They know my friend and would be glad to help me.

And indeed they were, when I talked with them in the company
of our friend. They knew that my wife had wanted to go to Rodez. I
should go to Rodez immediately and inquire there about where she
had gone. So I was once again given a travel assignment, this time to
Rodez, where I had spent the night in the barrack of the man with
the long beard. I felt no emotion whatsoever when given this advice.

Because I agreed to what they suggested, I was given a permit
to go to Rodez. I am blessed with official authorizations. I was
advised to proceed there without delay.

Miss S walked through town with me. It was no longer raining.
Miss S said she would introduce me to a woman who lived here, who
would get me the gasoline I needed to get to Rodez.

I declared myself open to any suggestion. What did I wish, was
there anything I wanted? she asked. But I found it pleasant just to
walk along with someone and talk.

We came to a lovely square just as the streets were beginning to fill up. Miss S led me into a small, exquisite restaurant; it was doll-like, really more a bar and food shop than a restaurant. The walls were painted with charming pictures of the region. We drank coffee and then I was alone; Miss S went to get her friend.

I sat, bewildered, at the front window of the restaurant and looked at the square and knew that I had now achieved what I had wanted. I am now in the place I had sought countless times on my red train map, a place I no longer need to inquire about.

I had done it. I had not arrived on foot. I even had my suitcase with me.

A pleasant spot. I could stay here if I wanted. But I was being sent on to Rodez.

Miss S appears with a smiling woman dressed in black. The three of us have lunch. What the two ladies then discuss, first alone, and then in the company of the proprietress, is done without my participation. They want to spare me the details of their plan. It concerns getting a car and gas for the trip to Rodez.

The lady in black disappears, then reappears with a healthy-looking man in his late forties whom I immediately recognize as the driver and owner of the car which will take me to Rodez. Yes, they have located him; the car and the gas, too. They rejoice, causing me to rejoice. But he will not take me as far as Rodez, his permit will not allow that, he will hand me over to another car owner, together with the gasoline, which I was to pay for on the spot. Everyone is pleased. I don't believe any of it. The whole thing is a comedy. But I pay for the gas in order not to give myself away.

An hour later the man arrives in the car. My trusty suitcase has already been loaded. I throw that rain sponge, my winter coat, on top of it. I say a fond goodbye to Miss S. I think (but do not say): Why can't I stay here? She has tears in her eyes.

Now I am leaving this beautiful city. I must leave it. I was here for a few hours only, but it seems so familiar to me already.

## Return

I am sitting in a car, under way, my coat and bag near me. We are stopped often but our papers are in order. There are soldiers everywhere. We encounter groups of civilians, tramping along on foot.

Alfred Döblin

It is fantastic that I am riding in a car. I don't like it. Everyone else is on foot, everyone is waiting around and I am in a car? It doesn't suit me. I belong on the street.

The driver had intended to let me off on the way, to turn me over to another car owner, a friend of his. But he thinks it over. He wants to take me to Mende. I agree to this.

And so I arrive in Mende, down from the mountains, along the river, past the camp. I see the barracks in the distance and the people in front of them. I press myself deep into a corner of the car and am carried past them. We cross the jinxed bridge. Wire has been stretched over the break in the railing. The pavement has been cleared.

Then he says he can go no farther, because there is just enough gas to make the return trip. I say, "We agreed that you will find me another car and turn over the rest of the gasoline." Yes, but there is only just enough gas for the return trip.

And already he has put my suitcase on the street and gone to ask at the garages. He comes back to tell me that he has no more time to ask questions; I will find someone. I protest. But he has the car and—can leave.

I stand on the street in Mende with my suitcase, my heavy coat draped over it.

I drag my suitcase into a shop and then walk along the street looking for a hotel and run into—my two criminologists, big Castor and little Pollux. Laughing ironically, their hands in their pockets, the two men see me approaching, I can't avoid them.

"So," the older of the two calls out cheerfully, "I thought you were in Le Puy." This time they believe me because I show them the names in my notebook of the two police officials with whom my family traveled to Rodez. When the tall one reads these names he says, "You don't need to go to Rodez. You can find that out here. One of them, P, has just arrived."

What a stroke of luck! I think. And I have the driver, the swindler who left me here, to thank for this. "Go to the prefecture right away." The commissar there, a young, stocky, well-fed man, has a bandage on his left hand. He receives me cordially: "P was here, it's true. You must have passed right by him. He left a half hour ago for Le Puy. Strange, isn't it?"

We are amazed at my bad luck. I can laugh with him about it without any trace of bitterness.

[ 75 ]

The young commissar takes an interest in my predicament and it occurs to him to call Le Puy to find out the whereabouts of my family from the policeman who has just disappeared so abruptly.

The call is put through while I am there, the connection is made immediately. The official is already there, he left my family in Rodez, they wanted to keep going in the direction of Bordeaux, and should I want further information, he says, I should go to Rodez and ask.

The friendly commissar advises me to ask the man in the next room, the press liaison, about means of transportation. I thank him and go to the press man.

It was as I expected: he proved to be a tobacco-smoking, dour figure, a bored lawyer. How, he purred, should he know anything about transportation or gasoline? He was absolutely right. There was no way he could know that.

Outside is the old, familiar Mende. The two criminologists who sent me to the prefecture have gone their own way. I have to find a place for the night before it gets dark. I ask at several hotels. I already know it is hopeless. So—to the camp.

I want to take my suitcase with me. But where did I leave it? I put it in some shop somewhere. I'm confused, as though I'm drugged. Some shop somewhere . . . I look around at them. I can't remember. I didn't take note of the shop. It wasn't on this street. I entered the prefecture through another door. I circle the building, unable to get my bearings. There is nothing for me to do in the end but go to the camp without my bag.

And so I walk along the river again in my old outfit, my heavy coat draped over me. The bridge is behind me. There is the school where I spent the night. There are the first barracks.

To the right on the highway I am greeted by the old poster: May 16, Circus Bureau, The Only Circus Without Illusion.

Well roared, lion. Here I am again.

In the reception room I am reassigned my old space without much ado. Now I am here. I won't be lured away again so soon. I bury myself in the camp.

# PART II

# STRANDED

# 4

# In the Refugee Camp

## *A Note on Delusion of Reference*

Before continuing with my report I wish to make a comment. This story, as I said at the beginning, is not simply a report on significant events from the summer of 1940. I would not be relating these incidents were they not of a curious nature, eerie and upsetting. Why? In what does the abnormality consist?

Is it that one loses oneself in a war? But that happens in peace-time, too. And it is more unusual to find oneself in war than to lose oneself. Think about it: the post office isn't functioning, the trains aren't running, and if they are, there's no schedule to guide one. On top of which, we are all scattered about. How, then, are we to stay in contact with each other? How many things have to converge to make possible the miracle of two people, moving toward each other from different points in France, meeting during a war? "Toward each other" is overstating it. Actually they're on a voyage into the unknown, moving by sheer guesswork. And they pass right by each other, of course.

The author—I will speak of myself as if of someone else—seems to be puzzled by the fact that a poster is hanging on the highway across from his camp: "May 16. Circus Without Illusion." For May 16 was precisely the day on which he received the first shock of news and lay down his pen. Now, it isn't that he had to encounter precisely that poster. It's possible there were other posters hanging there, too, and that he chose that one as "relevant" precisely because he is unceasingly preoccupied with his own misfortune. Perhaps next to it there was one about a steam laundry, or one that announced the opening of a butcher shop. But then he would have taken the butcher shop symbolically also, as a reference to the war. He would even have made something of the laundry. And why shouldn't there be a poster hanging there from May 16? The circus really had been there. Or does the author believe that the poster was deliberately put there because of him, left there in anticipation of his arrival, to point ominously to his own May 16, in case he, the author, showed up there one day to bury himself in the camp? What a ridiculous idea. Who would have deliberately kept the poster from being torn down after May 16, or from being dissolved by the rain, so that . . . it would be hanging there at the end of June in order to have a profound effect on the author? Who could have arranged something like that, could have foreseen it all?

And what does this whole long drawn-out process reveal to the author anyway? He buries himself in the camp and broods. He probably would have done that without the poster. You really cannot remain in a good mood after so much futile effort. The author seems to be angry at the whole world and his camp looks like a good place to pout.

There is much on this journey that is troubling. But journeys are never purely pleasurable. Bad connections, missed trains, are ironclad components of journeys. But the author, who forgets this, falls into melancholy, exaggerates, and looks for reasons in the wrong places. It is not an unknown occurrence at any train station that a fellow passenger suddenly loses his patience and rages at the totally innocent stationmaster because the train hasn't arrived on time. After tossing about a few invectives, everything quiets down again.

In this instance, in 1940, in wartime, the inevitable train scene falls in the author's lap and he wouldn't be who he is if he didn't come up with some theory about it and, due precisely to his moroseness, a demonology. He attaches deep significance to practically everything—pardon me, he selects only the bad things—that happens to him. He assigns a purpose to things in reference to himself, the author. It borders on the paranoiac's delusion of reference.

How can I defend myself? What do I mean? I really cannot, without being declared insane, maintain that the police commissar deliberately left Mende an hour early so that I would pass him on the highway and later, at the prefecture, be amazed by the perverseness of reality. The driver who brought me from Le Puy cheats me. Question: Why shouldn't he cheat me? The man took advantage of my predicament. After all, there's not a war on every day.

I admit it. It is all natural and quite in order. I only ask you to admit that the extraordinary circumstances could, if you will, lead to some crazy assumptions. And you must admit that it really was a great many coincidences to converge on one man alone. And that if I were to present the whole thing as a novella with even half as many coincidences, it would be rejected as incredible. I could even draw the conclusion that someone was playing a dirty trick on me, that I was the object of a bizarre, real-life conspiracy.

War, retreat, confusion, to be sure. In the end it was "not only" I who was affected by it all, but I was "also" affected. And I have a comment on this. In all modesty, in addition to the obviously significant things that were going on—the war, the chaos, retreat—I would like to introduce a new factor, and ask that it be accommodated for. I, myself, am this factor. If I am to miss trains, I at least don't want to miss my connection here.

I'm to have been undone by the general state of the railroad and the gasoline shortage, am supposed to accept it. But I won't be treated this way, the state of the railroad and the gasoline shortage are not that powerful nor sovereign.

In the world of the mighty trains with their massive locomotives that won't move, and the splendid cattle cars, there is someone who experiences them and suffers them (for a pleasure they are not), an *I*, a consciousness whose presence makes itself known at certain stages, at certain moments.

This *I* makes itself known when it takes the form of a person sitting in a rail car who establishes that it is not moving. It calls forth an emotion, and the railroad's significance withers away.

But this *I* makes itself known even more so when life retreats from all trains and all train stations, abandons this monument to itself, questions how its existence is of help to him and in how far.

And if this someone, this *I*, this person retreats even further, he suddenly finds himself in the company of exceedingly solemn, old, even ancient men, some are wearing wigs, from across the centuries, men who do not look crazy at all and who identify themselves as philosophers and sages. They say: You are right. The material world is spoiled, has been pretending to be self-reliant for some time. But that's no reason to let it drive you crazy, to fall for it. You're not doing the world a favor with that. For it cannot keep going alone, just as a train cannot keep going without passengers. The world and the *I* belong together, no matter how they act, no matter how many arguments they have or how many fights. The world cannot be separated or removed from the *I*. It is only under the careful protection of the *I*, of the person, that the world exists. There is no sign anywhere of an absolute, a clearly "objective" world. You can be sure that *the* world is also *our* world.

These erudite words support my position nicely, of course. I only have trouble in accepting that the ancient sages who stand by me so generously are serious in what they say. They don't do enough, in my opinion, to counter the arrogance of the locomotives, the wars, and cattle cars that is growing daily, to counter the madness of an "objective" world independent of us. They don't think through their thoughts, they don't bring them to fruition. They don't show how far, how powerfully, how deeply the *I* has sunk its roots into the world—and therefore how profoundly this world is dependent upon and permeated by the *I* in the type and character of its appearances.

Let the clever physicists and natural scientists show how much I am "nature," physiology, flesh, matter, a fragile, quickly wilting blade of grass (and even it shouldn't be dispensed with so quickly, even it wants to be experienced and understood). With or without the help of the ancient sages, we want to establish that the *I* projects more, ever more deeply into the world.

The events of the world, of nature, and history are our events more than we know. They are personal, more than we know.

We declare things to be causal and take pride in proving that nature is ruled by an intractable necessity, in which one thing follows from the next, one thing is the basis of the next, and no further questions need be asked. Goals, aims, intentions, feelings, thoughts are all banished from the scene, made to hide among the riffraff like unclean animals.

Alfred Döblin

I believe that paranoiacs suffer from delusion of reference and that normal people suffer the madness of a loss of connection.

## Day of Mourning

In the summer of 1940 it happened that I, like Robinson Crusoe washed up on the shore of a distant tropical isle, was shipwrecked in the interior of France.

I am in Mende. In the refugee camp.

The old woman is again sitting in the center of the barrack, disagreeable, alone on the bench. Other women sit at the door, knitting and gossiping. Two young boys noisily pull their squeaky wagons back and forth across the barrack floor.

I sit on the bed in my cubicle, my back bent and my head down in order not to bump it against the upper bunk. I am in a state of total disorientation.

## The Drummer

A drummer marches through the main streets of the town. When people gather around him, he stops and proclaims: "At eleven there will be an assembly at the town hall, a procession in honor of the dead. Today is a national day of mourning."

I join others across from the town hall and wait. In front of the hall several persons are greeting each other, shaking hands. A half-dozen clergymen arrive. Several officers. Now a number of elderly civilians, who have marched up together, mount the steps of the town hall. Three of them carry flags, war veterans from 1914–1918. The flags have little black streamers attached. Everyone has now arrived. An elderly gentleman with a commanding gait emerges from the building, he shakes hands with the officers and the clergymen. Now the procession assembles. It is led by the veterans with the flags, followed by the clergymen, the officers, a number of civilian men—obviously officials—and behind them a loose collection of those standing on the street, several hundred men and women, some of the women are holding children in their arms or by the hand.

When everyone was standing about at random, waiting, there

was not much to look at. But that changed when they formed the procession and moved up impatiently behind the flag-bearers. They walked along without music. But their silent, unified march is devastating. Many of them pull out handkerchiefs and daub their eyes.

It may rain at any minute. The first drops are falling. The marchers have reached the square and turn left. The square is large, but only its center is empty. Military trucks are parked on each side. They have been moved from the center and a large, square space has been left open, in the background of which a war memorial carved of stone can be seen. People silently fill up the open space. Soldiers have assembled in rows in front of the memorial. None of them carry weapons. The veterans line up at some distance opposite the soldiers. The clergymen and some of the officials stand next to them. The sizable crowd is held back by the police.

For a while nothing at all happens. Umbrellas go up. Back where I am standing, people are whispering. Then, commands sound from the memorial. A trumpet blares: the tribute to the dead, for those who died in action.

The melody is repeated, again and again. . . .

The mood of the crowd is somber. Cars move behind us.

The sounds cease. No one moves.

A minute passes. More commands. There is movement toward the front. The veterans' flags begin to move. The groups disband. It is over.


## *The Crucifix*


I wend my way through the busy side streets, across corners of squares, through the city until I am standing in front of the cathedral. It is an ancient building. Several people are going in. I follow.

The large church is practically empty. On the sides and to the front candles are burning before pictures of saints. What a nice way to pray, to supplicate. I slide along a pew. Soldiers are sitting in front of me. Some women on the other side are kneeling.

I sit for a long time. I don't think about anything. I have a lot of time, just time—I won't miss anything. I have nothing pressing to do. I could sit here till evening. I do not feel bored or tired, just hunted.

I remember my suitcase. It's sitting in some shop somewhere that I cannot locate. I can't look for it today, the shops are closed. The trip and that driver, the cheat. But maybe he saved me from something worse. I would have kept on with my foolishness, my search, my battle against the demons. At least that is now over.

I look around me, see the crucifix.

In Paris, I often stood before shops that sold crucifixes. I would stand there and try to think. The crucifixes intrigued me. As I stood with them before me, I thought: This is human misery, this is our lot, it belongs to our existence and this is its true representation. And the other thought I had was unimaginable: What is hanging here is not a human, it is God himself, who knows what misery is and therefore descended into insignificant human life. He assumed its form and experienced it himself. Through his advent he showed that it is not as senseless here as it appears, that a light shines upon us and that we also exist in a world beyond this one. Yes, this thought can make the earth more beautiful, richer—provided that it is understood and accepted. We shall be saved by it, it is written. This image, it is said, would illumine the earth and our lives with more light than that of all the suns of all the solar systems.

As I am sitting there I think:

If this were right, if this were true—for of what use is mere belief? There must be truth to it—if this were true, then for the first time there would be a basis for human existence.

Our existence would finally possess a truth, that is, it would be preserved, maintained, secured. As it is now, existence is merely accident, a fall into the void. As it is, it is an earthen vessel covered with dust inside and out, into which stones clatter. But the vessel will hold truth only when it is cleansed, washed out, and then anointed with water or wine.

A world without this, without substance of this type, without a concept of Jesus, cannot have been created by a true primal force. It would be merely a farce.

As on that street in Paris, I glance over at the crucifix and issue a challenge. My eyes seek something resembling an answer, a confirmation, a corroboration. But I must be on the wrong path, or . . . I'm asking in the wrong way.

My eyes glance over and come back empty. I remain seated in my pew with an ominous, painful cramp in my chest. I am being rejected. They say you must be trusting, have conviction. But that is precisely what I lack. That's why I look around me here, that's why I look over at the crucifix, to see if I can perhaps find something.

But there is something in me (even though it possesses neither strength nor certainty) that has long been fascinated by he who was crucified. When I read the New Testament and follow his sermons and deeds, there is nothing in them that does not inspire me or give me great joy. He is more real, more alive than an ordinary person, he is a human miracle, truly a perfect being whose appearance and existence is meant to consecrate time. The memory of such a being is handed down through time. We still draw sustenance from this memory. How understandable it is that people fell at his feet, that a poor sinner washed his feet. But did God send him? Is he God? That is my only question.

For in times of great trouble, when all else fails, neither golden words nor great men abide, nor do the miracles of man. I need to know for sure, and not merely as a fleeting thought, not merely remember.

I know that great beyond, beyond all human thought, a beyond we believe we can put a name to, beyond everything imaginable, that we signify with the word "God." But this also has its effect on earth, and on human beings. I know this, for without it we would not exist. We would not exist in and of ourselves alone, even fleetingly. But I do not know how he works, or where and how he will appear.

It is not enough to say he is "everything." But is it conceivable that he merely set this world in motion and then withdrew and left us to ourselves? Perhaps in grief or in anger about some corruption that had appeared, about the evil that was spreading? Is that conceivable? No. Whether the world is his reflex, his look, or gesture—in no way has he been separated from the world.

But how, what, and where is he in it? Or of it? Or of me, with me? What kind of thing is he? How can he be recognized? Our existence in general is imperfect, not to mention its ephemerality and fragility. Life, without any exaggeration, can be defined as hard and coarse and cruel. Human beings are persecuted, betrayed, and tortured. So if God has not abandoned this world, if he is involved in it—if it is he who pours life into it (and it is his life that makes this world's life, without his life we would turn to dust)—how is it, I ask, that he also takes the form of Nazis and builds concentration camps?

Yes, he builds them, who else? But it is inconceivable, incomprehensible, it makes me shudder.

No, I am unable to create a kind image of God. I have to take him, who created this world, as he (and this world) is. I have to swallow him whole. I cannot accept a cleaned-up, gentle God.

And then I think of the Old Testament and a few sentences I cannot repeat verbatim. Sayings that have often occupied me. God himself once says in the Old Testament, at the beginning, that his word is not somewhere off in the distance, such that we have to send out ships for it. Nor is it hidden behind the clouds or in some other part of the earth. Rather, it is quite close to us, it is in us, in our breasts.

In us, it says, inside us. But as I sit here I feel in my breast only pain and sorrow. My throat is constricted with the misery around me and within me. Where is God in me, in my breast? It cannot be that God speaks in this way. This cannot be his word, the word not hidden by him behind the clouds or in some other part of the earth. Oh, if only he had hidden it behind the clouds.

Or is he perhaps in some way also contained in this sorrow and this terrible pain? Is his word perhaps in them, too? It seemed to me the wrong turns I took on my journey were signs, clues. I am meant to heed them. Could it be that these wrong turns, this going astray, these failures and missed encounters are something other than evil, a mockery, like a game of cat and mouse (though with clues and signs, it is true), the willful expression of a primal force, but one for which there is neither good nor evil? This force is interested in me somehow, but in a way that seems demonic. I felt that certain things out there did not simply move past me but, rather, were connected to me, and that the connection was a mad, aggravating, and contemptuous one, and totally callous. I was worse than abandoned. And that added to my abandonment.

I sit in my pew in the cathedral. More people appear. A young woman, weeping, is led up the middle aisle by an older woman. They kneel beside each other.

Once again I cross-examine myself and the crucifix. But I get no answer. I don't make any progress.

However, the woman weeping at the front of the cathedral does me good. We are all like her. All of us.

I buy a notebook on the way back. I must organize my

thoughts. Perhaps in the process of writing I will arrive more quickly at enlightenment.

Sitting on my bed that evening I write: "The thought of death presses down on me. And always this wish to turn to a priest. The crucifix. Oh, this truth: pain, crucifixion—yes, we carry this heaven within us. But this is not the reason we have an *I*, or not the only reason, and we are inspired—by this terrible condition, by this loneliness."

Why am I disheartened? Whence this emptiness and lethargy?

I needn't look long for an answer. The emptiness was already there. It has only been revealed.

The futility, the fragility and ineffectiveness of everything I was engaged in has been revealed. I was traveling light. I did not know before how light. I had set my course on nothing.

The whole system around me that usually blinds me in regard to myself has been blown away. I lie on the sand as naked as Crusoe.

This has all been planned as a clever, precise experiment, this system and this exposure.

The philosophers' doctrine: these ropes are mere straws. How shall I build a hut with them?

Oh, the strange cunning, the shrewdness I was subjected to on my journey.

Why should "one" be interested in me at all? But one is. One cannot do otherwise. It belongs to the essence of things. For: I am, and that means that the primal cause, whatever that may be, has also created my *I*. It is as though I am being squeezed in a fist. This tension and oppression.

## In Search of My Suitcase

As soon as I awake in my cubicle and emerge from the abyss of sleep, my *I* appears, ill-humored and confused.

My *I* is obsessed with several ideas. They run in a circle like white mice in a wheel. These white mice, it seems to me, are basically me myself, my *I*. For I know of no other.

My white mice, my thoughts, my restlessness now center on my suitcase. It is laughable but true. The fact that I have lost my bag is yet another legacy, an echo from my glorious journey.

I walk through town. I am looking for my suitcase. It is absurd to report this. But what about this whole story isn't absurd?

Where shall I look? I know only that it was near the prefecture. For when I arrived by car and put down my bag, the two criminologists were standing close by and pointed out the prefecture, it was not far. So I will now search in the vicinity of that building. I enter various shops and make inquiries. No one knows me or anything about my suitcase. I slink back to the camp to get advice. I am advised to go to the office and register my loss.

There is a priest sitting at one table and at the table next to him is the head of the camp. They are speaking with a stocky man, a Belgian I already know. I greet him and wait. When the conversation seems to be over, I announce myself and receive a strong dressing down from the one-armed head of the camp. "You have to wait your turn. What's gotten into you, interrupting me." Their conversation continues for a few minutes more and then he turns to me. What do I want? he asks. It has occurred to him in the meantime that the tone he had used was uncalled for, for he then adds that he was giving instructions to someone on important "things" and did not want to be interrupted. I accept this, apologize, and explain my problem. The priest listens with interest and gets involved as well.

They ask how it is possible that I have left my suitcase in a shop and not noted which one. I relate the extenuating circumstances and admit to having been confused at the time. They want to send someone out with me who knows the area. The Belgian volunteers. I am satisfied at this, and leave. I have the feeling that after I leave there will be a great deal of discussion about me.

But by noon no one has shown up. I decide not to wait any longer and go into town alone. I've given up on finding my bag. I can't go on with this ridiculous search. I can't always be circling around the prefecture. I've been in all of the shops already. People will think I'm crazy.

I now avoid the main street, which I'm already sick of. I walk along the river beyond the bridge. Fishermen stand at the water, at street level, and below, at the shore. People are doing their wash in the river. I stop here and there. Then there are more people around, I've wandered into another area I don't know. Or do I?

This is a broad square with heavy traffic. This is the place I stopped the day before yesterday with that sneak of a driver! Yes, it was here that we got out, I paid him here, it looked just like this. I glance around, turn, and go into the first shop I see. It's the one. The woman has graciously put my suitcase in her living room.

As I am dragging it back to the camp, I ask myself: what was that really all about? As soon as I want something, and want it fast, antagonistic "accidents" begin happening. If I relinquish wicked "want," positive "accidents" result. Somehow my inner self is in communication with the secret world that controls "accidents." But are they accidents? There are connections, ties, between events and myself, my inner self. I think of the Biblical saying that the word is not hidden behind the clouds.

When I appear at the camp with my bag, the friendly stout man from the office informs me he has just told someone else to go into town with me.

# 5

# Scenes from the Barracks

*I* f you approach the camp from the highway, the first thing you
see is the laundry. Women stand next to each other here at all
hours of the day, doing their washing at a large washbench. Behind
this barrack lies the kitchen, a long brick building. The food carriers
gather there in the mornings, noontime, and evenings. Then to the
right comes a row of wooden sleeping barracks. A bridge of boards
leads to each door.

Each barrack is actually two barracks divided by a partition that
doesn't reach to the ceiling. The front section opens onto the quad and
the rear section onto the highway. Each section has a separate entrance, the food is delivered to both, and the inhabitants of the two
sections (there is a connecting door) rarely encounter or know each
other. But if there is no communal dining, there is communal noise.

For instance, we became acquainted with a large family on the
other side of the partition that sat quite near the door during meals, a
family consisting of parents (no, grandparents), and several grown
daughters with their children. No one in this family got along. It
started before the meals. The rest of us would smile at each other and
nod: the family across the way was cranking up. The loud female
voices were raised against each other, screaming at each other unself-
consciously, trying to drown each other out. They aired their griev-
ances for everyone to hear, criticized the food, the weather, their

surroundings. Occasionally one of the women would get up during the course of the argument and withdraw, defeated, into her cubicle, which we could ascertain because her voice would get weaker, but would not stop for one second. This murderously feminine battling was particularly bad in the evenings. It never appeared to come to fisticuffs, at least in public. During the debates between their mothers and grandmother, the children stayed very quiet, passive, like a theater audience.

Others sitting at their table had gotten used to the racket. Like us, they were a friendly group, they ate quietly and enjoyed the show, and as a result the contentious women—grandmother and mothers—thought they were alone. I never saw any of them. Perhaps I ran into them outside. They must have looked just like the rest of us.

In general, we all resembled one another. Whoever didn't look like his neighbor at first soon made up for it. We were dirty and got dirtier, from head to toe. We all took on the same dull, distressed expression, the same apathetic attitude.

Of course there was neither bath nor shower. We could wash ourselves in a barrack on the highway, right next to the latrine. In the washroom, water flowed out of spigots into a large tin trough. You stood before it, bare to the waist, and washed. The younger men did it with gusto. There were not many toothbrushes to be seen. There was no place for soap, no place had been planned for it. The latrines had been equipped as well as possible. For the men there was one large room by the street. There were toilets with stalls, set up on one side (toward the highway) for women (about ten), and an equal number for men on the other side. There was great confusion on the men's side, for a simple reason. The ten stalls for the women and children were inadequate, particularly in the morning. It was a lamentable sight, mornings, to see mothers standing there with their little ones, waiting. The mothers had to help the children. The toilets were badly designed and had been put into unbelievably narrow stalls. There was not enough room for the mother to go into the stall with the child, so she had to help it while standing in the door.

I often heard singing coming from a wooden barrack near the kitchen, and it didn't sound like French to me. At first I thought I was deceiving myself. Then I made out German words and soon found out that there were Alsatians living in the barracks. They had been evacuated from their homes. These women and girls (I didn't see any men) often stood out in front of the barracks in the evenings, talking. I would also run into them on the highway. Then I would walk past pastures and fields as the river flowed by below, a dynamic, swirling body of water. People were working in the pastures and fields, several of which were being mowed. It was an agreeable sight. Then you came to a small bridge in front of a barrack. Many of us strolled along this path in the evenings. Here, too, I heard Alsatian spoken, at the small bridge. These were upper-class women. It was strange for me being constrained to pass by them without greeting them.

Language had caused problems for me often since 1933 and I had lost much of my enjoyment of it, now that I had the land of the Nazis behind me. I had entered France as a foreigner, of course, but I happily would have liquidated—at least externally—all of what was foreign in my character, just as the Nazis had liquidated me by forcing me to expatriate. The only way would have been to speak French. And if I could not penetrate to the heart of the language, I would at least learn it superficially. That was difficult enough, but understandable in someone who continued daily to write in the German language. You have seen what happened during my journey, my flight, as a result of my French.

I did not come to know the other barracks. We all met on the large quad to fetch water, in the washrooms, at the latrine. We stood together in front of the office barrack and studied the announcements on the blackboard. Each morning a cheerful, clumsy Belgian from the office wrote the date on the board and then instructions and announcements. They concerned, say, condensed milk for newborn babies and small children, the only milk that was available. Or car owners were requested to register. Later, individual names were added, those fortunate enough to have received mail.

And one day a group of us rushed to the board to look through a thick notebook held together by string. It contained a long list of the names and locations of other refugees. At that point, the search for relatives began slowly to be organized. This list concerned Belgians only. They stood there leafing through it, searching, and then came back later to search it again.

There were well-off people in the camp, whole families who arrived in cars. They quickly continued south. An older man had arrived at about the same time I had. He would emerge from one of the rear barracks, dressed debonairly in hat and coat with a long scarf about his shoulders and, like myself, head into town. He was by himself, and clean at first. Day by day he deteriorated, got shabbier and more soiled, rarely shaved. His face became small and pale gray.

I would lie down on my bed for an hour or so after meals. The room is incredibly noisy. They clear the tables, push back the benches, wash dishes, and sweep the floor. In sweeping they stir up clouds of dust, so that I have to pull my blanket over my head. The dust comes from the dirt that dozens of shoes bring in from the damp quad. My window barely opens. I raise it carefully a hand's width. I could go out, but it is raining. I tell myself that everything has its end, even the sweeping and dishwashing. The women's arms will eventually tire and they will want to knit and talk.

It takes a long time. Then the children start up. It is time to get up. A refugee barrack is not a sanitorium.

But it is not only I who am lying on his bunk. When I walk down the middle aisle and sit down at the table to leaf through the newspapers, curtains part to my right and left. I can see a man here, a woman there, sitting on the edge of the bed. Mostly they just sit there, hunched over. None of them look pleased with the world.

The nights in the camp were difficult. The old woman in my cubicle went to bed at eight, eight-thirty at the latest. When I entered she would turn her face to the wall. Because of the cold I laid most of my things out on my bed, my two coats included. I covered myself with one of the blankets. I spread the second blanket over the straw mattress so that I won't feel my bones right away. The noise in the room, the cries of the children, went on until nine-thirty or so. But it was never totally quiet. You can't keep children from crying deep in the night. I heard mothers whispering, trying to calm their little ones. But children and babies have their complaints, they weren't comfortable, they hadn't eaten well, or enough. And so the mothers, who had taken care of them all day, were robbed of their rest at night.

In the cubicle next to mine, an elderly man slept splendidly. His sonorous snoring proved it. I could follow all the stages of his sound sleep through the partition that separated us. Occasionally there was also whispering. Then his wife would poke him. He would wake up. But it was hopeless. He was a bookkeeper.

In my cubicle the old woman suffered from emphysema, she gasped for breath, and the bad weather didn't help her chronic bronchitis. It was all right during the day. But the coughing fits started soon after she went to bed, when she had barely fallen asleep. They often lasted, in varying degrees, for hours, they tormented the woman and were hard on her neighbors, too. She coughed up a lot of congestion. I was particularly interested in where she coughed it up. There was a tin can under her bed, she must have had to empty it several times during the day.

She was a strong, resolute person. A tavern owner from northern France, she was seventy-three years old. She couldn't be judged by the mean expression on her face. Worn-out old women often look like that. She had definite opinions on things and expressed them uncompromisingly. As she was here alone, and idle, she liked to get involved in others' affairs, something that seldom went well. Occasionally the asthmatic old woman was addressed as "Grandmother," but more often as "the General." They cautiously avoided her. I once witnessed a loud argument between her and several women neighbors. Almost the entire barrack turned on the General. After that she got quieter, her expression more resigned. I came to know another side of her. We didn't argue. She showed me, when I first arrived, what to do, how to preserve my bread, how I could get my daily rations, and so forth. She often checked my bread reserves and occasionally, when she found them lacking, added to them some of her own. As she had trouble walking, I had to fetch water from the fountain for her at meals, and each time she also gave me her cup to wash out. Often in the evenings I heard people to our right and left complaining about the old woman. And they called me "*ce monsieur-là.*" They weren't wise to me, they thought I was a "*professeur,*" were polite and as helpful as they could be. The old woman's latest act of maliciousness was reviewed each evening, along with the fact that she considered me, "*ce monsieur-là,*" her messenger boy. She listened silently from her cubicle.

She was a strong old woman, accustomed to ordering others around. But she couldn't get away with that here. She often complained to me about it in our cell. She would explain her predicament to me, sitting there on the edge of her bed, dressed in a black dress with a black apron she never changed because she had nothing else to wear. She would frequently reach up to her upper bunk and bring down, trembling, her soiled black handbag (it was full of papers and photos), put on her steel-rimmed glasses and begin, whether I wanted her to or not, showing me what was in her letters. I had to look at her pictures. There was one of her standing in front of her tavern, she was a square-built woman, obviously difficult to get along with. To her right and left stood younger men and women, vigorous-looking people, her children—they were scattered all over the world now, she said, even her grandchildren, they had either been evacuated or were fleeing from the German bombers or were soldiers somewhere. If only she would hear something from her sons.

She often proudly showed me pictures of each of her sons, in civilian dress or as soldiers, and also the pictures of her grand-children. I marveled at the strength of them all.

I sat beside her at table. My situation became both difficult and comical following a particularly violent quarrel that the old woman had started or that someone had started with her. As a result, she decided to distance herself from the people sitting next to us, partic-ularly the person in the cubicle across from us. She decided this in the afternoon. And that evening, going to my seat at the table, I found everything changed. The old woman had moved from the middle of the table to one end of it. This time I sat at my old place. Then that changed. For the two of us (at her insistent request) had bought a bottle of red wine together and the bottle now stood at her place, and she had taken it without asking me. But I couldn't side with her declared enemies and continue to room with her at the same time. So I, too, had to move to the end of the table. I was sorry to do so, for I liked the people I was sitting next to.

To my left there now sat an entire family, consisting of father, mother, and three small children, all working class. I did not know how or why the man, who was in his early forties, had arrived at the refugee camp. He must have had a complaint that made him un-suited for the military. He was a powerfully built man who talked wildly and attacked everyone politically. After having carried on for a while he would relent. I noticed that he didn't take any of it very seriously and that he liked to end his declamations with a long, happy, conciliatory laugh. These people were bitterly poor. Their clothes were in terrible shape and the children were undernourished. The woman was pale, her hair unkempt. She had a flat nose. She treated her children quite maternally. But if they wouldn't eat, she would clout them without much thought. And whoever didn't eat after that didn't eat at all, for as soon as the woman noticed it, the child would be given a good shake and sent to its cubicle under a stream of curses—all of which she performed without gusto.

Alfred Döblin

The seven-year-old boy of this family sat next to me, befriended me in his own way. He was mischievous, roguish company. And it was he who was the cause of a fight between the old woman—the General—and his family. For one day the old woman ordered him to go into town for the bottle of red wine for us. When he returned with the bottle, I gave him ten centimes, which he took to his family's cubicle with a whoop of excitement. The old woman found out the reason for his yell and lectured me sternly not to be so free with my money after I openly admitted having given him the ten centimes. I should have given him only five, she said. On top of which, the boy should know that he had earned only five. I tried to calm her. But she didn't like this "pack" anyway. And soon I heard the fight outside. She was lecturing the entire family about the five centimes. The father got involved. It wasn't long before it got down to basics. The old woman returned to her cell red in the face and didn't say a word, even to me. She had been repeatedly called an old bag among other things.

Before the seating arrangement at the table changed, a very sweet young woman sat across from me with her daughter, a cute two-year-old. The woman was in her mid-thirties. Living with her in the same cubicle was an intelligent, white-haired woman who wore glasses. At first I thought the white-haired woman was the grand-mother. I later found out that they weren't related, and hadn't known each other at all before they had been evacuated. They had met during a heavy bombing raid, had helped each other, and had remained together. The young woman didn't know where her hus-band was. She came from a middle-class background. I didn't ask her anything else. She poured out her sorrows to me once when I met her at the door of the barrack, where she was trying to clean the little girl's dress. The girl wasn't really dirty, she said. But children fall down or sit on the ground—and look at the floor of the barrack. The older woman came up. She said she couldn't stand to look in the mirror anymore, they had been here for weeks without a bath, how were they to keep themselves clean? The little girl's mother com-plained how hard it was to get warm water, her little girl wasn't doing well here.

This young woman was very gentle with her daughter. From morning to evening they cooed to each other. The mother would call, *"ma chatte, ma cocotte,"* and each time the daughter would answer, *"maman."*

[ 97 ]

They sleep in a cubicle catty-corner to mine. Each day begins early with the chirping sounds of *"ma chatte, ma cocotte"*—*"maman."*

## Scenes from Childhood

I am a little more relaxed. The pressure has let up. I no longer want to think about the trip to Le Puy.

I have a roof over my head. The war, the killing, have ended, at least for the moment.

I take walks in the afternoons. The town is swarming with fishermen. They are soldiers, primarily. There are shops for anglers in the narrow, badly paved streets of town, and in front of these shops soldiers and civilians are talking about fishing. The soldiers buy things, particularly postcards, pencils, and shirts.

The inner city is teeming with life. Among the passers-by, two types dominate: peasant and middle-class. I see only a few educated, sophisticated faces. Everyone is robust and lively. There is no hint of the "situation" in the air. Some of these people—refugees—occupy themselves, other than with eating and drinking, with finding a place to stay. I hear the lodging question posed several times, and the world is divided into those fortunate enough to live here and those who want to live here. Once again I hear that there are other refugee camps than the one I live in. But they don't sound much different.

The refugees want middle-class, single rooms. But there aren't any available. These kinds of discussions are held in my barrack, too. Some people even made up their minds to do something about it: they go to the prefecture and find out where there are empty rooms to be let. They then rent them and begin the search for furniture. They are planning a long stay in Mende.

To this end, a young, attractive woman disappears with her two children after my first few days in the camp. She was a blonde with a stylish hairdo. She was in her mid-thirties and when her children weren't there, she conversed normally. But she was a problem at mealtimes, when her two children were with her. Hers were like all the other imps: they sometimes refused food (and there was a good reason). The children—they had been here for a while—went on strike as soon as they saw a spoon. And their mother immediately

[ *98* ]

got angry and the battle began. Her blond curls would fall across her face and the children would slide away from her.

The threats started. The food wagon got closer and closer. The children saw disaster looming. They inched farther and farther from their mother on the bench. The mother used her long, strong arms and pulled the rascals back. They used every break in her attention to slide away again. And each time that the food battle began, the mother began a conversation with the woman sitting across from her—it was usually one-sided—in which she drew attention to her children's ingratitude. Now that there was a war on they should be satisfied with anything they could get—and the noodles were excellent, nutritious. There was even a piece of meat in them. And then came the intimidations, and threats of calling the police. She would telephone them if the children refused to eat, she said. The boy looked sharply to his right and to his left. He couldn't escape. It was clear to see that he wasn't going to eat voluntarily. He faces a world full of enemies and hardhearted adults.

The serving woman stands there with her bucket full of noodles, laughing. There is a huge ladle in the bucket. The boy hunches his shoulders. Mercilessly, the ladle dips into the vessel and comes up with a thick blob of noodles for him. The server immediately wants to plop a second blob onto his plate. But the mother stops her, wagging her finger: "First he has to eat this. If he doesn't, I'll call the police."

The little scamp sits there rigidly. The space between him and his mother has grown once again. The mother grabs him and pulls him over to her. And now it really begins.

The boy has pressed his fists against his mouth. His mother puts her left arm around his shoulder. With her right hand she navigates the spoon filled with mush. She holds it up in front of him with a stream of reassuring words, seconded by the camp's female members sitting nearby. Now she bends down to her tiny victim. The steaming spoon hovers in front of his mouth. And his mouth—stays shut.

The woman shakes the boy's shoulder from the left. She orders him to open his mouth. It stays shut. The boy is sitting twisted at an angle; his mother has a firm grip on the upper part of his body— because his mouth is located in the upper part—but below, he is slipping away on the bench, his legs pumping so powerfully to the left that the woman next to him has to move over.

[ *99* ]

As she holds the spoon, the mother's tone gets louder. She repeats: "You must eat. You *will* eat now, you ill-mannered brat— *you will eat now!* You'll eat with everyone else, you see that everyone is eating. I'll eat soon, too. The noodles are good. They're soft." She tries them. She turns to the others for reassurance: "The noodles are soft. The noodles are good!" This is eagerly confirmed from all sides.

Her resolution grows at this. She turns to the little scamp, the spoon pointed once again at his mouth, held before his lips, ready to unload. Suddenly the boy moves his knee forward and the spoon tips, noodles stick to his chin. He bawls.

Beside herself, the mother shouts, "What are you crying for!" And she turns to her neighbor, who knows the game already and is waiting for her moment: "Please, madame, call the station now. The police should come right away."

The woman immediately gets up and leaves the barrack. The boy doesn't say a word. He knows this game. I think that she underestimates him. The mother broods darkly for a few minutes, ignoring him. He waits nervously to see how things will go. The woman reappears and nods to the mother from a distance. The mother resumes her role. "So. Now we have called them. They will be here soon. Open your mouth up fast or they'll take you away."

He doesn't budge.

She now takes her napkin and energetically cleans the boy's face. Noodles are still stuck to his chin. The boy again begins crying loudly. The mother appeals to her tablemates, imploring them: "The police will be here soon. They will take the boy with them. That's what he gets. It's his stubbornness. He's always been like this. The opposite of his sister. Him and his monkey business."

An elderly man sitting at the table says complacently, "A sound thrashing would do him good." The woman nods enthusiastically. "Did you hear that? A sound thrashing."

The little boy is howling by now. He believes he has justice on his side, now that his mother has wiped his face so hard. But his mother has waited for just this moment to try it again. He's bawling, his eyes are full of tears, and he can't see. Attacking him from the side, she shoves a spoonful of noodles deep into his mouth. She tilts the spoon. The noodles fall into his cheeks. He has to swallow.

As he is making choking motions and getting ready to let loose with a mighty scream of protest, his mother, with another of her sneaky hand motions, pushes up his chin. He swallows. He cannot do otherwise. He has to swallow and he does.

But scarcely is his mouth empty again when he raises his voice in a horrible scream. The woman laughs. The others laugh too. He is done for. After five spoonfuls more she has had enough fighting and lets the little boy go—only now to look at her daughter's plate. The little girl has seen what they have done to her brother. She also understands why he is on strike. And she sees that many of the grown-ups have refused to eat the thick paste. But when she sees her mother's reproving look she digs in and swallows. At this, the mother eats her own food contentedly. She has completely changed and chats cheerfully with her neighbors about apartments, about furniture.

One morning the father joins the family. He is a brawny soldier. He sits at table with us only once, and he pushes away most of what he is offered. Then the family goes off to wander around town. The woman becomes much more affable and well-mannered. When her husband appears he has only bad things to say about the food, the sleeping quarters, the noise at night, and particularly about the warm morning drink. He is familiar with all of it from the military. One evening the family moves out. They have found a small, empty apartment—a room and a kitchen. The family departs amid admiration and envy. It is amazing how the mother has changed. She looks almost elegant in a Parisian sort of way. And the two children are suddenly well dressed and walk behind their parents like well-behaved, calm, ordinary children.

What memories will they have of the camp? A week later I meet the mother and her children in town. While she is buying vegetables at the market, they are looking sharply at the world, and behold, now they spot me, they recognize me. I nod to them and smile. They look at me strangely and whisper to each other.

## This Is the Time of Deprivation

There are no radios in the camp, and seldom are there newspapers. I get hold of one once and read the terms of the cease-fire. So far as they appear in the paper, they are quite general. The occupation of the Atlantic coast was to be expected. But without doubt there also must be conditions concerning the surrender of weapons, airplanes, cannons, concerning the dismantling of fortresses, perhaps of the Maginot Line. There's nothing on this. There's no need to make people even more depressed.

I come across Article 19. It contains provisos that Germany will demand concerning the extradition of certain persons from France and from the colonies. A misleading article. I say to myself that these are conditions applicable for a limited time only, during the cease-fire. They can be revised. I try to convince myself of this, but I can't.

At home, in the camp, when I sit on my bed or stretch out after meals, or at night when I'm awakened by the old woman's coughing, I think about things. I brood.

This is the time of deprivation. My *I*, my soul, my clothing have all been taken from me. I don't know what is left of me, really. My apathy, my skepticism are intact and justified. And for that very reason I am at the same time indifferent and helpless, impassive and nervously lethargic. Something in me isn't cooperating. So I think and think. . . .

Nothing of what I had endures. I could build myself a raft and sail away. It's comical really. Insignificant creature that I am, a rubber ball floating on the waves, how could anything that I create support me?

Over and over again I ask myself what causes this condition. Am I frightened because France has been defeated? Am I frightened for my family? Am I frightened for myself? My anxiety leaps from one object to another. Afraid of the Nazis? I seldom think of them. I don't want to think of them, I don't want to see pictures of them. After I left Germany I was able to view Nazi publications only with disgust. I remember the nausea I felt at seeing a group of Nazis standing with their flag in front of the Charlottenburg exhibition hall in Berlin. This hydra from the German swamp extends its polyp arms even here. Germany has brought disgrace and shame upon itself in producing something like this. I am certainly no Hercules who can slay the hydra in its swamp. What, I ask myself, have I done, or could I do today, to annihilate it? Disgust alone is not sufficient.

I have seen the hydra's presence grow in the last few years. I have learned what Nazism represents and how feeble the so-called

Alfred Döblin

propaganda against it was. What tangible weapons did I have against it? Was that supposed to have been the Herculean battle, against a hydra that one couldn't get at with clubs and fire? I always asked this question; I never saw any weapons.

These thoughts occupied me in the camp for hours. They remain unresolved. I can't bring them to a point where I am satisfied, can't find that point.

# 6

# I Test and Question Myself

*T*here is nothing we have any reason to be proud of.
    I walk around, and I sit, and sit some more. I feel compelled to sum up my entire life, to settle accounts with myself, as if I were confronting my own death. I have to find out how I have gotten to this point, what I have done and left undone.

I have been like a plant growing in the earth, have taken my nourishment here and there and remained as I was. I have never seriously examined what drove me to want this or that. I was driven, and I assumed without ceremony that it was I who was the driving force. I have never been concerned with what my *I* claimed to be, what it wanted or didn't want. Consciously. Socrates taught: Know thyself! But how can I know myself if I am simultaneously that which knows and that which is to be known? I have always looked about me, have observed and judged things critically and gathered experience, and when I lie down to die I will have protected myself from feelings that I consider to be weak. I have been active, moved among people for years, was a person like they, a minor being, a microbe swirling in the waters with millions of others.

I wish to, I must, now look at what is at my back and beneath my feet.

Judgment Day? No. It is not I who can pass judgment, least of all on myself—I just look around, sum up.

What was it like?

[ *104* ]

## Alfred Döblin

I was born sixty-two years ago, in 1878, in Stettin. My father ran a tailor shop, my mother was from a well-to-do family. I wrote a little book twelve years ago, at fifty, describing how it was between my father and my mother. What have I brought with me from my family life? My father worked—and then went his own way. My good mother was occupied with running the house and raising five children, and she suffered. We all were on our mother's side. There were terrible scenes at home.

I attended school in preparation for the high school for modern languages and was in my first year there when my father, who was then forty, deserted his home and family for a girl from his shop who was twenty years younger than he. He went to America. I do not wish to comment on the misfortune that befell my family as a result.

In 1888 we left Stettin and moved to Berlin, to the eastern part of the city. We were poor, and my mother's brother supported us. My memory of that trip to Berlin in 1888, of our beggar's existence that followed, of our poverty, has never left me. And so I grew up. That is what home meant to me.

The notion that we, that I, belonged to the poor has stayed with me. It has determined my entire way of being. I belonged to the nation that was the poor.

I was sent to the parish school at Friedrichshain, and three years later I was accepted at a high school for the humanities as a scholarship student. I was always three years older than the other students in my class. And so I was at the high school until I graduated in 1900. What did I experience, what did I absorb? Our teachers were Prussian civil servants, professors, and they provided our so-called humanistic education, in addition to our Prussian orientation, which included discipline and hard work. I learned a lot at the school, including a great deal about classical Greece. I also studied the German heroic epics and German literature. I learned them well. There was instruction in history, in Prussian and German history. I was young, I took it all in, it was a state education that we received at the high school and it was valid for its time.

And what about Judaism? I had been told at home in Stettin that my parents were of Jewish origin and we were a Jewish family. That was about the only thing concerning Judaism that I noticed about our family. I encountered anti-Semitism outside my home as a matter of course, as did my other schoolmates who had been told the same thing I had been told at home. So I didn't take instruction in the Protestant religion. The instruction in Judaism was equivocal and more voluntary. I didn't go to school on the Christian holidays and got two or three of the Jewish holidays off. This was noted by the other students. My parents celebrated two holidays: New Year's and Yom Kippur. They dressed up and went to Temple, usually in the evening and in the morning, and didn't work on those days. The books they took with them to Temple had prayers and excerpts from the Old Testament, as well as the Psalms, they were bilingual, in German and Hebrew. During my occasional religious instruction I learned a little Hebrew, no more than the basics. Why should I be interested in learning Hebrew on top of Latin, Greek, and French, when I had always found linguistic instruction disagreeable? What with the *Iliad* and the *Odyssey*, the lays of Edda and the Nibelungen and Gudrun, I had little interest in the early history of the Israelites, who later dispersed and disbanded. As for the teaching, the actual religious teaching—I read it and listened to it. It was, and remained, superficial to me. It did not affect me emotionally, I felt no connection to it.

My mother could read Hebrew, and it was touching to see her, she who worked so hard and cared for us and hardly had time to read a newspaper, sitting off quietly to one side of a room on the high holidays. She would hold one of her books in her hand and read Hebrew for a while, softly out loud. Sometimes it was only a murmur. When I think of Judaism, I think of this image of my mother. She ran around exhausting herself for her children, whose father, her husband, spent all his time in Hamburg with his girlfriend, only occasionally remembering his large family with a letter. My mother could have had a pleasant old age, but she developed Parkinson's disease, and she died at the home of my eldest brother, who had assumed the role of father to us. On her tombstone we engraved: "Love never ceases."

And so my soul went out to hers, as she sat quietly in a room with a book in her hand, praying.

But oh, how I came to life—and it was the first sign of that dark being I carried with me as the self I thought I knew, and I thought that what I knew was really what I was—how I came to life when I first encountered Heinrich von Kleist's *Penthesilea*, and how angry I was at Goethe who, so cold and so reasonable, had rejected it. To Kleist, whom I took to my awakened bosom, I added Hölderlin. Kleist and Hölderlin were the gods of my youth. "You shall have no other gods before me, I am the Lord your God"—I had heard and read that before, but it had stopped at that. For in what had he proven to me that he was God? The external world was visible, ascertainable, calculable without God, according to the laws of nature. It worked "naturally." I had not yet come to question what "natural" was. And history took place within the framework of nation and society. And if the followers of God, of he who wanted no other besides him, believed in him, that was their affair, it was a private matter. My own private matter was different.

I carried a copy of Hölderlin's *Hyperion* around with me between the years of 1898 and 1900, until it fell apart. It was not then common to read Hölderlin so closely, so intensely. Both Kleist and Hölderlin became my spiritual godfathers. They stood with me against what was lifeless, bourgeois, self-satisfied, and mediocre.

Was I led by these two? Could I follow? I know that they never aged for me. And now, when I think of them, I know that they were the first to awaken me, and they remained my friends. They could not lead me. But I continue to love them as comrades, as brothers, these two splendid, ill-fated men.

This was the path I chose. At the beginning of my university studies in Berlin, in 1902, I made two discoveries close upon one another. In a small rental library on Schönhauser Street where I occasionally browsed, I stumbled across Dostoyevsky, and then Nietzsche. I was then twenty-four years old and studying medicine. Richard Wagner had already risen in my musical heavens, his star competed in brightness with that of Johannes Brahms. Wagner quickly faded. Then Hugo Wolff had appeared. Then I got my hands on Dostoyevsky's *Crime and Punishment* and several titles by Nietzsche. I was tremendously moved by *Crime and Punishment*. It was far more than stimulating reading. It wasn't just a novel, the book transcended the boundaries of literature without even being stylistically innovative. After Hölderlin and Kleist I had been introduced to new territory. *Crime and Punishment* was an event; it created a reality, as had *Hyperion*.

And Nietzsche. I remember sitting in my room, having read the

*Genealogy of Morals*, and laying it aside, covering it with a notebook, literally shaking, shivering, and I remember standing up in my room and walking up and down, beside myself, and standing at the stove. I didn't know what had happened to me, what had been done to me.

Did I know God, in spite of it all? God, who was the subject of the conflict? Did I know him? Did I feel his presence, long for him? I don't know. But I saw that it was a terribly serious subject and that it concerned God, and that I was involved.

As with my poor friends Kleist and Hölderlin, what I was dealing with was neither *belles lettres* nor even philosophy. Once again someone was forcing his way back to the beginning. In reading these works I became like a man who is suddenly required to organize a perilous expedition to the glaciers. He is not an alpinist himself but he survives the adventure, finding out during the climb, and especially afterward, what he is really made of, what his strengths are. For life is like that in our bourgeois society, no, in every society, really. We only partially express ourselves, we are asleep for the most part, there are a great number of questions we don't even pose, life plays itself out in a small, restricted circle. We curl up like porcupines. Where are the problems in that, what are problems, anyway? Other than the search for food, housing, comfort, and respect? When hunger and cold, love and shelter, and perhaps ambition, are taken care of, what is left?

A veil covers the rest of existence—and what an enormous remnant it is.

So I drifted and I studied. The prosperity in the country where I lived increased, and I found myself well-off. Then a lightning bolt fell from heaven, struck right in front of me, and in its blinding light I saw something I had never seen before. The lightning was Dostoyevsky and the conversations of Raskolnikov and the Karamazov brothers, and then the *Genealogy of Morals*—thunder, an immense storm, lightning bolt after lightning bolt, so that I longed anxiously for the old, familiar blue sky.

I began to study medicine because I wanted the truth, but not the kind that had been strained through ideas, diluted and worn down by them. It was not mere philosophy I was in search of, and still less the delightful illusions of art. I had experienced hard times by then and did not appreciate the things that the well-to-do found amusing, and the artistic life, at least what I saw of it, appalled me. Everyday life, in contrast, was filled with solemnity and energy, and nature, which we were a part of, was marvelously brutal and cruel. And then came Nietzsche, he had not studied medicine and didn't know much about the natural sciences, but he knew what to make of what he did know. He was honest, he demanded truth and only truth. (It was, rather, the obsession to pursue truth, which as a result turned out not to be truth.) I followed what he wrote breathlessly and thought about his ideas. I neither embraced them nor rejected them. I let them have their effect on me. It brought enlightenment and emotional shock to me.

There are two types of encounters one must be grateful for. One is the encounter with persons who fulfill our wishes and answer our questions. The other is the encounter with those people, or books, or events or images, that create wishes in us and cause us to ask questions. Those are the encounters reminiscent of a spring shower in the desert that causes luxuriant greenery to flower from a ground that yesterday was only hot, yellow sand, that had never given any suggestion of such plentiful, splendid growth.

We are exposed to the light of the world in these two ways. The magicians I have mentioned appeared to me in such ways. I grappled for a long time with figures and characters from the works of Kleist, Hölderlin and Dostoyevsky, and with Nietzsche's teachings and then abandoned them. But they did not disappear, and whenever I approached them in the future I did so with affection and gratitude.

I sit on my bed in my cubicle and ask myself how it has come to this. And it becomes clearer and clearer to me: if I were like many others with whom I was exiled and whom I have met since, I would by now be as hard as steel and totally sure of myself. Nothing at all has been proved by our misfortune of having been driven first from Germany and now from the country of our asylum. Those who carried the flag with an iron fist carry it still. The flag, it all has to do with the flag. Which flag have I carried? Which flag do I carry? And the others, can they tell me which flag they are carrying, have they answered for that flag?

I have always been on the side of the poor; that is the one thing I am sure of. From time to time, for this reason or that, I have followed this flag or that one. But I was never capable of going into battle for it.

I met one other magician, rather late in life, around 1935 in Paris: Kierkegaard. I struggled with him, too, as I had with the other gods, but less forcefully and without result. This unfortunate man reminded me of Heinrich von Kleist and the confusion he felt on encountering Kant. Kierkegaard wants truth at any price. He says he wants it—but he doesn't. For he has it already, not the truth, but his truth. And he clings to it. He doesn't dare tear himself from it. His conscience forces him to keep searching. He insists that his conscience forces him to keep searching. He insists that his conscience keeps him from finding it. But it isn't his conscience at all. It is his obstinate pride. And so he acts like a dog on a leash, he barks and barks, runs in circles, but gets nowhere. He denies himself access to the truth. And what a pathetic effort, what wasted labor. He would be so happy if someone would come along, take him by the hand, liberate him with some words of comfort, and lead him away.

I do not want to forget.

In the first half of the twenties, something resembling pogroms were taking place in Berlin, in the city's eastern section, on Gollnow Street and its surroundings. This happened against the paramilitary background of those years; Nazism was in its infancy. At that time, representatives of Zionism in Berlin invited a group of men of Jewish origin to meetings at which these events and what led up to them were discussed, as well as the goals of Zionism. As a result of these discussions, someone came to my apartment to persuade me to take a trip to Palestine, which I found strange. His attempts at persuasion had a different effect on me. I did not, to be sure, agree to go to Palestine, but I found that I wanted to know more about the Jews. I discovered that I didn't know them. I could not call Jews those of my acquaintances who called themselves Jews. They weren't Jews in their beliefs, in their language, they were perhaps the vestige of an extinct people who had long ago assimilated to their environment. So I asked myself and others: where are there Jews? I was told: in Poland.

I went to Poland. I have written a book about it. I went there and for the first time in my life I saw Jews. I was deeply touched by the sight of them. I have never forgotten what I saw in the ghettos of Warsaw, of Wilna and Krakow, and particularly what I saw in the town of a great rabbi, in Gura Kalvaria. There they wore the costume of the German Middle Ages, the long black coat that is called a kaftan here. Their language had clearly been arrested at Middle High German, it was mixed with words from their region and their wanderings. I sat on the street with a group of schoolchildren, ten to twelve years old, with their hanging locks of curls at both sides of their faces, with shoes and socks like pages wore. They were a strange people, from another world altogether. They had their own religion, their own language, their surroundings. I had as little in common with them as they had with me.

My interest in the Jewish experience was heightened by this journey. The plan to create a land for what remained of this homeless and persecuted people made sense to me. Perhaps the Jews, having been uprooted from their own land and having floated among the peoples of the world for two millennia, could once again find land upon which they could develop in their own way, utilizing their own strengths. I rejected a nationalistic Zionism; it was too European for me and too bourgeois. So I joined the "territorialists." I even tried to learn Yiddish. I traveled, wrote, and spoke out in support of this movement. But I remained outside it. My words meant nothing, and I felt nothing. It was yet another flag I could not carry.

The long years in Berlin during Socialism, following the First World War and for a long time afterward . . . the workers' world was my milieu. I embraced socialistic thought, the true idea, the basic feeling of a human brotherhood. I observed party politics and saw— boss rule. That's what happened to socialist thought. And in the end I was part of a small group of men in Berlin who had all split with one party or another, basically we were all disappointed and disillusioned. We splinters continued to meet until the Terror drove us apart. Which cause was my cause?

Am I stranded, now?

I built myself a rowboat that was too light to carry me across the ocean. Its sides were battered in, of course. Its bottom proved to be of paper, and dissolved. I dragged myself along as long as the storm permitted, then came one blast of wind after another and the boat capsized and my sea journey was at an end.

I also wrote. Did it help me? Did it make me secure? What was it? It formed a climate in me, a meteorological situation that corresponded to a definite spiritual need. I could not rest until I sat down in front of the blank page and filled it with words and sentences. I had to open a secret door and enter a quiet room that belonged only to me, close the door fast behind me, and then I was totally alone and something began to happen, something coupled with excitement and tension that was good for me and that often filled me with dizziness or happiness, a quiet event behind closed doors.

This writing (for I was writing) had nothing to do, however, with contemplation or clarification. It was a reality in itself, it did not need legitimation from any other reality, even if it brushed up against it. I see myself placed before backdrops, pushed into landscapes and situations that surfaced in me—I cannot say that I thought them up or created them. I could neither summon these phantasies nor ward them off. Nevertheless, I never entered that world alone, even if it seemed that way to me. I never sat alone at my table. I was always surrounded by a large gathering: of words, of language. The words accompanied me. But the words inside here were something other than words outside that facilitated understanding and denotation. The words that entered my room served to construct, to play, to depict. They wore a kind of ghostly attire. They were not permitted to come in otherwise; and that was all they were permitted to bring with them. It is an odd thing, writing. I never began until my ideas took on a certain degree of ripeness, and that was reached when they appeared clothed in language. Once I possessed this image, I set out on it, my pilot boat, from the harbor, and I would soon see a ship, a great ocean liner, and board it and continued sailing and was in my element, I traveled and made great discoveries and only months later did I return home from my long journey, satiated, and could once again set foot on land. My journeys behind closed doors took me to China, India, Greenland, to other eras, and out of time as well. What a life that was.

But did I bring back something with me from these journeys?

I had "traveled" with words, had used them to construct images and phantasies. What could be brought back from such travels? In the end, a book. And I was satisfied, placated, until once again I was beset by restlessness and emptiness and got the urge, and the urge grew in me and became an addiction, the addiction to traveling, to wandering, to escape, to change. It wasn't enough to assume only one form, to be one single human being. . . .

But I remember, too, and do not want to forget that this single human being had, and knew, something else between his adventures and quick changes. A stream flowed through his landscape. And he never tired of walking along its banks.

He knew of the secret from early on—the secret of the existence of the world. Without having been taught he knew that in the face of the secret there was only one human response—and that was to sink to one's knees. I knew this. And when I wrote about and contemplated nature, my only consideration was to get close to this secret and to pay my respects. And all my works were a part of this respect. All my adventures and travels occurred under its sign. To a certain extent they were all prayers.

But at the same time I had to accept the fact that I was considered to be an atheist, because of the company I kept and, furthermore, because I talked only of "original meaning" and sought it in nature and history alone. I kept my distance from the great names invoked by the pious.

As I sit here now I discover that the catastrophe has not robbed me, it has revealed me. And that I profited in my poverty. One end result of "original meaning": to it belongs justice. It is not only the natural world that is constructed purposefully, but also events, history. The true depth of history is inaccessible to us. And if at present there is no sign of justice—and justice is the only thing I possess in the aftermath of the catastrophe and the revelation of my poverty—then I have to recognize that this is not the only world.

The lack of justice in the world proves that this is not the only world. Original meaning does not extend itself to our world, our senses, alone. Its effect, and its justice too, encompasses and permeates the visible and invisible worlds.

There are other worlds, yes, invisible ones. What an obvious idea. The moment this occurs to me I no longer feel so driven. From invisible worlds omens and coincidences and signs flow into the visible world. It is a sort of "softening" of reality. Reality becomes transparent. It always is, actually. But there are not always eyes to see. We content ourselves with our trees, our animals and cities—the surfaces, the superficial planes.

# 7

# A Newspaper Article and Other Things

*T*wo terrace cafés lie opposite each other on the main street: one is called Café de la Paix, the destination of my afternoon walks. Others like me lounge about on the terrace. The ones to be pitied are the military personnel, they are driven away if they appear before six, the waitress whispers something to them, even to the officers, they look bewildered, pay, and leave. But a compromise has been found. To the right of the café's property wall is a garden wall painted green, with a garden table standing next to it. It has been decided that this table is extraterritorial and does not belong to the establishment. Although the table is not served, soldiers can sit down there and read newspapers or write letters.

The flow of refugee traffic has abated. The whole street scene has changed since the cease-fire. It is dominated by soldiers awaiting demobilization. There are officers, too, walking around in the afternoons and evenings in full uniform, but without weapons, a sad sight. I once saw two soldiers carrying out a secret mission on the broad lawn of the Grand Hotel: one of them is kneeling in the grass searching for something. The other has two thin branches he holds like a fork. What are they doing? Now they've got it! They have . . . caught a butterfly. The one with the branches holds up a struggling insect and proudly shows it to those of us at the wall.

Other soldiers take walks along the river and fish here. They avoid the women washing clothes, who have set up their clotheslines down from the anglers, ruining their spot. Now and then a soldier triumphantly yanks a little fish up into the air.

The soldiers' attire is beginning to change. It is progressing toward the civilian. One of them is wearing plain white linen trousers, another is in military pants and a uniform cap, but he is a civilian in between. It is strange to see fully outfitted, heavily laden soldiers in steel helmets among these groups of half- and quarter-soldiers—a song from long, long ago.

I manage to get my hands on an issue of *Paris-Soir*, sit down with it on the square in front of the church, and study both pages—for the newspaper has only the two.

I find an article by Gillet, a member of the Académie Française. He writes of visiting his son, who has been wounded, and what his son had to say about the Germans. What he writes is also what I am hearing in my barrack and from the people I meet in the mornings in front of the bookstore, waiting for the papers. We often stand there for an hour, the papers are delivered by car. They glorify the Germans now. Even the soldiers glorify them, adding, of course: our leaders are no good.

Gillet, in *Paris-Soir*, strikes this same note. From his son's descriptions he has formed an idea of the other side's "elemental energy," he reports. He says France is now being inundated and overrun by "a new Islam." In the last war, the war of 1914–1918, the Germans were, if I remember correctly, called Huns and barbarians, at the very least *Boches*. And it was the same in 1870–1871. Now they are spoken of with respect, even with envy.

The French spirit, Gillet says, is deficient in force. I will ignore the question of whether or not France has really been overrun by the force of some "spirit" and whether a defeat necessitates bringing religion into it. There were, and are, in France many kinds of "spirit." There are many kinds of plants growing in this great and plentiful garden, there have been for a long time. In recent times there have been fewer towering figures, but the old supply was large. There was Catholic, Protestant, Calvinist, neo-Catholic, neo-

religious, classical-religious, lay and Voltairean thought—all existing side by side, all French. It was irrelevant whether or not any of
them constituted a mass movement. It was enough that "France"
was a domicile, a historical given. Politics and social life were carried
out within the domicile, it was a question of individual happiness.
All attempts to transplant the collective hysteria and mass psychosis
of dictatorships outside France met with failure here.

This meant we were badly prepared to wage war against a
military and police state. Precisely because of French individualism
there should have emerged from the débacle a determined will to
fight. But we saw what rolled in: a monolithic human machine, just
the opposite of what is appreciated here.

But behold: in the newspapers and among the philistines, at
least, the human machine is revered! These people are so "objective"
that they can admire how efficiently the machine crushes them.

And to this human machine is imputed a new, praiseworthy
religion, à la Islam. This is no longer individualism, but a mixture of
stupidity and masochism.

What sort of Islam is it that Gillet speaks of? We have been
neatly duped by the Nazis. Many people considered it too simple-
minded to think that the Prussian drill book and discipline formed
the backbone of Nazism, and that Nazism in general is Prussian
militarism dressed in new clothes, drilled in a new way. Apparently it
was necessary to live in proximity to it, and to see columns of Nazis
in the streets to recognize that the old Prussian parade ground had
expanded and, having swallowed up Germany, had then devoured
half of Europe.

This time it was a different form of Prussian militarism, a
modern version. The barracks lackey had freed and democratized
himself and chased off the officers from the old school. It is no
accident that the whole thing is led by a former corporal.

The November Revolution has been continued here. In that
case, too, it was not the workers, the proletariat, that headed the
movement, but the petty bourgeoisie. And why them? Aside from
their numbers, because they can work both sides, and they hope to
profit from both. They are, as Gillet correctly notes, fanatics, but
what kind of fanatics? Is theirs a religious fanaticism?

Prussian militarism was not destroyed in the last war, at least
not as a caste, and the principal goal of the war was therefore not

attained. Prussian militarism not only was allowed to survive, it was given a new stimulus—the stimulus of defeat. This caused several reactions. It heightened the petty bourgeoisie's energy and combative intellect more than a victory could have. It enabled the leaders of this group to reduce all the misfortunes Germany had suffered to one common denominator: unwarranted, undeserved defeat, to which was added moral dishonor. They succeeded in spreading the message that Germany had not been defeated at all in 1918. The sting of surrender was overcompensated for by a colossal notion of national grandeur. This concept had been around for a long time in Germany. At first, it was purely the psychosis of defeat, then the concept appeared under the guise of compensation, followed by the rise of the military. This movement donned the Nazi uniform, then put the disastrous economic conditions and unemployment to work for itself.

What does that have to do with Islam?

The whole thing only demonstrates, as Foch had already said, that no one knew how to take advantage of the victory of 1918, and therefore Prussian militarism was given time to rearm itself.

And we should not be so shortsighted as not to recognize who it is we have before us in new armor, in new costumes. We should not be discussing Islam but should be beating our breasts instead. Do we find our lethargy and inattentiveness praiseworthy? By doing so we merely obscure evil, lauding it as a new religion.

## Surprises

Time passes slowly in the camp. I have settled here because I can get no farther. I dread mealtime. You have to eat what is put in front of you, you can't refuse it without being looked at askance; but the food kills your appetite. The dishes are tasteless. There is no variation: noodles, beans, potato soup, lentils. Once we are offered sweet, hard rice that has been unpleasantly scorched. A little chunk of meat is served—not always—and a piece of soggy bread. I force myself to swallow it all.

I often consider the possibility that my wife made it to Bordeaux and took a ship to England. If she did there is no way I can get word of her. But what plan will I then follow for myself? My daydreams, my waking phantasies, become more and more feverish as the days go by. I try to shake them off, but they overwhelm me, they devour me. My life is without plan or goal; I am vegetating. Perhaps writing would divert my phantasy, "lance" it, but except for the two pages of the daily news, I want to read and write as little as I want to eat.

I am often obsessed by the question of what I will do later, alone. Where will I go? And if my family is still in France, what will become of us if the country is gradually occupied by the Nazis? We will try to hide somewhere, under the sword of Damocles.

My mad daydreams—particularly the ones I have while sitting in my cubicle, but also ones that come during my lonely walks— often assume a predatory, savage character. When I leave the camp I see the poster: "May 16, Circus Bureau, the Only Circus Without Illusion." My phantasies rob me of awareness of my surroundings. They make me absentminded. My barrack mates tell me that they have met me along the way somewhere and said hello, but that I walked by them without even looking up. Sometimes my imaginings terrify me. I decide I must pull myself together. But then, quick as lightning, I'm again sucked down into the vortex.

Once, as I came to myself at the café, following one of the appalling phantasy episodes, it occurred to me that I was acting like Goethe's Torquato Tasso. The same demented, self-punishing speculation, the self-torment, the same breathless race up the misty mountainside, to be blown back down by a gust of wind.

I am pleasantly surprised on one of my walks to see "my" two criminal commissars. It is not unexpected that I run into them. The town is small and, like me, they wander around. Now and then they sit near me at the café, observing and eavesdropping on passersby. On the street they ask me about my situation. They praise the camp and advise me to be patient.

Each evening I wait for the moment when the old woman will lie down, then I swallow a sleeping pill and lie down myself. Each hour I can rob from time is a victory.

I often see before me the horrid image of the man crushed to death on the bridge. At least he has it behind him.

Once, around six in the evening, as I returned from my aimless walking and sitting about—I had walked up into a soothing, wooded area that did me good—I read on the camp's blackboard: "Is there a Madame Döblin in the camp?"

I go to the office. A telegram has arrived—not from my wife, as I had assumed, but from someone else. I am told the telegram is at the post office. I am given a slip of paper so that I may pick it up. I later find out that someone is opening my mail.

The telegram I am given is mystifying. Miss S advises me to contact a certain agency in Bordeaux for my wife's address.

So the next morning I go to the prefecture and ask the commissar, the one with the bandaged hand, to telephone Bordeaux for me. He is disinclined to do so. First, it is not possible to call Bordeaux, and second, the agencies, as I could read in the papers, are in the process of moving, some to Clermont-Ferrand. He sends me somewhere else: there I am advised to come back in two days. By then maybe they would know where the wandering agencies have settled. Though I could send a telegram myself, they say, but if and when it would arrive was another question, of course.

I telegraph Le Puy that the Bordeaux address is no longer valid, and ask the sender how she knew that the agency had my family's address. The entire telegram business was pointless anyway. I only did it to have something to do.

It is Sunday in the camp. There was a great deal of activity last night in the barracks. A group of bicyclists took over the vacant beds. When they got quiet, the children began coughing, almost all of them have whooping cough. The attack begins first in one cubicle, then in another. I lie awake and struggle to stay calm. I am plagued by thoughts of death and dying. I try to assume a positive attitude about death. The hours pass slowly. This morning I hit the street. I follow the churchgoers, sit in the cathedral.

I look at the crucifix. I try to hold on to "Thy will be done." And then I reflect on what the sermon was about and what the mass proclaimed: "The world is unhappy and wanting because of our guilt and our weakness. But mercy, love, and salvation were sent to the world. God knows of our condition. He takes us unto him. We must only approach him and want him." I say this aloud. Only approach, only want. I would like to. I would like to. But I am unable to. The balm of tranquility does not flow in me.

Back to the camp. I walk past the blackboard suspiciously. That afternoon as I return, I am handed two telegrams: one from my friend, who with his wife is home in the Midi, he will do all that he can for me, he says, the other is from the girls' school we stayed at in Cahors: there has been no word from my family.

It is probable that they have gone to England.

My thoughts have taken on a stumbling, oscillating, pendulum-like character. I have no way of stopping them. My thoughts no longer even have the character of thought, they are like pistons in an engine.

That evening as I take a walk in the warm air, I am comforted by the sight of "my" poster.

But why? Later, I write in my notebook: "We should not oppose the secret forces that guide our destiny." I feel this. At least this. I own it. Yes, and it possesses my whole being, my soul. I am in total harmony with this thought. It expresses me perfectly.

And it allows me to breathe. It allows me to watch the harvesters in the fields. Soldiers in shirtsleeves are helping them. The women from Alsace are chatting on the little bridge.

## Waking Dreams and Thoughts

Demobilized soldiers are returning. They bring their families to the marketplace, where there are vegetables and fruit, sometimes eggs, but never butter. This is peace, a tranquil world.

Until yesterday we could see the trench they had begun to dig on the town hall square—today it is filled in.

For the last few days a large covered truck has been parked on the square. It served as a residence for well-dressed officials. They sat on chairs inside, slept on straw-filled mattresses. When they lay down on them, they hung their chairs outside on the truck. The truck is gone. Military personnel idly stroll through the town's back streets. They are gradually being demobilized. Crowds of people can be found each morning at the prefecture, waiting for the newspapers, the *Éclair* and the *Petit méridional*. It is my only intellectual nourishment, too.

Ambulances have gathered here in recent days. They are positioned around the city. There are fully operating X-ray and surgical trucks.

The unarmed soldiers, the ambulances, the empty military barracks by the bridge, the motorcycles rattling by—the whole thing is a bad dream. The town, with its crooked streets, its rough cobblestones, and pots and baskets of vegetables set out before the shops, with its soldiers plodding about, it's all a nightmare to me.

"We should not oppose the secret forces that guide our destiny." I say this to myself often. I have long held these words within me, first in one form, then another. They express an old, essential feeling of mine. When I articulate them I have formulated my entire belief system. But the words are lacking, and that is what keeps me going. I am unsuccessful in connecting with the crucified Jesus, though my emotions almost force me to. I have only the secret forces that guide my fate.

It often occurs to me as I am sitting in the empty cathedral that I must bring together the secret forces with the reassuring thought of Jesus. I try. But I can't.

A new day.

Yesterday at Sunday mass, it became clear to me why my feeling about the secret forces and the idea of Jesus are so difficult for me to reconcile.

I see Jesus on the cross, with his crown of thorns, as the incarnation of human misery, of our weakness and helplessness. I do not deny this truth. But it is not what I am seeking. For of what significance is it to me now? It is a truth that serves situations other than my own. The crucified Jesus is a vision for the "heart hardened to happiness." But wasn't it also said that he was the Saviour? That he would bring glad tidings, that he was the son of God, was sent by God to transform human misery? Where is the evidence?

Instead, I am tormented. The account of the Passion is told to me. But we don't need God to appear and tell us our existence is full of suffering. What we need is a reason, a justification for our condition, a message that we do not suffer hopelessly and in vain.

But everything is being associated with the stations of the cross. What remains is the Other, the Real, that which we all lack, and which no science teaches: the eradication of misery and weakness through exaltation, the victory over mortal need.

How glum the priests look at the altar. How quietly the faithful walk about or sit. But why? We are in a Christian cathedral, no one has died, someone has risen!

The Church, for reasons I cannot ascertain, is neglecting something here. The priests are glum. Maybe it is necessary to heighten people's empathy with one another, the strong and healthy tend to be unfeeling and aloof, they are concerned with their own burdens. People who are unfeeling and joyful tend toward cruelty. A model must be created that will connect that sort of person to what is humane: the suffering Christ. What do we require to make us strong? We experience misery and hopelessness. We are defenseless against all kinds of threats in society, in the State. People are ever more prosperous, yet feel poorer as the decades go by. What did they expect of Socialism, of Communism? What is it we need? We need a new basis for our existence. But upon what foundation?

There is only one foundation: the eternal source of all being from which we were created. We cannot comprehend what lies behind that creation, nor what we signify. But understandable and certain is that the eternal source of all being created us, together with this world.

It is impossible to accept the idea that this world now exists separate from the eternal source of being. That is a superficial view of mortal beings according to which they live, thrive, die, and rot among other mortal beings, without foreground or background, without ground.

Then Jesus appears.

I see Jesus as a counterpart to the Prometheus of antiquity. Prometheus brought fire to earth, drew people out of their caves, and became ruler over a number of natural forces. To be Promethean is to attain human nobility; not to understand the limits of the Promethean is human folly.

I again sat in the cathedral for a long time and tried to merge my thoughts with the secret forces that guide our destiny, with the eternal source of being that supports and maintains us—with the image of the crucified Jesus.

There must be something that takes us to this source, that connects us to eternal life, or, to be more precise, that illuminates the ever-present connection.

The crucified Jesus will not let me be. I am fascinated by him and by the religion formed around him. But I cannot manage to meld his image with what I feel is true.

[ *122* ]

Alfred Döblin

## *Once Again, an Objection*

I must interrupt myself. How would someone following this line of thought from the outside argue against it? Possibly in this way:

The outsider finds himself in a physiological and psychic situation that is abnormal for him. The man (a physician) should have recognized this, actually.

Two weeks in quiet surroundings with enough to eat would be sufficient to liberate the man from his theology.

I really was undernourished. I lived in an unhealthy environment. At times I fell into a sort of hallucinogenic state of agitation; one afternoon, for instance, as I was sitting on my bed, thinking of nothing, I heard my wife, speaking in a normal tone of voice; after this I heard another voice I could not identify. Both said something that was totally ordinary. Perhaps it was simply a conversation taking place in the distance. I wasn't frightened by it, afterward I merely rubbed my ears.

Malnutrition, detachment from external reality, the obliteration of normal attachments, however, constitute only the frame of the picture. For if you sit around putting on fat, if you drift along through everyday life, you experience only the commonplace and the banal. Your ears are attuned to the mundane and you will hear nothing else. It is necessary to be jolted out of the daily routine, it was for this reason that ascetics went into the wilderness and monks locked themselves into cells and fasted. Hunger and malnutrition counter the fat, the lethargy. Comfort and routine strangle what is alive in us and that which wants to live.

What is this quotidian comfort that makes our lives easy, what is its meaning, its role? We are told that it encourages contemplation and profundity. But in fact it leads to frivolity and aestheticism. We dream, we let ourselves be shown the tragic struggles, the suffering and the fate of others, the martyrdom of ancient and modern heroes. We watch them, desiring to buy ourselves out of our own fate. We accompany these heroes with a feeling of guilt and a bit of self-incrimination but, above all, with self-satisfied enjoyment because it is not we, after all, who have to deal with the situation. From a distance we cynically enjoy the dramatic suffering of others. We think that heroes will act it out for us. These martyrs and heroes represent our *I*, are our ersatz *I*—just as in olden times one bought a poor peasant to send as one's substitute into battle.

We lead a tightly regulated life, but it is actually chaotic. We long ago ceased to do anything but manage external reality. But who is it who regulates, who orders things? Who and what is it? We think we can dispense with the eye that is watching us, from ordering what is internal.

Is there such a thing as guilt? I remember encountering a sentence from Nietzsche that goes something like: "Guilt is a totally foreign idea to me." Nietzsche expresses with this something that many people feel. But guilt, contrition, doubt, are things that no man, unless he has shriveled up, escapes. No one who has experienced life as a human being escapes them. Anyone who says he has no feelings of guilt or contrition has withdrawn his *I* from life and hidden it, or has not looked within himself, or is hiding from himself.

## *Accidents, Omens, and Signs*

Under my coat on the empty bed above me, near a sack of tomatoes I bought, and next to my towel lies the red train schedule with the map, which I brought with me here. Sometimes I cover it up, sometimes I leave it in the open.

How happy the people in the camp are! They never stop talking about going home. Is there such a thing for me as going home? For a long time now we have scarcely had a home. And now this other thing, this other thing in me.

Patience. I never would have believed what strength patience requires, and what patience really is: tireless work, holding out against suffering, not allowing oneself to surrender. I relax for a few hours.

I stand in front of the post office, observing the people. Trucks drive by in spurts, letting off soldiers. They storm the post office with questions about letters, and immediately telegraph the whole world their new address. I see what a hurry they are in, they empty the receptacle that holds the telegram forms and write their message. Yes, it is comforting to have written. At least that is something. Everything else is doubtful.

A sign hangs on the wall: "Telegrams are very late in arriving."

And if you take a look at the clerk behind the counter, the one with the flushed face, you understand why. A huge pile of telegrams lies beside him. Now and again an assistant appears, picks up a bunch of them, shaking his head—the clerk shrugs his shoulders—and carries them off somewhere. The soldiers are not discouraged, they continue to write and send off telegrams anew.

The weather is lovely. The ambulance attendants sit, lie down, and sleep in their ambulances. Doctors walk around town; stagnation. And what will happen, what could happen, when everyone goes home and the country, half of it occupied, is under armistice?

"Accidents" continue to occur. They happen and I notice strange things. This is no "normal" time we are in. A man appears on crutches. I spot him in the camp located next to the ominous bridge. He is dragging himself into town. Another man moves across the bridge toward us; he, too, on crutches, his right knee in splints. I know that this will not be a good day.

I continue along my way. A grotesque figure appears in the street in front of the Grand Hotel. At first I cannot make it out. Only when I come quite close do I realize that it is a deformed old woman. She can barely move. Her torso is bent at a right angle to the rest of her body. Her head is bent down sharply. It looks as if she is searching for something on the ground. She creeps along like a snail. Movement is unbelievably difficult for her; she can't pick up her feet, she shuffles along, advances by pushing one foot in front of the other. It is hard work, a terrible sight. Probably Bechterew's disease, a spinal condition.

I have several days of such experiences. Then at some point, perhaps in the evening, or around noon, things change. A transformation occurs, the "power lines" (as I call them) change direction, or other power lines take over. And then everything heats up.

On one such difficult day I receive two letters after dinner. They are delivered to my barrack (I didn't get the idea they had been opened and read, but others in the barrack expressed surprise that they took so long in arriving). My friend writes to me of his futile efforts on my behalf. And the second letter, from Miss S in Le Puy, contains a telegram from an agency now located in Vichy, which my wife had turned to while in Bordeaux, requesting my address. Miss S will undertake to answer this. On the evening that I received these letters, down as I was, I did not give them much thought. It was enough to have heard something from the outside world, from the world at large. It hadn't given up on me yet.

As I am leaving the barrack I am addressed by the old, white-haired woman with the glasses, who sat across from me at table. She tells me her woes, her stories. And once again I find myself in my old accustomed role of letting others talk.

As I cross the bridge in the soft evening air under skies tinged pink, and turn into the main street, a group of city people come toward me. I usually encounter only peasant types here, both male and female, cattle dealers and such. Now the city is coming toward me; it, too, is a letter from another world.

I sit down on a bench across from the Grand Hotel. Across the way, among the civilians, there is a tall young officer with an intelligent face. He is reading a book in the twilight. What a gesture: reading. He is sporting a short goatee.

As I walk on, three officers pass me in lively conversation. The one in the middle is odd-looking; he is an army priest; I had never seen an army priest. He has a wise face, wears glasses, is about thirty-five, has on a regulation military cap with two peaks, but the cap is black, as is the rest of his attire. He wears soldier's boots with high leggings, the long, wide robe of the priest that reaches to his knees and has wide pleats and is belted at the waist so that it falls in a bell shape. A large white crucifix hangs from a chain on his chest. They are walking past me into the center of town. And later, as I return to the camp from the opposite direction, they appear again in lively discussion. They marched along with large strides and stopped from time to time to argue with each other.

I arrived back at the barracks later than I ever had before. On the way I run across pairs of lovers and hear them laughing.

Night came slowly. The heaven's bright magic slowly faded.


## A Memorial Service

A service for soldiers and evacuees in the cathedral.

The church is almost empty when I arrive. A stand in front of the altar holds French flags. I sit in the back, next to a middle-aged soldier. Nuns come over to us and ask that the back pews be kept free

Alfred Döblin

for orphan children. A group of boys and girls come in, led by a priest; they drag over benches and chairs from the front and sides of the cathedral and sit down in back. The church slowly comes to life. First soldiers arrive, then well-dressed civilians. The families of the little town come in. In front of me a mother sits down with her son, a large boy. They are cracking almonds. The boy is holding a new prayer book. The church fills up around ten o'clock; people are standing in the back and at the sides.

The organ begins to play. It is an awful moment. I must be very nervous, I can scarcely contain myself. Then the feeling subsides. The candles are lit. An ancient Gregorian requiem begins. All over the church, people are weeping. A man sitting behind me sobs loudly.

I become attentive as the "Dies Irae" approaches. I expect a dramatic burst of music, Verdi's punitive storm. But it is kept simple, honest. It is chanted in the same intonation. This is not wrath; this is a human voice that knows wrath, anticipates it, and speaks of it humbly, a "Dies Irae" of great integrity. The "requiem aeternam" and the "Amen" are deeply moving.

The bishop, dressed in a violet cassock with a violet skullcap, mounts the pulpit set between pillars, followed by two priests.

He speaks. The centuries-old cathedral receives its congregation today, he says, in one of the most painful moments of its history. He praises the army, its courage and spirit of sacrifice. Honor has been upheld. He quotes Marshal Pétain, that the enemy was so much stronger in manpower and weaponry. He calls for courage; we must think of rebuilding. "Let us pray."

The service is not yet over when I leave. The heat outside is scorching. The bishop's talk was meaningless. He talked over us, not from among us. I buy a newspaper. There are reports that the Germans will attack England. They will certainly try it; the English are alone, they won't have it easy.

I sit on a bench behind the church.

I will leave the camp soon and make my way alone. What will happen? Should I find some corner somewhere and continue to write in my accustomed way—but for whom, in German?

Writing has had its time and its place—now fading. It is not a matter of finding this or that person to base it on.

[ *127* ]

The natural world of which I, too, am part, sends forth its charms in an irresistible, indisputable, powerful way, it penetrates my being. It scatters its blessings as a flowering tree powders its surroundings with yellow pollen. The blessing of the air, the wind, the sky. I feel them, sitting on my bench.

And, later, as I walk along the river, the water flows by below me, the fluid, elastic element of which the little stream, and the Amazon, the oceans, waterfalls, glaciers, hail, rain, and fog consist. What a miracle water is! And the whole of nature—like the *I*—product, act, sign of the primal force. And what a force it is! And how spiritual. Water showed me this long ago with its transmutations, its treasures, its crystalline beauty. Am I to believe that it was some awkward, some senseless thing that arranged this and put it here, that appears in this costume? Brutal, cruel nature is not only brutal and cruel. The brutality and cruelty do not exist for themselves alone.

We live amid many positive things. And no matter what happens: mankind is a solid, well-formed, and intelligent thing, despite all its madness and wickedness. We are complex, and, it often seems to me, not quite completed. We are still on the way.

And we are at home in too many worlds, in even more worlds than is water.

So I am a child of the world in spite of everything! Why shouldn't I be, I ask myself, when this world, with its verdant nature that speaks to me, reveals the sign of a divine hand? Why should I close my ears to the music of the spheres?

## The Telegram

My name is listed on the blackboard when I return to the camp for lunch, feeling safer and calmer than usual.

I hear that a telegram has arrived for me. The messenger took it back with him, however, when he couldn't locate me.

It must be the telegram I am expecting. My newfound composure is momentarily shattered and in no time the old, frantic apprehension takes over.

I am almost prostrate with anxiety. I take two pills to calm myself. I eat in distraction. The post office will open again at two o'clock. I will use the time till then to calm myself.

Alfred Döblin

As I sit on my bed during the bedlam of washing up and sweeping—the dust forces me to use my blanket as a mask—I try to think. My futile anxiety confuses me. The confused phantasies of the past weeks return obsessively to take the upper hand. Nothing I concentrate on has any effect.

I try to hold back the storm. My present frame of mind, which had so pleased me this morning, doesn't stand the test.

At two o'clock I am at the post office. I am told to come back in half an hour.

Protest rises up in me. I do not want to be made to feel dependent on postal deliveries. I should wait and pick up the telegram that evening. I return to the camp, the heat is insufferable, I sit around wearily in the barrack. Someone asks me about the telegram. I go back to town.

As I near the post office I feel determined, firm. I am prepared for anything, like the time I arrived in Le Puy in the storm and rain.

Several people are waiting at the counter; the clerk looks up and sees me at the back of the line. The telegram has arrived. The others make way for me. She gives me the piece of paper. It is marked with a red stripe that reads "urgent."

I open it. The word "happy" leaps out at me. I read the signature. The telegram is from my wife. She is staying in Toulouse with our child.

# 8

# The Spell Is Broken

## *An Hour in the Café*

*I* felt nothing resembling strong emotion. The telegram is like a wind blowing in fog, scattering it. Phantasies disappear. I become cheerful and clear-headed: the surge of energy that precedes action.

A small map is hanging at the post office. It hangs in a dark spot. I try to locate Toulouse; how far is Toulouse from Mende? The dreaded problems of destination and transport raise their ugly heads.

As I am standing there with my nose to the map, a man asks me what I am looking for. I tell him. He laughs. I won't find Toulouse here. And he points to a spot a foot from the map: "Toulouse is here." I ask him how I can get there. He answers amiably, informatively, that there is a bus. It is either nonstop or I have to change. At any rate, he says, I should inquire at the small café I already frequent. The proprietress would know.

I wait for the proprietress and note that I am already in a new fever pitch of anxiety. I sit on the terrace with my glass of black coffee and fret:

They are in Toulouse. It's strange. When I could proceed no farther in Rodez there was a bus parked at the marketplace. I asked where it was going and I was told: Toulouse. But I decided against it. My head said: Le Puy. When I went to the prefecture in Mende the first time to ask for a travel permit, and was asked where I wanted to go, I said "Cahors"—and the next stop after that, oddly enough, would have been Toulouse. But there was no reason for me to go to Toulouse. And on my permit, on the *sauf-conduit*, my destination was given as Cahors or Toulouse. And when I went to the train station for the last time in Mende, to find out when the trains were departing, people were hurrying across the tracks, civilians with suitcases, and when I followed them they said: This is the last train leaving, and it is going to Toulouse. And again I stood there, and couldn't decide, and did nothing.

It seems to me that we receive signs that come in waves, in currents. Sometimes we prove good, sometimes bad, receivers. We comprehend the signs or we do not, or we misread them. If I look into it more deeply, I do not stop at the physical image of "resonance," for we ourselves are somehow actively involved in the appearance of these signs. We are surrounded by them constantly, we swim in them as in a nutritive broth and receive certain things, but also transmit them. So it is a correspondence, a secret conversation with an unknown partner.

The proprietress finally arrives and tells me that there is a bus that goes in the direction of Toulouse to a certain stop, and from there I will have to take the train. But whether the train is actually running . . .

At this I go to the train station and have a long talk with the man in charge. He refuses to allow me to take a train with my *ordre de mission*, which has long since expired. If I take a bus to the Canourgue station I will get stuck there. They wouldn't let me onto the train. The man tells me I need a new *ordre de mission*.

I go to the prefecture. Without discussion the word "granted" is stamped quickly and contemptibly onto a certificate of safe-conduct. That's it.

I end my action with a telegram to my wife: I am not yet certain of the date I will be able to leave.

I am exhausted from running back and forth in the heat. That evening, a small revolt breaks out at the camp.

## The Revolt Against That Evening's Spoiled Soup

It involves the soup. The soup is terrible. Of course. It has always been terrible, that is to say: watery, without substance, lukewarm. But until today that was enough for me and for the others. Suddenly it wasn't enough. I don't know why this changed.

At any rate, by the time I sat down on the bench next to the old woman, the change had already occurred: the soup was no good. Everyone along the entire length of the table was in an amazingly uniform fury about it, there was absolute unanimity: *the soup is bad*. I cannot find it anywhere on the table at this moment. It swims only in my and my neighbor's bowl. All of the other soup bowls have been turned upside down, the tin vessels lie bottom up all in a row, a revolutionary sight.

When I taste the soup, I find it innocent as charged. It had been singed a bit at its inception. But it has never tasted otherwise. "They're making us sick," is the word. There is no answer to that one. Some will feel sick and blame the soup. That's better, at least, than blaming the Jews. The father of the three proletarian children, the one with the flat-nosed wife, is particularly incensed. His features are twisted. These people are always protesting, but they are not evil. Today they are happy to have something to be furious about for a change. Basically, it's a nice alternative. The working-class man and his wife have stood up and are in loud discussion about it. They are giving speeches. The city council contributed ten francs a day per person at the camp, they said. We should demand something for that money.

While we are swallowing down our lentils and bread someone suddenly says: They're in the kitchen. Who? At any rate, everyone jumps up and storms the door.

Strange, this soup story. The rumor of spoiled soup has been spread in the other barracks, too. No one knew where or with whom it originated. But now the entire camp is in revolt. The courtyard is filled with people, all of them cheerful and pleasant, their faces reflect happy news. There's nothing better than spoiled soup.

The crowd swarms in front of the kitchen barrack. It is said that the head of the camp and the camp physician are inside, and are at that moment testing the soup. The crowd parts and the one-armed camp chief—veteran, Legion of Honor, chief magistrate—appears. Beside him is a quiet younger man, people are addressing him from all sides. He is the doctor. He does what he can under the circumstances: he looks serious and says nothing.

Then he is compelled to say something, and his answer spreads like wildfire across the courtyard: *the soup is good!* Everyone repeats this angrily: he has tasted it and says it is good!

The whole camp is outraged. They crowd in noisily on the two men. The soup is bad! What will happen? Suddenly someone announces that the police are coming. The noise level grows. Just let them come! A few people withdraw cautiously to their barracks. Not long thereafter two large cars pull up to the camp and stop in front of the office. Gendarmes jump out, and a police commissioner as well. The crowd stares at them, mocking, combative. The gendarmes plant themselves before the kitchen barrack, the commissar goes into the kitchen, into hell's kitchen, with the head of the camp.

The commissar emerges from the kitchen. The insurgents crowd up to him, protesting the soup. The soup was bad. They complain about the food and about other things. The gendarmes get involved, question people, and ask several of the more vociferous for their names. The people don't like this. The woman with the flat nose, who had demanded action, is questioned along with her husband.

This goes on for some time. Endless palaver from the kitchen down to the highway. People gradually begin to slip away. The timid ones have already retreated to the front of their barracks, or are inside looking out through the windows, the cowards. The gendarmes have now taken charge at the office; it is said they will soon go to each barrack and question the occupants individually. In the end, when nothing occurs, and the tables have been cleared, I act as though nothing at all has happened and take an evening walk—only to find out that by nine o'clock everything is quiet in the camp.

A single police car is still there, two gendarmes are smoking and talking with a few of the camp's inhabitants, who are also smoking.

## Who Is to Blame?

A swarm of young bicyclists has again arrived during the night and appear the next morning at coffee, loud and exuberant. These people appreciate the stale, dry bread that we shove toward them, they dunk it in their coffee. They have come from St. Étienne and report to us on what it is like there. They ridicule the ineffectual barricade constructed there to hold back the Germans, who had made quick work of it.

Those sitting near me at table nod their heads. All agree in denigrating the French war effort. But they don't spend much time discussing the question, that's what newspapers are for. And nothing can be done, anyway. All discussion ends with the statement: *If only we were home again. . . .*

The young people notice that their stories don't count for much here. They are among adults who have other worries.

But the tales fascinate me. I already had the impression on the way here that a war had been lost against an enemy who had allowed us only one initial move against him. We were checkmated before the game got started, and were left with most of our pieces still on the board.

People, even those here in the camp, tell themselves cock-and-bull stories about treason committed by highly placed officers who don't want to fight, etc., etc. They go so far as to maintain there was a conspiracy among officers against the Republic—they didn't want it to win.

## The Miserable and the Contented in Our Camp

The revolt of the spoiled soup was not without consequences. The people at table maintained it was owing to their action that the soup improved afterward. I found no great difference. One unarguable result of the revolt was the removal of the combative proletarian family. All five of them were abruptly summoned to the office, put into a car, and driven off to another camp.

Also connected with the revolt was an announcement that appeared on the blackboard with the message that anyone who had relatives or friends in another camp, or who would rather be in another camp for other reasons, should notify the office.

The departure of the proletarian family was mentioned at table without commiseration. An aside: An unusually fresh, bright boy belonged to the family, a seven-year-old who sat at my left during meals. He was lively and rebellious like his parents. He always greeted lentils with a whoop of joy and swallowed the first spoonful yelling, "*Les cailloux*" (gravel). Then he would rub his stomach to set the stones clattering. The malevolent grandmother with whom I roomed had given the boy the task of fetching us a bottle of red wine from town every three days. I gave him ten centimes for this, which was reduced to five when the old lady objected. The boy knew that the grandmother was responsible for this reduction and told his parents, who had then gotten into a terrible fight with the old woman about it. She, however, was used to pain and grief. She told me of her battle with the mob. Her decision was: either the boy would take five centimes or he would no longer fetch the wine for us. I had to bow to her decision. And the boy, as a true son of his parents, did what they had forbidden him to do, secretly, of course, for five centimes.

But the old woman begrudged him the five centimes. And sure enough, when the gang left, the old lady came to me and asked if I would agree that she fetch the red wine! Of course I had nothing against it. My eyes nearly popped out of my head the next day when she showed me the bottle and drew up a bill. She added five centimes to the price of the wine. I gave them to her, incredulous. She accepted them solemnly and drank most of the bottle herself, as is befitting the proprietress of a tavern.

Poor and miserly as she was, the old woman was always ready to help me. Every day she poured out her heart to me. I heard the same stories over and over again, looked at the same pictures.

As for me—my telegram would have excited me a few weeks before. It signified the end of my wanderings. Now my wanderings were no longer wanderings.

Now I wasn't moving at all. I had set foot on new land.

Two souls dwelled, also, in my breast. While the one listened to the new tune, the other thrashed about, jostled me to keep me distracted, urged me to act. It forced me to go to the square from which buses depart in the direction of Toulouse. I met a young man there who was talking with the driver. When he realized that I was interested in going to Toulouse, he tried to talk me into leaving with him within the hour. We would get to Canourgue and would "figure it out" from there. He was of the opinion that it would be easier for two than for one. He tried to persuade me. But I was lethargic. I was blocked internally. I didn't want to start the old game of hunting for cars and trains all over again.

## Some Curious Events

There are Spaniards in the camp. They have come from a camp for Spaniards that has been closed. They arrive in cars, spend the night, and hurry off the next morning to the south. The Belgians and French are talking of going home. On the board is a notice that French citizens should come to the office to report on their status. A morning breeze is blowing. There is supposedly a notice posted at city hall concerning the return transport of all people from unoccupied territories. It applies to only a few of us, but it gives us all courage.

The grandmother has received a letter from one of her sons. She tells everyone about it, and her neighbors respond in a friendly manner. During the day she now sits on her bench or by the door of the barrack, proud and content, quasi-rehabilitated. She even calls the children over to her. But they stay clear of the General.

The gentle young woman is worried about her little daughter. The child is spoiled, and is sick. The doctor comes. The mother says her husband is at the front—where could he be now?—her child is everything to her. She doesn't appear at meals. And the old woman with the glasses, who shares her cubicle, is also in low spirits. The nights are cold, the windows don't close, and the children lack proper care, hot water, and much else.

One woman in her thirties has two small children with her, a boy of four and a boy a year old. Neither wants to eat, both have whooping cough, and they look miserable, including the mother. But I watch the mother when the children have a coughing fit. The child can cough till he's blue and she won't pay any attention. When the child has finished coughing, she picks him up to wipe his face. Once, the bigger boy didn't want to eat, he sat back from his food, rocking on his bench, which was otherwise unoccupied, the others having already finished eating. He tips over, of course, together with the bench, there is a crash and a loud scream. Everyone rushes over. The boy is lying there, howling. The bench has landed on his foot and squashed his big toe. His mother stands up, grabs the boy by the arm, yelling furiously, and, had we not been there, would have given him a sound thrashing. He knows this, and as soon as he can stand, he flees limping and whimpering into his cubicle—while his mother seats herself again with an expression of outrage and continues to feed the other boy, who now does not want to eat either.

She's having a hard time of it, she gets no rest day or night. Her nerves are giving out.

And no one here does anything for her. The more I look around this barrack, the more astonished I am that each person keeps to himself and has little to do with anyone else. I run into the head of the camp outside, and we discuss the soup revolt and the case of the deported proletarian family. It is his opinion that perhaps the soup was not ideal, but that agitators have to be gotten rid of. Barracks morale demands that. People here had problems enough, they didn't need troublemakers.

I ask him if other inhabitants of the camp help each other out. He shakes his head no. One should have no illusions about that. Everyone is concerned only with getting his or her own share, and with seeing that the next person isn't getting any extra. No one gives away a crumb.

This was official pessimism speaking. It was a superficial view. People are forced to look after themselves, to get their share, but that doesn't make them egoists. They behave differently when things are better. I need only look as far as our barrack grandmother. She was ridiculed as malevolent and stingy, and everyone avoided her. She was poor as a beggar and was treated badly. But how should the old woman have reacted? She behaved differently toward me. We are not living under normal circumstances here. Everyone is ill-humored and becomes uncooperative. I am not the only one with my head in the clouds, everyone is like that. And who would want to have both feet on the ground at a time like this?

There are also those in the camp who are content, even happy. The young men from St. Étienne, for example, are comfortable here. They should have been home long ago. But they remain, playing cards, sleeping late, and lounging about. People poke fun at them, but they take no notice. I'm convinced they will stay here until they're kicked out. They are still there when I leave the camp. They're making a vacation of a necessity.

And my neighbors, the bookkeeper and his wife, these two (both around fifty) are happy, they say so openly. It was hard here at first, the woman admits to me; they were despondent. But they didn't know the town then, the river, didn't know what they could buy at the market. Now they have looked around and settled in. She has gotten her hands on an alcohol-burning stove and she goes shopping and buys all kinds of things for herself and her husband. She even has someone who sells eggs to her. At first they were not alone in their cubicle, but now it is their apartment and they are more satisfied than they have been for a long time. Her husband, she says, had always suffered from headaches owing to his work as a bookkeeper, sitting over his calculations every evening, the numbers had pursued him even in his sleep, and their summer vacation had always been too brief. I should see him now, she says, how rested and cheerful he is.

And it's true. He looks tanned and fit. I often met him at the river. He had bought fishing gear and spent half the day by the water and was delighted to be able to bring home a fish for dinner. These people did not need to worry about rent or food. They are literally blossoming. You could not discuss politics with the husband. He often sat placidly on the bench next to his wife while she knitted, smoking his pipe and reading a paper someone had left there. You could tell by looking at him: he was reading, as Goethe put it "of war and battle cries, when far away in Turkey the peoples fall upon each other."

I am being interrogated.

One afternoon, when the post-lunch noise and dust become unbearable, I flee the barrack and outside, at the door, run into the small, white-haired woman with glasses. The child has still not improved. But the doctor has said it isn't anything serious. She then begins chatting, telling me how peaceful it is here. She had left the town where she lived under a terrible bombing attack. The bombers had been German and Italian. Even when the bombing had gotten farther away the reverberations were so awful that her garage door had been knocked off its hinges. One of her sons is a soldier. She has not heard from him, but hopes that he will return safely. She lost her husband and her elder son in the last war. When the bombs were falling and she and her neighbors were so frightened they didn't know what to do, she happened to remember a man who lived nearby who had something to do with the transportation system. He took her along with him in his car and let her off here. He himself had continued to the south, but she hadn't wanted to, it cost too much.

I find a meadow beyond the soldiers' barracks. I spread out my coat and spend a good hour there. This is a day when I get nothing done. But when I return to the camp that evening, I am handed a telegram from Le Puy, from Miss S, who repeats my wife's address in Toulouse and I am asked—no, "requested"—to appear at the office. They want to talk to me.

In the office, in addition to the one-armed chief of the camp, there is a civilian unknown to me sitting at the desk. The head of the camp tells me, "The director wishes to speak to you."

The director is a government official. He seems to have had no other special characteristics, for I can no longer recall his face. But I still remember his cold demeanor and the suspicion that he exhibited toward me. He asks me about the letters I have received, and particularly about the telegrams. I am dumbfounded. What business are they of his? But then I catch myself in time: I am in a camp.

I describe my situation. Apparently he has heard all of this already but doesn't believe a word of it. I recite my litany. I present all the papers I have in my possession. The camp chief explains to the director, when I refer to the sender of the last telegram, that this woman is the same lady who sent the earlier telegram. The director wants to know more about her. He states that he opened my last telegram himself, in his official capacity.

It is clear to me that, as a native of Stettin, I am suspect, and that the telegrams have made me more so.

Nothing comes of the interrogation.

My barrack friends are amazed. But I cannot explain it to them; I can't say that my mail is being opened or that I was born in Stettin and am therefore suspect. I am again summoned. The director has now spread out a large form on the table and takes down my pertinent data. I am questioned about my family, my occupation, my entry into France, etc.

As the result of a foreboding I had felt at the beginning of my journey, I had brought along all sorts of papers with me. So I can now present them. The gentleman fills whole sheets. It is obviously a report and he wants to cover his back. I am allowed to go. They barely nod at me.

Under normal circumstances I would leave the camp. But then I risk the chance that someone else will pursue this elsewhere. I must stay, though there is the chance that I will be sent away in a few days' time.

## A Series of Agreeable Events

One of the following afternoons goes better. There are, as I am already aware of, currents, waves. At no other time in my life have I experienced this so clearly.

That morning, as I am on my way into town to buy a paper, I hear radio music coming from a window, Rossini, the William Tell Overture. It makes me happy, cheers me up. But things don't progress much further. At three o'clock, as I am sitting on the terrace of the café, having written two letters, I think, this is the high point of the day.

Then an officer sits down next to me and borrows my newspaper. I see a cross hanging on his chest and ask him about it. No, it's not a war medal, but a medical cross. He's a doctor. He tells me all about the cases he has observed involving lack of discipline. They call for strong measures, he says, which are already being set in motion.

The time passes so quickly in talking to him that I am surprised to look at the clock and find it is already five-thirty, and I must be back at the camp at six. When we say goodbye he comments that perhaps we will see each other again the next day, or the day after. That is fine with me. I've got nothing but time.

As I am leaving the barrack after dinner, the camp boss is crossing the courtyard toward me, carrying something in his hand. I have received mail again, two telegrams. I don't look to see if he has already opened them and resealed them. I immediately hand them to him to read. He doesn't refuse, reads them (probably for the second time), and listens to my explanations. In one of the telegrams, an urgent one from my wife, she asks why I have not yet left, the trains are running again. The other is from my friend, who gives me an address to turn to with my inquiries. The head of the camp, at least, believes me.

Alfred Döblin

Then, as I cross the highway to the left of the military barracks, I see officers camped in the grass by the small bridge, smoking and talking. A young officer from the group gets up and comes after me to say hello, to address me. He knows me from Paris as it turns out: and then I recognize him as well. He is a young, aspiring editor with a Paris newspaper. We often saw each other in the bookstore of a mutual acquaintance. He has been on duty since the beginning of the war, but not at the front. Now his unit is being demobilized; they are just passing through here.

It sounds magical, remote to me, what he says, and how he talks about Paris, about meetings and books, as if we weren't all on a polar expedition. He mentions acquaintances and tells me about them. The world broadens. I feel like I am lying in a well.

As we are walking past another camp (they know me there; I am literally ashamed to be seen in the company of an officer), we are joined by another young officer, a friend of the first, who also knows me. I am amazed at all that has happened to me today. We stroll about.

They are talking about places they have been and where they are likely to go now. The first officer asks my advice on what he should do following demobilization. Whether he should go back to Paris, his home. I think it through with him. I advise against it for several reasons. They seem to make sense to him.

Then the two discuss the grand old town of Mende, which they have recently discovered. As I listen in astonishment, they talk about the enchanting old back streets, the squares, and the ancient cathedral. I don't want to spoil their pleasure and so only listen, pretending interest and curiosity.

But I don't agree with any of it. I reject it totally. Later I tell them something and they immediately object: I say that the little streets aren't enchanting, but are filthy and cramped. That the people living in the dilapidated buildings in these alleys, in dark, comfortless rooms, would not work up any aesthetic enthusiasm about them either. Those who live in such conditions think differently about medieval towns than do tourists.

My feelings keep changing during this conversation. First I am happy to be able to take part in a "normal" conversation, then the two men's state of mind oppresses me, then I merely think: how good it is to have encountered them. It makes me grateful for my camp and my stay in it; I have left these men's opinions far behind me. They have not even comprehended the defeat, no, they have barely heard of it!

When we stop somewhere along the way later—it is the fork that leads to the train station—I look around and don't know where we are.

It has gotten dark.

But the street is well lit and in front of us is an inviting tavern with a terrace on which people are sitting peacefully, drinking and talking. I've never seen this place before, though I pass by here daily. After the two officers have taken their leave of me—they promise to come by the camp for me if they are not transferred the next day—I again examine the strange, lively, cozily lit tavern and then I recognize it. It is beautiful in the evening. Otherwise it is a sad-looking corner bistro, next to the bridge.

But it is not only the bistro, which now looks like a swank nightclub, that has changed. Even the street produces a dreamy, secure impression, with pedestrians strolling up and down it. What a transformation. As if I had leaped out of time and were traveling through a landscape that had ceased to exist long ago.

I returned to the camp quite late that evening. It was nine-thirty. Everyone was in bed. The barracks were dark. It was like coming home from the theater. A mysterious change had taken place.

I have been inundated with a wealth of pleasant events.


## Church and the National Assembly

On Sunday I climb to the porticoes of the cathedral. But then I can get no farther. At that moment priests in their vestments, and a boys' choir emerge from the cathedral in antiphonal song, to assemble outside. The church doors remain open.

The priests and choirboys face the open square, rain is pelting down. I do not understand what it is they are singing. The choirboys are swinging their censers. After ten minutes have passed, the singing priests, walking two by two, lead the procession into the church again, the congregation is standing. I am delighted by the ceremonious act performed before the town as the rain is pouring down. It is a consecration, a blessing of the town. A mass, a service to God, it is a combination of many things. Man must come to know "him," must draw things closer to him. The streets, the buildings, the fields—it is good that everything, including things dumb and without consciousness, is included, that nothing is left out.

A man hangs contorted in pain.
Who is Jesus? A historical figure?
Is it conceivable that the eternal source of being would focus its attention out of turn, so to speak, to human beings in particular, would meddle in its own creation?
It could be argued either that he is God and created the world in its perfect form, as it now exists—or it isn't perfect and he, therefore, is not God. Can Jesus be understood as a historical God, an additional God?
The figure of the historical Jesus, a Palestinian like thousands of others, is not very significant. If I ask myself, "Why do I rely on him?" the answer is that I want to hear that he is God. It has nothing to do with human esteem, but with the establishment of fact.

I sit within sight of the crucifix.
When I close my eyes I feel the crucifix above me to the right, radiating warmth.
The world is incomplete. It is incomplete as a natural world. It moves, progresses, comes to no resolution.
It is also incomplete as an *I* world. And at that point it becomes fate. The source of being did not produce a perfect world, for what moves within it has not yet attained its goal. And because fate, which also has not reached its goal, is equally imperfect.
Nor have we been created to be destroyed by this imperfection, to go to waste, to be ground down by the meaninglessness of existence. It would be incomprehensible to place feeling, thinking souls in the center of the world only to have them deplete themselves in a roiling broth of matter.
Even "matter" is not just matter and not just roiling. I have known for some time that the matter found in crystals, plants, and animals is full of meaning, alive, and equipped with amazing capabilities and facilities. Everything was given us in the beginning, was connected with our nature: pleasure, the joy in existence, the feeling

[ *143* ]

of achievement, unison, harmony—and as for the rest, that which is painful and disturbing: we have the chance and the inclination to know that this is what has not succeeded, and it will fall away.

And "Jesus" is not an "additional God," a corrective to existence, but (I would speculate) an addition to our knowledge, to our understanding about what existence, and the world, really is.

Understanding means: the eternal source of being that created us has also not given up on our relationship to him in this fallen world. Do we feel lost? We must not believe that we are lost, but merely unfortunate "individuals."

"Jesus" says: "The world is bad, but it has history and we have a destiny that extends beyond our earthly existence.

"As a creature, man tends to regress to the bestial and to doubt. He knows not of himself and his salvation."

Who, therefore, would Jesus be, he who hangs there on the cross? I have often looked to him to no avail. My eyes went to him empty and came back empty.

He is God, he is one and the same with, united with, the source of being. He is total meaning, meaning created in relation to the world and to ourselves. He is the call that pulls us back from the two chasms between which we live out our existence: the swamp of organic vegetation, and doubt.

"Jesus" is more than knowledge—he is a new voice. "Jesus" says: We are on the path, and he provides the light of clear passage.

It is impossible to perceive the "eternal source of being." It must appear as the word "Jesus" in order to draw near us.

We experience the world as human beings. If we are then to draw toward the truth we have to acknowledge "God" by bowing our heads silently and reverently—and acknowledge "Jesus" by raising them.

These are my thoughts in the cathedral, and I note them as such sitting outside on a bench, and later that evening in my room.

# 9

# And This Was the Camp

## Last Days in the Camp

The bookkeeper from the neighboring cubicle looks refreshed and relaxed and has spent the day fishing. He tells me he is living here in Mende as in a dream.

Women wearing field-gray uniforms and soldier's caps appear on the streets. They are ambulance drivers. Otherwise everything military in town is sinking from view, disappearing into civilian life. Soldiers are still everywhere, cigarettes in their mouths, their hands in their pockets. Their uniforms are becoming increasingly shabby, and are taking on a greenish sheen.

A true "camp life" is developing. The weather is balmy and everyone is enjoying it in the quadrangle, in the open. Chairs and tables are placed outdoors. The women sit at the embankment in the greenery by the river. They have their children with them as if they are on an outing. Some wash clothes, a young woman with her three small children sits in the grass, it is the woman who loses her temper often at meals, who yells, "I'll kill you, I swear it!" when one of the children won't eat. At which the child blubbers and the mother either yells even louder or goes off to eat by herself. The sight of this woman among her three little ones at table is indescribably comical. The children sit there with their large, blank bird eyes, looking at their mother and screaming *"Du pain, du pain!"* (Bread, bread.). It can only be a matter of one or two days more. I see people at the train station, go over myself, and find out that a few of them have permits, the others don't. At any rate, the man at the counter is selling tickets. I ask and he answers: he is not concerned with permits, he is selling tickets. I don't question him any further, but ask when a train is going to Toulouse the next morning. "At 6:05 A.M." Hearing that I buy a ticket. My major task is accomplished.

I have the ticket, an ordinary train ticket. It looks like the one I bought in Moulins on my way to Le Puy. But this train ticket will take me into the normal world. I go to the post office and telegraph the news to Toulouse. I have to change trains in Beziers. So there is the chance that something will go wrong.

It is late afternoon. I go back to the camp, and as I walk by the bridge and the school, I am suddenly overcome by a feeling of sadness on seeing them for the last time. I give notice at the office that I am leaving. The head of the camp is not there, I had wanted to say goodbye. I ask if there is anyone who can help me the next morning with my bag. A young man, a Belgian, will do it for a tip.

I go to bed at eight-thirty. The old woman gives me the rest of her bread to eat on the way. I bought cherries this afternoon, and give her the sack, it is almost full.

I get up at six, the old woman is awake and shakes my hand. She wishes me a good trip and whispers: "It's a great day." A gendarme is walking up and down the platform. He looks closely at everyone. He doesn't stop me.

We depart.

And that was Mende.

From the train I see another camp in Mende, its quadrangle is just coming to life.

## Toulouse—Again

We travel into daylight. After an hour I have to change trains. I wait, sitting on a raised terrace in a sunny station restaurant, like a vacationer, drinking coffee. I no longer belong to a camp.

I cannot adjust to my new circumstances. Doesn't it once occur to me that what I am doing is running away? That's right, running away. Something like treason. . . .

I can see all of them in the camp in Mende. I had my coffee and left as if the camp meant nothing to me, went my own way. Which way is my own?

There was something positive about the camp, it occurs to me. It was good for me, revealing. It opened something in me, but it was only a beginning, it is not yet finished. I should have stayed longer.

I travel. I look back out of the window often. I travel; but everything here is settled; here I will encounter no accidents.

We travel toward Beziers, an interminable journey. It took the whole day. There were only two civilians in the full car, the rest were trainmen who had been evacuated and who were now being repatriated. There was nothing for them in the south (for we were traveling south), they belonged in Paris, most of them, and talked about it the whole trip. But they were to assemble somewhere beyond Beziers, from where they would be taken north, into the occupied zone.

How happy these people were for the entire journey. They came well stocked with wine (in large wineskins) and food. I was persuaded to share their wine once. But otherwise I kept my distance, in order not to be drawn into the discussion.

There was an older official with a thick moustache, a good-natured man who drank a lot, and a younger man who delivered political speeches off the top of his head that no one listened to. He was talking about the "money" that must remain in the country. For he had heard that the rich were now in the process of taking their capital abroad. It had to be held on to. His suggestion: get rid of money altogether. But what then? the others asked. How would commerce function—abroad? That's as far as it got.

For hours the bottles with various red wines were passed around. We emerge from the mountains onto a warm, even hot, plain. There are gray, flat stone structures here, they have a southern, an Italian, feel to them. This trip had a largely epic character, it swept across epochs.

In order to be left alone I hide behind the little book, as I don't have a newspaper, that I bought just for this purpose in Mende, *Merlin the Magician*. The title attracted me and I was not disappointed. I enjoyed reading it not because it dealt with remote, irrational things, but because it had breadth, diversion, richness. I swallowed the book in small doses. As it got darker and darker in the train I began to get worried: I didn't want to arrive at night and have to sit at the train station. But they said that Beziers was a real city and that the station was right next to the town. Soldiers sitting across from me mentioned that there was a *centre d'acceuil* right by the station.

We got off in the dark, and at the exit each person was asked for his travel documents. There was to be a connection to Toulouse at midnight, but it was doubtful that it would take civilians. I decided to spend the night here and went in search of a room.

I remember the total darkness that surrounded the large square in front of the station. But beyond it were bright signs: large hotels. Having been turned away at two, I arrived at the third and found a room with running water. I put down my things.

And I stood there in the room and thought of Mende, of my barracks and the cubicle with the old lady.

For the first time in weeks I could undress. I could hang up my clothes. I lay under a proper blanket on a mattress covered with linen. I slept deeply until morning.

That morning I washed my shoes with water, a practice from the camp. But the thick mud was not easy to clean off. My trousers were caked with the same mud. I packed them in my suitcase. I had one other suit. I put it on. A fresh collar, a new tie. My collars had gotten too big for me and I had to draw my belt in tightly.

Things were lively in the breakfast room. And when I went to get a newspaper, a nurse I had seen in the train called out to me: "You better hurry if you want to make the connection to Toulouse. It leaves at nine-thirty!" It was nine. So much for drinking coffee and reading the paper. I paid and ran to the station.

Looking around the hotel room in Beziers, I had already felt that I had left the shore, the wilderness behind, and was being sent back into the world of cities. I began to recognize things from my former life. The globe of my memory began to fill. But my emotions didn't respond. There was no *I* to respond to the memories. The last weeks had passed as if I had been ill and they didn't leave me as I had been before. I knew myself better. How far away all of that was, what had happened before June 10, no, before May 16. A normal express train stood at the station, and left on time. It stopped only where it was supposed to. It didn't detour and didn't go back from where it had come. It was foreseeable that I would arrive on time.

As I sat in the smooth, speeding train the experience of my

collapse accompanied me. I had not left it behind. The longer I traveled, the closer I got to the "normal" world, the more it seemed to me that it was not my collapse that was accompanying me, but I who was accompanying it, it took me along, was my unknown *I*.

The farther away I got from Beziers and therefore from Mende, and the longer I sat in this orderly train among orderly men and women (they read newspapers, looked past one another, as is befitting cultivated city people), the more I felt my experiences being transformed, coming at me, filling up my empty inner being.

I feel grief and sorrow: Why did I leave? Why didn't I wait? Things were still in a state of flux. Everything had just begun, nothing was ended. Why run away?

I asked myself these questions as I approached the orderly world that I had so wanted to reach and hold on to so desperately, with such longing and fear, when I left Cahors. That's why I had left, after all, that's why—or wasn't it?

No. Under the appearance of this journey I had been invited to another. To destiny's journey.

In one hour I would see my wife and boy, for whom I had undertaken this sad, bewildering journey. I will arrive properly, in an express train. No, the speed of this transition, this end to my worldly/otherworldly adventure, even if provisional, was something that I found a little shameful.

It is not finished, I said to myself. I swear it to myself. It cannot be finished.


## Reacquaintance

Then, in Toulouse, I drag my bag through the ticket gate, it is midday, people are waiting at a barrier, I look around.

My boy comes running up to me joyfully and kisses me and then my wife comes. We are together.

We walk slowly to the exit.

# 10

# Another Escape

Now my wife will relate what happened to her and our son from the time we were separated in Paris, at the dark train station teeming with people, until that afternoon in Toulouse when I stepped down from the train from Beziers and my son ran toward me at the gate.

## The Calm Before the Storm

One afternoon I wandered up to the cathedral in Le Puy and sat down across from it on a bench on the sloping street. From there I had a view of the town and surrounding countryside. My thoughts wandered. I pulled letters from my pocket. A short time later I heard a voice ask: "Good news?" And before me stood a woman in native costume with a lace cap, wide black skirt, and large white apron. "News from your husband, your son? Is peace coming soon?" When I replied that the situation was critical, she was surprised. It couldn't be critical in Belgium, the Belgian people were brave and dependable. I explained it to her, she listened in disbelief. I asked her if she read the newspapers. "Newspapers? No, never." But she listened to the radio often at her neighbor's. Then she calls across the street: "Mrs. X, did you hear? Things are going badly in Belgium, oh God, oh God!"

Alfred Döblin

I take many walks with my friend. We keep each other calm and discuss everything with each other. She is afraid for her relatives in the war zone. She is a Catholic who had distanced herself from the Church. She loves her country so much that she now is asking herself whether she should become devout again. The whole thing seems to be a test. No, if there is still any meaning to existence, France cannot fall.

We attend a curious event.

A meeting of the English-French Society at the theater. The room was full to bursting. When the curtain opened two bald-headed elderly men in black suits, one small and stout, the other tall, thin, and elegant, were seated behind a table. The stout one stood to greet the audience and to say that he was proud to have today in Le Puy such a respected man (a flattered smile from the tall one). He praised the English-French Society and welcomed those who wished to join. Then he turned the floor over to the tall one.

He walked in front of the table, smiling. He wanted to talk about England, he said. His topic was: Freedom in England and France. The two countries not only spoke different languages, they had different customs and institutions. There were no cafés or terraces in England. The meals were different. Drivers passed on a different side of the road. Gentlemen walked on a different side of the lady than here. He went on like this for forty-five minutes. The war showed how good it was that the two countries understood each other. He spoke a good deal about parking and restaurants and cafés.

We shook with laughter. Then things improved. An orchestra of schoolchildren played the English and French national anthems. The mayor announced there would be a demonstration of folk dances. The little orchestra fiddled away with gusto as ten-to-fourteen-year-old girls danced. They were charming in their tartan skirts and blouses and matching caps. They were so happy. Tension was growing.

My neighbors at the boardinghouse, older people with a grand-son the same age as our boy, were asking everyone for advice. Their daughter was still in Paris, she owned a large jewelry shop, and their son-in-law was fighting in the field. If the daughter left Paris, she would have to close the store. Was that necessary? A few days later the old man decided to go to Paris himself.

More and more refugee families were arriving. They were

[ *151* ]

housed wherever there was space, in rooms, garages, basements. They came in trucks, in cars loaded with mattresses, a particularly large number of young people arrived on bikes. We listened to the radio deep into the night, discussed things on the street and in the shops.

My own nervousness grew when a telegram informed me that my husband had left Paris, gone to Tours, then news from Moulins with the hint that he would not remain there. The streets are swarming with people. The newcomers are given bread, warm soup, the children, milk. Whoever doesn't have relatives in town is transferred to the countryside. People sit for hours on the steps in front of the train station, hoping for a seat on the trains that depart at irregular intervals.

## Panic

Then came the day when I was driven out onto the street by an internal state of panic.

Behind the park I see the prefecture and the street in front of it, full of people. Trucks are parked on the large square. Soldiers are jumping down from them. They are unbelievably dirty and covered with sweat. Other trucks follow. The soldiers are squatting and lying everywhere. They're standing on the running boards, hanging from the front and back of vehicles.

The townspeople stand there in shock. "What has happened, which regiment are you with?" Most of the soldiers aren't wearing insignia.

We are all seized by an indescribable confusion. Some begin looking for family members, perhaps a husband or son is there, perhaps someone has information about his regiment.

When I turn onto the street it is full of military trucks, more trucks, tanks. Small cars tow farmers' wagons in which everything is jumbled together: uniforms, civilian clothes, dogs, cats. A huge number of fleeing civilians are pushing their way through. You couldn't exactly say that the soldiers are bewildered, they keep saying: We are only regrouping, the Nazis haven't beaten us yet! The grocery stores are under siege, everything sells out quickly, only the soldiers can get bread.

After lunch I sit down at a terrace café. Everyone is watching, talking, the waiters included. The number of retreating military and civilians is growing. Trucks roll by with dismantled airplanes and others that appear ready for use. There are more and more tanks and a plethora of strange-looking vehicles. On the trucks winding their way through the streets, soldiers lie half stretched out, some of them are rolled up in a ball, asleep. They say the Germans are only a few hundred kilometers away. St. Étienne is threatened. They say the resistance is fighting them and that the Germans won't be able to advance more than fifty kilometers a day.

I return home exhausted. My landlady comes looking for me, she wants me to give up my room. She's already housing relatives in the garage. For the first time, I consider leaving town.

The heavy vehicles rolled through all night. We lived on a hill. On the other side of the hill, at the top, they drive through endlessly.

The troops drove and marched through for three days. They were traveling south for the most part, though to my great surprise not all of them.

The situation was becoming eerie. We were losing our ties to the outside world. Mail wasn't being delivered, telegrams were transmitted at one's own risk. In spite of this, everyone still hurried to the mailbox at the garden gate, hoping for news. A train passed by now and then, mostly train workers fleeing occupied territories.

Then the schools closed and the hotels were requisitioned.

## Preparation for Flight

The Germans were still some two hundred kilometers away when I had another talk with my friend. She was also of the opinion that I must leave. I went to the station and spoke to an officer who had a position with the Red Cross. He introduced me to two young people who had escaped from Lyon in a small car and wanted to leave for Bordeaux the next morning. The administrative authorities had gone to Bordeaux and if I wanted, the young people would take me and my boy with them. They were leaving at nine the next morning from the train station. But it would be difficult without a permit.

So I appeared before a military board to present my case. One officer explained that civilians could be issued such permits only if they had an official mission to perform. I should appeal to his superior. His superior told me I could not receive an official order. I went to another office with the same result. I was advised to seek out a civilian agency.

At the municipal agency, I was received by several friendly and sympathetic gentlemen, one of whom advised me to go up into the mountains and hide in a farmhouse. Nothing would happen to me up there. I asked how long I should stay. They couldn't answer.

I went to the station the next morning to thank the young people and explain why I couldn't go with them. I waited for an hour or longer. They never came—and then I heard they had left the night before because the situation had become too dangerous.

At noon we were sitting in a large restaurant that had a powerful radio. When I heard the announcer's voice I ran over, as did a young officer sitting nearby. Marshal Pétain was speaking. He was announcing France's request for a cease-fire.

Then they played the Marseillaise. Everyone in the restaurant, soldiers, officers and civilians, men and women, stood up, the soldiers saluted. Many of us were weeping and standing there as if paralyzed. Never again shall I hear this anthem without remembering this moment, the loudspeaker, the terrible news, the soldiers saluting.

I sat down with my friend and said to her: I don't know what will become of us. I won't go up into the mountains. She comforted me, gave me a glass of liqueur. I should go lie down, she said. In the meantime she would ask around. Late that evening she came by to tell me excitedly that perhaps something could be done after all. She had an appointment the next morning with some influential men.

At seven the next morning there was a knock at my door and my friend stormed in urging me to get up, and my son as well. Then she ran out.

I stood there befuddled, then tried to wake my son, who wanted to sleep longer. Soon there was another knock at the door, and to my utter confusion it was my friend again. She was panting for breath. She had been running around like crazy. At the same time the housemaid arrived with our breakfast tray. My friend insisted: "You have to leave in fifteen minutes at the latest, to pick up your permit. No breakfast, no washing up, just go!"

I threw on my clothes. My son was still dozing, both of us started shaking him and helped him get dressed. My friend got out my hand luggage and my son's rucksack and packed a few things in them, two blankets and a few items of warm clothing. We left everything else—jewelry, letters—behind.

She explained everything to me as we ran downstairs. "You'll be traveling in an official car. But hurry, otherwise they'll leave you." My permit was ready at the agency, they quickly checked the dates, wished me good luck, and we hurried down the stairs.

A large truck stood ready to leave, it was filled with massive boxes of files. My friend was happy to have been able to help us. Two men and a woman with a five-year-old girl were already sitting in the truck on the piles of paper. They helped us up. An elderly, funny little man sat up front with the driver, apparently he was a draftsman.

And we were off. We waved and called out our thanks.


## The Trip to Bordeaux

We stop once in front of a building to pick up an older woman and her daughter. Then the truck rattled on.

Our fellow passengers are painfully cheerful, making droll jokes about our journey. These people are the relatives of officials. No one knows where we are headed. We are driving at high speed and constantly fall off our stack of papers.

The roads lead uphill and down. Our fellow passengers begin unpacking their provisions—bread, cheese, wine. We have brought a small package of cakes and chocolate with us. Someone offers us a piece of army bread, it tastes stale. My son has eaten practically nothing and the rattling and shaking and constant slipping from his seat have taken their toll on him. The others help me to bed him down on some straw. Around four in the afternoon we stop at the edge of a small town. We go into a little restaurant and drink a cup of hot coffee without milk or sugar and, actually, without coffee. When we continue on, the others are tired and quiet. Around seven in the evening we approach the city of Rodez.

We get out at Rodez and say goodbye to the others on the street. I go to an office building to ask what their hours are. But everything is closed. When I return, the truck is standing there empty and locked. Our fellow passengers have disappeared.

We wander around looking for a place to stay and ascertain that our only possibility is the *centre d'acceuil*. We soon locate it. It is almost eight o'clock when a man with a long beard appears. People on motor scooters drive up, he has the key and assigns places to everyone. As soon as he opens the door everyone dashes in. The cubicles are all alike, none have doors, they lie to the right and left of a wide central corridor.

We soon fall asleep, to be awakened in total darkness. Soldiers are turning on lights, stomping around the barracks with their heavy knapsacks, sticking their heads in our cubicle.

We fold up our blankets around seven. Soldiers still lie asleep on the bare floor of the corridor. My son complains of pain and doesn't want to walk. I coax him into drinking something, then it will be better. We are in a café among soldiers and civilians. The child doesn't want anything to eat. We walk the streets slowly, passing the main post office.

As my son was getting more and more upset and complaining of pain, I took him into a large apothecary and talked the woman who worked there into giving him some drops of something, which she at first didn't want to do. We begin talking and she offers to watch my son until I can take care of my errands.

So I proceed alone to the office that was now open, explain my case and present my authorization, which mentions Rodez, and above all inquire as to where I should now turn in my search for my husband. I am given a precise answer: Bordeaux. But how can I get there? I tell them how I arrived from Le Puy. They express their regrets, for just the night before the same type of transport left here for Bordeaux.

When I suggest I take a taxi, they tell me they will provide the gasoline and a permit to travel to Bordeaux, and assign a man to personally escort me to the taxi stand. The taxi driver doesn't want to go, he had driven someone there the day before and had gotten caught in machine-gun fire, people to the right and left of him were hit, and he doesn't want to risk that again for any amount of money. We talked and wheedled until he gave in. He would leave at one o'clock, he said, and we would be in Bordeaux by eight; but if there were any incidents along the way he would turn back immediately. The cost was 1500 francs, and I have only 1800. But I don't care.

My son is overjoyed when I pick him up at the apothecary—he has made friends with the clerk in the meantime—and tell him that we have a car and will be in Bordeaux that evening. The drops have worked, his pain is gone and he is so excited: eight hours in a private car and that same evening in Bordeaux, with Papa!

We hurry through town and have something to eat at a hotel. But just as we're making ourselves comfortable at a terrace café, the friendly proprietor explains that unfortunately we can't sit there, the terraces must remain empty by official decree.

Our driver was a good one, he knew his city and its surroundings, but he had never been to Bordeaux. And he reiterated that he was afraid. He would return from Bordeaux as soon as he could, even if he had to travel all night. Who knew, perhaps the Germans were already there. I allowed him to drive as fast as he wished. We were stopped repeatedly by police and gendarmes and asked for identification papers. The permit got us through every time.

We made long detours and drove through a lovely, peaceful stretch of countryside. One would never guess that a war was being fought only a few kilometers away. Our driver clearly could not use his map for the detours, he got lost and had to ask directions of the farmers. Time passed. The man had hoped to reach Bordeaux by eight o'clock, he got nervous and returned to the main road. We were allowed to take the *route nationale*. There were no civilians on it, and only a few military vehicles.

Two hours from Bordeaux we were again driving through a village and were stopped by a policeman. We immediately took out our papers, but that wasn't what he wanted. The lady beside him had been standing by the road for hours, he said. The military couldn't take her along, could we? We were the first civilians to come along. Of course I said yes. A plain, middle-class woman in her forties climbed in with a small handbag and thanked us. She sat next to the driver, but soon turned around to tell us about herself.

Her son was in the hospital in the town we had just passed through. It was the first time in months that she had seen him. She had received a telegram that he had been brought here because his parents lived in Bordeaux. The twenty-year-old had been wounded several times, most of the wounds had healed, but he was blind. She had spoken to him. He was calm and had comforted her, saying she shouldn't grieve, he had merely done his duty and paid his dues toward his country's freedom. Others had died. He would learn a blind man's trade, he wouldn't be without work. And he had placated his mother by saying that she, who loved children so dearly, had a small child once again.

[ *157* ]

The woman wept for a long time. Her son had no idea what shape France was in. She had gone to see him three days before, on the local train.

I wanted her to tell me something about Bordeaux, but she was too preoccupied. I would have a hard time of it if I didn't have a place to stay. The government and its agencies were there. There had been a bombing, the Germans had known precisely in which buildings the ministries were housed.

## Bordeaux—Cease-fire

As we approached the city at eight-thirty we saw many military men and barracks and army hospitals. Every few minutes we had to present our papers.

I immediately inquired about the agency my husband had left Paris with. They didn't know anything at the prefecture. One official laughed: "Agencies, ministries. God knows where they are, in Africa perhaps." I was directed to the bulletin board. They called another official over, who explained to me that the agency had dispersed for the most part. But some of the officials were working in the city, at the theater, for instance.

So we went to the theater, but no one there knew anything about my husband or his friends. We drove to the employment office. The driver pulled out his watch and declared it was nine o'clock, he had to return. Who knew whether he would get home safely? I was told to make inquiries on the fourth floor.

I paid the driver his 1500 francs and have 300 left. The man carried my suitcase up the steps, put the rucksack beside it, and disappeared.

Straw has been strewn about the large vestibule of the building. Soldiers are settling in for the night. I am allowed to go upstairs.

On the first floor I encounter women and military personnel. I am instructed to keep going. I climb another flight. I receive only negative answers to my questions. Even on the fourth floor.

As I'm standing there not knowing what to do, I hear a woman's friendly voice calling me by name. And truly, she knows my husband. He isn't here, nor does she know where he is. But she is sure I will find him the next day. She calls over a lieutenant, who greets me saying, "You won't remember who I am. I was in your lovely apartment once in Berlin, on the Kaiserdamm, it was a long time ago." And he describes our apartment to me. Then he says it is late, but tomorrow he will place himself at my disposal.

I stand there with my child. The woman who spoke to me is Polish, she speaks French fluently and tries to help us. The city is overflowing with people, there are no rooms free, every bed is occupied, requisitioned. There is someone everywhere.

"There's only one thing to do. You'll stay here. They can't put you out on the street with a child in the middle of the night. We have some straw mattresses, I'll have two of them carried to an office for you. In the meantime go out and get something to eat." We are told to return before ten. Downstairs, soldiers are already bedded down on the straw, snoring. They're lying in their shirtsleeves, covered with their jackets and coats. As we leave the building the soldier standing guard recognizes me and asks, "Did you find him?" And steps into the totally dark street to show me a dim light across the way where we can have something to drink.

We soon return to the building. This time we are allowed to use the elevator. Just as we're getting in, an officer comes running through the vestibule and storms into the elevator, then greets us. He too is going to the fourth floor. Radio music and voices can be heard coming from every room. We drag our things into the room where the friendly Polish woman is staying and begin talking to her, when to our surprise the same highly placed officer we came up in the elevator with enters the room and looks around. The woman apologizes and explains the situation. He nods curtly. There is a knock at the door, it opens. A soldier enters: "The lines are working again. The cease-fire has been agreed upon."

The doorway immediately fills with soldiers and officials. Everyone is very upset. We want to leave the room but cannot get out. Finally the entrance clears and we push our way through. The Polish woman quietly brings me my coat and quickly excuses herself: at the moment she can do nothing for me. But she calls to someone on the floor who can help us.

So we stand there in the corridor in the general excitement and confusion. A cease-fire. I am flabbergasted. What does it mean, what will it bring?

A soldier approaches to help us. He leads us into an office nearby. The door closes. Straw mattresses have been placed on the floor to the right and left of the door. The parquet is filthy, nor are the mattresses clean, straw is sticking out in several places. There are no curtains on the windows. The furniture consists of a table, an armoire, and two chairs. The door cannot be locked.

We spread out our blankets, lie down on top of them, and cover ourselves with our coats. Radio music can be heard for hours to come.

Early the next morning we return to the café from the night before and wait for the Polish woman. The young officer from last night appears between eight and nine, the one who had mentioned our apartment in Berlin, and informs us with a joyful smile that he knows where my husband is: we need only go to the theater nearby. Though I was already there yesterday, I make for it straightaway— and find no one, of course. And as I wander about the different floors and walk down corridors, I land in an office where, though no one knows anything about the agency I am looking for, they send me back to the prefecture. So I go.

And there a truck is just entering the courtyard. Four young women and several men in civilian attire get out and take the same direction I am taking and enter the same office. They are greeted happily and I hear they have come from Cahors, where a few of the departments of the agency I am seeking have converged. I join them and find out that the agency has been disbanded and its members scattered all over. But they know my husband and our mutual friends and it is an odd feeling to be standing there among them, because they know him and he was with them.

But when I ask where he is now no one can answer. Someone says: He is definitely not in Cahors. Another says: He didn't go on with his friends, but went alone to Le Puy, to look for you. I look at them in astonishment. That cannot be true. That would be unthinkable.

The head of the office appears in the meantime. The young lieutenant introduces me. The man knows my husband, if only in passing, we have mutual acquaintances. He is kind and comforting. He will do everything in his power to help. He will now try to reach Cahors officially, by telephone. He hopes to get through. I am to come back in a few hours.

With that I leave the prefecture, badly upset. What should I do, whom shall I turn to? I get an idea: I go back and ask for information about another agency. There is a man, a high official working for it, who has been kind to our family for years now, and who helped us during the many difficult years of immigration. I go to the school I am directed to and walk into the large schoolyard. And I spot him in the distance. He is standing in a group.

He recognizes me the moment I walk up. "My God, what are you doing here?"

And as I am explaining it to him, he interrupts me: "No, you would be better off anywhere but here. The Germans will be arriving in a few days. We know nothing further about the cease-fire, that's true. But the Germans will occupy the city. The administrative agencies will have to leave. They'll be safer somewhere else. I can only advise you to leave, get away from Bordeaux. Yes, even from France—just get away!"

I am horrified. I can't just run off. I know nothing of my husband, my sons, they are all I have, and what kind of transportation is there, anyway?

He sticks to his opinion that I should leave. He is only trying to be helpful, he says. I should not have any illusions. I would find my husband anywhere but in France.

I return to the prefecture, crushed. It is eleven o'clock by now. Groups of people are standing in the streets, everyone is discussing the cease-fire.

Lines are forming outside the shoe stores. They are practically storming them. It is primarily women, but there are also elderly men and soldiers. A painful sight. On this day when the country is awash in grief, people are standing in line whose only care is getting themselves a pair of shoes.

They have placed a call for me to Cahors. I have to wait awhile. Several hours go by. My son waits on the street. Finally Cahors calls. They repeat what the young woman has already told me. My husband is no longer in Cahors. He has set out alone, he wanted to go to Le Puy.

## Helplessness

What should I do? What should I do now? I have no connections. No money. We can't keep spinning around each other, circling each other like tops. It seems I must stay here no matter what.

I wander through the streets of Bordeaux, bewildered, distressed. It is three o'clock, the lunch hour has passed, on top of which the restaurants are so crowded that you have to stand in line forever to get a simple meal. That isn't important now. We don't want to eat. I must be very careful with the rest of the money.

We take some refreshment at least, a cup of coffee and a sandwich at a café on one of the main streets. It is Sunday and the café is filled mainly with townspeople. Outside, hordes of pedestrians stroll by, a few in uniform, almost no trucks. A tram passes by from time to time.

After a brief pause we again go to see our friend the official at the school. He is not there. We wait on a bench in the courtyard lined with plane trees. It is good to sit there, but I am terribly depressed. There are many people sitting here, including entire families. The inner courtyard beyond the gate is filled with cars. Someone addresses me: "You look so sad, can we be of help? Have you had bad news?"

Someone else tells me about a boarding school where many people are staying more or less comfortably. They figure they will soon be ordered to leave. The Germans will be in Bordeaux by Saturday. These people don't know where they will go—but one thing is certain: they will be all right. They will be taken somewhere or other, crowded in a truck with their families, that's all. It's more difficult for those with sons and fathers in the army, for no one has any news and everyone is worried about the defeat.

After my friend the official enters the schoolyard with his wife and says hello to people on all sides, we proceed to a large classroom in which he has his office. Each high official has his own classroom.

He shrugs his shoulders when I tell him of my decision to remain here after I have found out that my husband has gone north to Le Puy to look for me.

Soon I am again under way with my son, tired and having accomplished nothing. We slowly walk to the building where we spent the night, they know us there and let us pass. Upstairs, music and voices are coming over the radio from various rooms. We locate the office we spent the night in without encountering anyone in the corridor. Our bags stand in a corner, the straw mattresses are spread out on the floor. We remain here. It is evening, there is no one to ask permission to stay the night. It is Sunday. We simply stay.

We look out the window, we are fairly high up. We can see the cathedral. Both of us are unspeakably tired. We lie down on the straw sacks, fully dressed like yesterday and the day before.

Alfred Döblin

*  *  *

Before eight the next morning a man in uniform enters our
room without knocking and apologizes when he finds us there. But
he says this is his office. We gather our things and depart. We run
into the Polish woman, who says she is sorry things are so confused,
but unfortunately she must ask us to find other quarters, everything
here is taken. I can leave my bag here, however.

So I go looking for our friend for help.

When we arrive he is talking with a high officer. He turns to me
with the comment that he will leave here before I do, possibly this
evening, in the direction of Vichy.

I am devastated. This man is my last support, he has known us
for years, he is an honorable man who not only offers advice and
assistance, but is someone I can talk to openly. And he wants to
leave. I fall apart. I go into a classroom and sob. Everything is
collapsing around me. It is horrible.

When I pull myself together I ask him where we can stay. He
gives me a letter of introduction to another man from another office.

Crowds have already gathered at that office. I present my letter
and am allowed through. The man isn't there. When he appears after
a long wait he tells me in a friendly way that all the rooms have been
taken by the military. Only they can tell me if anything is available.

I can't go on. I've had it. I've heard how people resent their
rooms being requisitioned for others.

Back to the school. "Find us a place anywhere," I implore, I
plead. This time he gives me a letter to the director of a school.

So we go there.

The school is far from town, a half-hour walk. The director tells
me she would like to help us, but she has no rooms left. An entire
agency is being lodged there. She calls in a teacher who is just passing
by on the street. They have a long discussion. They can't simply send
me away, they make a phone call. Finally the director says, "Well, if I
may make this offer . . ." She hesitates. "I'm a little embarrassed." I
tell her that I'll be grateful for anything, for a roof over my head. In
that case, she says, she has a small kitchen that is not in use at the
moment, it's located in an annex on the ground floor and is therefore
somewhat damp. They can set up two metal cots there and find some
mattresses, and the sinks have running water.

We are delighted at this offer, and go back to town to pick up

[ *163* ]

our bags, then walk back with them the same way, dragging them along. My son is exhausted. There is an electric tram but it doesn't go directly there and comes only every twenty minutes. We continue on. It is evening already. We pass by a small place to eat. It is full of men and women. I ask my son, "Shall we try and get something to eat? We haven't had a hot meal since Thursday evening." Our intake has consisted solely of several cups of coffee and a sandwich a day. The boy doesn't want to. We have so little money, he says, and where would we sit? All the seats are taken.

A man passes by and I ask him if he is familiar with this place, we would like to get something to eat. "Come with me. They know me here. You'll get something, but you might have to wait awhile."

He speaks to the owner, a woman standing at the bar. The room has long tables with benches, all of them occupied. If people move over a bit we can fit in, but we'll have to sit at separate tables. My boy doesn't like this, he doesn't like the atmosphere.

So we leave and walk on. I buy our evening's provisions: a piece of bread and some fruit.

In the meantime beds have been set up in the tiny kitchen that houses us for the next few days and nights. They've even given us towels and a piece of soap. How good it is to be able to wash again.

Next to our room on the ground floor is the school's main kitchen. An elderly, affable cook greets me. When she leaves in the evening I have the roomy kitchen at my disposal. I can boil water. Cars park in the garden in front of our window. My son soon goes out to talk to one of the drivers, who is waiting for an officer.

Before we go to bed the director appears, not only to look in on us but to say that our friend has called. He wasn't leaving after all, he would stay for a few days more. That did me a world of good.

How happy we were to be able to undress again. But once in bed, which was a delight in itself, things were less pleasant. A humming noise began, something was biting us: gnats. It was quite warm but we had to pull the covers over our heads. The gnats hummed and buzzed. The next morning we were covered with bites. The kitchen is located in a damp garden and is itself damp. All of the rooms but ours, the vacant kitchen, were protected by netting.

At eight o'clock we were on the street. This time we had to find a new café to eat breakfast in, which didn't look too promising in this "popular" area. We walked a bit farther to the huge square. It is

Tuesday. Today must be a special day, for the shops are closed. When we sit down at a terrace café we are told they are not serving. It is a national day of mourning.

On the main street we walk past a small shop that sells oriental and South American items, and also serves coffee. I am happy to get two small cups of black coffee after ordering several times.

The streets are deserted. Everyone is going to the service at the cathedral.

We wander over to the prefecture. The man I want to speak to isn't there. We chat with the others. Someone asks us where we eat. My son says: "Us? We just drink coffee with a croissant or a sandwich. We don't have any money."

"Is that true?"

Someone immediately brings over a box of sweets and urges my son to help himself. And when the boss appears, the whispering begins. He says, "They tell me you have no money and aren't eating. Is that right?" I say yes and tell him how much I have left.

"That won't do," he says. "Take your money and promise me you will eat something today. And I assure you that I'll get together some money privately. I don't know you and am only barely acquainted with your husband, I met him once briefly in the company of a friend. But the friend spoke affectionately of your family. My friends' friends are also my friends. You can count on me, I will do what I can. It will be noon soon. How much do you have? So—go and get something to eat now."

A young woman offers to accompany us, she knows a little restaurant where the food is cheap and you don't have a long wait. It is only somewhat difficult to reach, she says, the neighboring buildings have been damaged by bombs, and a cleanup action is under way in the neighborhood, the police have closed off a few streets. But for precisely this reason one could get something to eat there. It was a twenty-minute walk.

Soon we were sitting at a table with place settings. Our new friend began talking about herself and her family. She was no longer on salary, she belonged to a department that had been dissolved. She was from Paris and had heard no news of her parents. She had asked to continue working for no pay so that when the agency left Bordeaux she would be taken along, it was her only chance for advancement. But they had told her that her office would remain here for a while and that she would probably witness the arrival of the Germans.

She ate with gusto. She was ecstatic about the excellent salad served as an hors d'oeuvre. She scolds my son, who is fussy and doesn't want to eat. No one has the right to refuse food in times like these, she says. Everything tastes so good. She goes out to eat only once a day, she says, and that is her main meal.

Late that afternoon we briefly visit my friend at the school. I see official telegrams and ask if they can inquire in Le Puy whether my husband arrived there. He warns me against being too hopeful. It will take awhile for a reply to arrive.

We sit in the garden that afternoon until the gnats chase us inside. On Wednesday everyone returns to work. The shops open, people stand in line at the shoe stores, now almost bare. Even the display windows are beginning to empty out. Now and then a woman walks out with a pile of shoes. There are lines here and there in front of the grocery stores. From a distance you can often see signs on the windows: "No . . ." butter, milk, sugar, chocolate, etc. Oil, soap, and meat are scarce as well, but available. There are plenty of vegetables and fruit and bread if you don't wait too late to shop.

People are lined up at the curbs as though a parade were passing by. They say that the Germans have arrived. They were fabulous-looking, they say, strong men beautifully outfitted, motorcyclists. They were waiting, perhaps others were coming. . . . The onlookers wore pleased expressions.

At the school our friend confirms that motorcyclists had passed through Bordeaux. That was against the terms of the treaty, but . . . Was I sure I didn't want to leave?

He suggests that I leave my son behind in Bordeaux under another name. Nothing would happen to him here. I couldn't come back for him until the end of the war, of course, but he knew of a good foster father for him and a good boarding school as well. If I were alone I would have a much better chance of escape. My son was listening. He begins crying loudly and clinging to me. I tell our friend no.

## The Germans Arrive

That same day, at two o'clock, I spot Germans on motorcycles and in small cars.

The people stare at them, their equipment, their order. Yes, they admire them—but to me they look like figures made of papier-mâché. Their faces all look alike, expressionless. Many wear little moustaches like Hitler's. People reassure one another that they won't hurt anyone. A few officers went into a shop on a side street, they say, and they spoke excellent French. They paid what was asked and gave something to the children standing around. Everyone is envious of their raincoats, which are truly waterproof.

Something wonderful happens at the prefecture: the man who yesterday asked so pointedly if we had enough to eat tells me that he has succeeded in interesting a man in the city in my case. He gives me an address; I can go there now, the man will be at home.

It is not far, we arrive a few minutes later. I do not wish to go into details, but will say only that this gentleman in Bordeaux, whom I did not know at all, offered to help us. He named a large sum and asked, "Will this get you by for a while?"

Of course I said yes. I offered to pay back the money as soon as I was able, but he waved away this suggestion. He was familiar with my case. He himself could not participate in the war, but at least he wanted to make this contribution. I cannot express how I felt, how grateful I was. It was a load off my mind. Not only were my financial worries over for the near future, but I dared to have courage again. What an amazing encounter. Now to leave the city. The sight of the Germans had given me a shock. It was clear that Mr. L was correct, it was pointless, even dangerous, to stay here any longer.

I take my son and we walk to the train station. It is a long way. A mob fills the square in front of the station. When I come nearer I see that they are in uniforms—soldiers and sailors. They're standing in front of the station and on the steps leading to the entrance, waving identification papers and yelling. A dispatcher stands at the top of the stairs, selecting people and letting them pass.

Is there a chance we can go with them?

We mingle with the crowd pushing forward. It soon becomes clear to me that it is hopeless, and besides, they are not taking civilians. These are soldiers and sailors they want to ship out as quickly as possible before the occupation. Someone mentions the possibility that civilians with proper identification papers may be transported the next day.

On Thursday morning more German troops arrive. H. L. tells me he will stay, he doesn't know for how long. Others are already preparing for departure, everything is chaotic. I have not received an answer to my telegram.

I decide to leave Bordeaux in any case. I want to, I must, and I shall. If I remain here any longer I risk being captured by the Germans. My husband can't come here: for days now no one has been allowed to enter the city, he wouldn't be able to find transportation, and it would be madness to rush into the arms of the Nazis. But how will we escape? Our friend H. L., helpful as always, thinks it over. He knows of no one at the moment who could take us along. And anyway, everyone who is leaving is heading for the countryside and we must get to the border.

At the prefecture they tell me that there is only one direction I should be going in: Toulouse.

So I request a permit to go to Toulouse, and receive the necessary papers. But transportation cannot be arranged. I try to see a higher official, but it is noon and waiters are hurrying up the stairs with covered trays. The officials are so busy that their lunch is served here. Who will have time for me now? I go back downstairs to the office. "Help me," I say.

The man thinks for a while: "I really want to, but what can I do?" He thinks further. "I'll ask Mr. X. He's interested in literature. I'll check with him, please wait here."

Fifteen minutes later he returns smiling. "You'll leave at two. Be at no. X on Y Street at two o'clock and don't be late. I'll be there as well. They'll take you along. Ask for Mr. Z."

We arrive on time with our bags. We don't know exactly where we are going or with whom. People are standing around, everyone is curious about the Germans. Trucks filled with newspapers are stopping in front of the building, they are carrying heavy stacks of papers inside. A while later they carry identical stacks out again and load them onto other trucks, which drive off immediately. I ask for Mr. Z. He is here, but busy. We will be driven to Toulouse, but we must wait until they find a truck, the ones here are going in other directions.

We wait for four hours, four long hours in this courtyard and on the street. From time to time I turn to the man in charge. Has he forgotten us? No, no—but all the trucks are full, and besides, not one yet has been going to Toulouse. My son is getting more and more impatient. It doesn't help matters, we can't make demands, this is a stroke of sheer luck. We try to figure out what is going on with the newspapers, why so much effort is being put into first dragging them inside and then back out again. They are being weighed and counted.


## To Toulouse


Finally departure time arrives. Someone comes over to us with a driver. He will take us along with his newspapers. He is not happy about it, he has only a small car. The backseat is removed, to be left behind. The space is filled to the roof with newspapers, our blankets and coats are added to the pile. We climb up front next to the driver, with my son in the middle. He holds his rucksack between his knees, my handbag serves as a foot pillow. The car is going to Marseille through Toulouse.

It is six o'clock. The driver's main concern (and ours) is avoiding the Germans if at all possible. It is better to bypass the *route nationale* and travel a bit longer.

We have difficulty getting out of the city. Wherever we turn we encounter German vehicles.

He says: "I've got to go back, I forgot my map of Bordeaux. I can't stop at every corner to ask directions."

We turn around. We've been driving for fifteen minutes. The man jumps out of the car and comes back with his map, satisfied. Now we can proceed out of the city.

We find a road that runs parallel to the *route nationale* and make good time in the quiet countryside. Each time we approach a town, a gendarme jumps out and stops the car; he sees what we are carrying, his face brightens, and he allows us through without looking at our identification. He asks only for a copy of the paper. He's posted here on a country road near a little town and would also like to know what's going on. He asks us if we have seen any Germans and advises us on how best to avoid them.

We use the side roads and travel one hundred kilometers an hour outside the towns. We encounter more and more gendarmes, we give them newspapers willingly, the driver sets aside a number of them for this purpose; occasionally a gendarme asks for an extra copy for his colleagues.

Twilight descends at eight. We have to cross the *route nationale*.

We are on a bumpy dirt road when a gendarme waves us over. There are two small farmer's carts in front of us; an old man jumps down.

There are Germans on the *route nationale*. We have to wait for entire regiments to pass. They are traveling in troop transports interspersed with cars and motorcycles. They sit in the trucks in their waterproof raincoats, apparently taking no notice of their surroundings.

Some farmer's wagons roll along the broad road amid the Germans, irritating them. Right at our corner an officer jumps down and begins giving orders, waving his arms vehemently: civilian vehicles are expressly forbidden to interfere with military traffic! They are directed to the other side of the road and kept there. Satisfied, the officer jumps back up on his large truck and yells, "Forward!" And a gendarme at the crossroads not far away yells with him—in German for some reason—"Forward!"

Our driver keeps murmuring, *"Dear God, dear God,"* words I hear over and over again whenever things become critical.

Finally the Germans have all paraded by. One time a German officer jumps down from his vehicle and looks sharply at the civilians, but does nothing.

We take the *route nationale* on the correct assumption that we will encounter no more Germans. We have lost over half an hour. It was almost nine and getting darker, but it was a clear night and the driver knew the way.

We traveled in darkness through Montauban without difficulty. It was here, on our way to Bordeaux, that we had been accompanied by gendarmes because the transport was French. The city was quiet, there was no one on the streets. Our driver said he had enough gas, but wanted to fill the tank to be safe. We would reach Toulouse much later than he had thought, perhaps in the middle of the night. We stopped at the two or three gas stations in Montauban, but no one wanted to give us gas, they would sell it only to the army. All we could purchase was a liter of oil. *"Dear God, dear God"*—it would have to do.

## Toulouse

We arrived in Toulouse between one and two in the morning, stiff from the long drive. The driver assured us on the way that he would take us to a hotel—he didn't know where the *centre d'acceuil* was, and if there was one it was certain to be full—but there was a hotel lobby where we could spend the night.

We found ourselves at the square in front of the train station in Toulouse. The driver rang the bell at the hotel and asked that we be let in. We were. Then we said goodbye to him. I offered him fifty francs, but he refused them. He had already been paid for the trip, he said, it was his job and we—we were a matter of honor.

We stepped from the pitch-black street into the hotel lobby, which wasn't much brighter. It took awhile to orient ourselves: people were lying on the floor or sitting on seats of straw. The hotel clerk offered us a straw bench and we spent the hours till morning on it. My son soon slipped off to the floor.

When it got lighter we could make out our surroundings. People were even lying under tables. A Belgian soldier was snoring on the floor, his wife asleep in an armchair. She later said they had been fleeing for a long time. Where would they go? The lobby had to be cleared by seven A.M. People disappeared one after another to freshen up. I heard some of them say, *"A ce soir."*

Once again we found ourselves on a strange street, this time in Toulouse. The cafés opened a while later. We were happy to get some refreshment. We walked through the city in the direction of the cathedral to a school to whose director H. L. had given us a letter of introduction. The man was there and received us. He apologized when he showed us the room we would be staying in: he wasn't to blame that the school was in such a miserable, dilapidated condition.

But for us it was a privilege to have the room, a real room of our own with two beds, a little table, and washing facilities.

I immediately continued in my search for my husband. I sent a telegram—telegraph services had been reinstated—to Miss S in Le Puy, asking if she had seen him. I looked for acquaintances in Toulouse who might perhaps know something of him and also went to the university where they had opened a center for university members.

At noontime I searched the restaurants. Perhaps I could also locate the soldier my husband had stayed with in Paris before his departure, who supposedly lived near Toulouse. We studied the slips of paper pasted on the city hall and looked at the bulletin board in the public square nearby. And indeed, a young woman who had previously belonged to my husband's agency was sitting at a table with lists of names. But she found nothing for me on her list.

There was a very friendly family staying on the same floor with us at the school. I had long conversations in the washroom with the woman and her daughter. The woman complains about the people of Toulouse, the city is overcrowded and is housing twice the peacetime population; there are too many Belgians, whole Belgian regiments were housed in the city and its suburbs, and Dutch refugees as well, and many Frenchmen from the north—but the people of Toulouse weren't treating their fellow countrymen well. They should be trying to help those who had been driven from their homes, who had no home and were on the run, as I was, I who had experienced horrible things and was under incredible strain. They didn't see us as sympathetic fellow citizens but as unwanted mouths to feed.

But food really is scarce. There are plenty of fruits and vegetables, but a shortage of oil and fat. Everywhere you look you see written in large letters: "No more . . ." "*Pas de* . . ." In Le Puy they lacked specific items but here there are long lists of things they don't have.

The prefecture is nearby, and across from it they have set up an agency for the support of destitute refugees. People start lining up at five o'clock in the morning. First they pick up and fill out forms, then if their information is correct they are given ten francs a day per person, surely a large sum for the State, but precious little to those who receive it.

I envy the concierge at the school, whose booth I often pass by. She has a home, a kitchen, a real stove. I haven't had these things for months. She is an old woman who is from here, and wherever she goes people know her and treat her better than us refugees. One evening as I walk past her booth and ask as usual if there is any news for me, there is a young woman with her, her daughter-in-law, and then her son walks up. How fortunate she is.

After five days go by, the concierge hands me a telegram one afternoon. I open it very nervously, cannot read it at first, it is totally misprinted, with one entire line of text on top of another.

I run into the school to the teachers, who are in the middle of a meeting. They help me, and after a while we have decoded the message. It is from my friend in Le Puy—and gives the address of my husband as a camp in Mende.

I don't understand what he is doing in Mende, in a camp. And when I tell the director I want to write to my husband right away, so that he will know where we are and will come to Toulouse immediately, the man looks at me with a strange expression. "But how? How can you? He's in a camp, don't you understand. Perhaps your husband is a prisoner." I angrily reject that idea. He is French. Perhaps he is there, the man says, trying to placate me, in some official capacity. I don't buy that either.

At any rate I must wait for an answer. The days pass slowly. Then finally there is a telegram, this time from my husband, giving news of himself. Others follow, then letters arrive. It is wonderful to hear from him. But I get the feeling that my husband is in difficult straits outwardly, and even more so inwardly.

# PART 3

# RESCUE

# *11*

# In Toulouse

*M*y wife and son are standing there at the station, pale and worn out, and here I am, as pale and thin as they.

We sit in a restaurant by a window. Then we walk along the street and once again I encounter my former existence, the sight of a big city. We take a tram to the school. It's an old structure, all right, and the rear building with its now empty boarding school is run-down, dark, and dank. From the room we are staying in I look out onto a narrow yard covered with a green fungus. We have three beds, a table, and chairs, there is electricity, and because it is summer we needn't worry about heating. The carpet is ripped, the air in the damp rooms is musty. But how many refugees have better quarters?

The journey into the unknown is ended. If fate wants something of me, wants to get to me, now there are three of us. Things have changed, the point of attack is larger than before, the blows will be better received.

My wife takes me into the city, to the area around city hall where there is a broad, square plaza, one side of which is taken up by city hall itself, a magnificent building. The other sides are lined with restaurants, cafés, shops. Trams circle the plaza (on that first afternoon the plaza was almost empty, on the following day it would become a marketplace, boisterous and colorful).

[ *177* ]

The heat was strong. A well-shaded café lay hidden behind rows of columns. We sat there as if it were peacetime, and then my wife began talking to me.

I had brought my suitcase with me to Toulouse in addition to myself, shabby and inwardly changed. I had been through a great deal and had thoughts in me that I had not yet dealt with. I carried them inside me as something private, like a coin that you hoard for yourself.

Now, as we sat in the café, or walked back and forth through the marketplace in Toulouse, my wife began asking me how I saw the future.

I no longer recall my answer; it was a testy and indifferent one. It is possible I countered it by questioning how she could ask me such a thing at that moment.

And then she came out with a definite plan of action. It seemed crazy to me. But fifteen minutes later—we were still at the marketplace, it was before we returned home—it seemed less absurd to me, and within half an hour I had agreed to it and was committed to carrying it out.

She said: "We cannot remain in France. We are German emigrants who have become French citizens, our sons are in the French army. The Nazis will hunt us down. Toulouse is in unoccupied territory today but that can change tomorrow. We are not safe here. On top of which we are broke."

I said: "And . . . ?"

"We must leave France as soon as possible and go to America."

This seemed preposterous to me. I had been to America the previous year, as a guest of the PEN Club's international conference during the World's Fair in New York. Who would pay for our trip this time?

"We must telegraph Peter and tell him."

Peter, our eldest son, was twenty-eight at the time. He had gone to America shortly after we had emigrated, and worked in New York as a book designer and illustrator. The idea of "going to America" was totally foreign to me. But in the course of the conversation I realized we had no other choice, we had to leave. I was ready to take the first step. My wife had been waiting for me to agree to the plan before sending that first telegram to America.

I had arrived that very day and now wanted to draft the telegram and send it right off. Why this haste? I remember it well. I was not pleasant company at that time. I don't know if I ever have been, but in those weeks following my Robinson Crusoe existence I was not easy to be with, and my wife's words rekindled the feeling that I was being hunted down. I insisted—that's how I was—that we go to the post office right away and send the telegram, our cry for help, to America.

We went to the post office, it was swarming with people. As in Mende, everyone there was writing, everyone was looking for something or waiting, it was like an anthill that had been tramped on. My wife wrote out the telegram in English, giving our address and asking that three visas and three tickets be issued to us, our son was to alert our friends in New York, and the PEN Club.

It was done. It was reviewed and stamped by the police—and sent. It would be in New York in two days, in four days we could have an answer.

## Refugees

There were many Germans in the city—searching, inquiring, disoriented; well-known people among them. They had been released from camps, now they were sending wires to every corner of the earth. I remember one young married couple. The man, a robust type, talked of forming a collective for refugees, as we could not help ourselves individually, but he always got stuck in the details of this idea. His wife was sitting across from him in silence, she was familiar with the plan. She joined in only at the end of the conversation: oh, she had had enough of it, enough! The escape from Germany, the misery here, the camp, and now defeat. She'd had it up to here, she said, she wanted to slit her throat. The young woman was pale and undernourished as were we all, she was not sick, only broken.

One man was stout and prosperous-looking. He had been doing auxiliary service and somehow had gotten out of it—I don't know how. He had no idea where he would go either, but he had a private plan and he reveled, yes reveled, in what he had "experienced." It had all been an adventure for him, a priceless, novel adventure. This man was enjoying everything that happened, as if it were already history. He was living out his future as a former

military campaigner. He felt it an honor to have been able to participate in world-historical events. The march through some town at
night, the fear, the panic of the civilian population, all of this was for
him nothing short of the Thirty Years War.

One young woman I had seen in Paris, eight days before the
collapse. She had been pushing a baby carriage at the time and she
had spoken of her husband, who was in a camp. Now both of them
appeared, husband and wife, and the man was pushing the baby
carriage.

And then I saw a well-dressed gentleman whom I didn't recognize at first. It was the man I had met at a train station on the way to
Le Puy, the one with the two suitcases hanging from a rope stretched
across his shoulders. He was looking for his mother then; it was the
industrialist from Paris; he had found her in Mende and had returned to his wife in Toulouse. And there beside him was his wife, an
elegant woman. We had returned to civilian life, to peacetime! We
shook hands and laughed: "What a time that was!"

We also ran into a professor from Paris whom we knew well.
He had become a spontaneous and affable man here. He was enormously confident: the Germans wouldn't allow things to continue
like this for long. For no matter what one thought of the Germans,
one thing was certain: they set great store by order. He was sure of
that.

He would return to Paris within two weeks at the latest, he said.

We strolled about the marketplace. And saw a monument there
that bore witness to the misery of this time. It was city hall, and a
good half of its façade had scraps of paper pasted on as far up as the
human arm or a ladder could reach. Each piece of paper carried an
inquiry about someone. Its lower half had gone blotchy, spotted as if
with a rash—by the scraps. As befitted a solid building, city hall
stood there placidly when the weather was calm. But when the wind
blew, the scraps fluttered and ruffled up like feathers. It was as if the
building came alive and the bits of paper were sending their cries out
into the wind. It was as if they wanted to lift the building and carry it
away—searching, always searching.

The conversations I had with my Parisian acquaintances did me
no good. I noticed that I had calmed down only on the surface, that I
was becoming agitated again. My anxiety resurfaced. I tried to avoid
these conversations. In the end I could neither offer the others
comfort nor could I discuss what preoccupied me, what was churn-

ing about inside me. What would these democrats and socialists have to say to the thoughts that had preoccupied me in Mende? They would fall silent, then ridicule me.

I give myself a shake now and then. But my self-disdain is not enough to silence those thoughts. They appear without summons. I carry them within me, sometimes they are a thorn and sometimes a treasure.

As if to torment us, German planes fly over the city every few days, intentionally low. They couldn't care less that this is unoccupied territory. A plane once flew right over my head as I was sitting quietly one morning in the small park by the church. It roared over the marketplace and frightened people, women fainted.

## *Waiting Period*

We had taken up residence within ancient, damp walls out of the cracks of which gnats swarmed in the evenings. If we opened the closetlike room next to ours we were met with a musty blast of air.

When we opened our wooden shutters in the morning we saw below us the greenly shimmering yard, and across from us other refugees were opening their shutters. They were housed in emergency quarters like ourselves. It was not easy to locate the washroom. But it was there somewhere. You merely had to go along a short corridor, then through a long dormitory with about twenty beds, then cross several more corridors, none of them particularly well-lit, and then in the distance you saw a blue light and had to make for it fearlessly. There was something eerie, mystical, about it—but it was just the washroom. Its windows had been painted blue.

It had sinks and running water.

But if nature called, you had to continue your march even farther, open a door of the magical washroom, and step through it onto a gallery. From there you could look down onto the narrow, dripping courtyard, a shaft, a pit, a breeding ground for gnats. But at the end of the gallery—small, forgotten, secluded—you found what you were desperately seeking, what the gods had barricaded with so many corridors and hallways and galleries.

The three of us left our room each morning, often after our son had gone on his solitary patrol. We headed for the café.

The café was located a few minutes away, across from a church, on a wide street that the tram ran on. It would be base ingratitude if in the midst of this report on difficult and distressing events I failed to mention this café in Toulouse and to sing its praises. It offered an excellent coffee with cream, whipped cream, and sugar. This hot elixir was drunk while standing. It is obvious why the establishment offered coffee only while you stood. If you sit down, you tend to relax and talk, but if you have to stand to do something, it demands all your attention. That is why the café served its wonderful coffee only to those who exhibited through their upright posture that they knew how to appreciate what they were being given. In Toulouse, as far as I know, this coffee was served only in the unassuming locale across from the church in the center of the city. And in praise of Toulouse, and as a tribute to its people, it must be said that the tiny space was never empty.

Here, in the early morning hours, we reached the high point of the day in terms of an enjoyable repast. For there is little to report of the other mealtimes. There was a restaurant on the marketplace at city hall that served, at a middling price, an equally middling meal. To get one you had to line up at the door, starting at noon. The proprietress would open the door from time to time and a crowd would push in. As there were many customers and only a few waiters, lunch took over an hour, starting off with an hors d'oeuvre only mysteriously hinted at, followed by a discreet course of fish or meat, and ending with a vegetable plate of great potential, and a pitiful amount of cream. It didn't add up to many calories, but that was made up for by the number of plates and by our cheerful anticipation and desire. The meal was an aphorism. As suited the time, it was a highly spiritual meal.

You could fill up with bread and drink your fill, as well. You could wash down everything you wished you had eaten.

The evening meal was taken within our narrow domestic circle. We bought bread, cheese, and a bit—"bit" in the truest sense of the word—of fruit and tomatoes. As there was no butter or margarine for the bread, we energetically spread on a "bit" of cheese for glue. In those days no one had any illusions about quantity. Even the smallest amount was acquired only through cunning.

Our days passed harnessed to these frugal meals. I was, as I mentioned, not pleasant company in Toulouse. My wife told me this only later, she showed little reaction to my sullenness at first and then became increasingly sullen about it herself. I was oppressive, like the small town and the stale air of the camp that I had brought with me. I said very little, was stilted, I was ready for the museum, as they say. But when I did say something my remarks were not very helpful. I often repeated, for instance, the sentence I had brought with me from Mende: "This is not the only world." My wife, preoccupied with finding food and other necessities, had more to do than sound me out on this metaphysical statement.

I had lost almost twelve pounds, but had taken on a hundred-weight spiritually. I dragged myself through Toulouse.

What else did I do other than get on the nerves of everyone around me? Nothing. A thinker can always say: I am thinking.

I often sit here beside a fountain in the little park by the church and watch the fish in the pool. Or I lie down after meals, as I have become accustomed to do, usually with a newspaper or a book—still *Merlin the Magician*, from Mende—with all kinds of things running through my head. But my thoughts no longer focused on Mende alone. No, I rebelled, I had no stomach for keeping that up. I was often terribly angry with myself and had the feeling that I had acted in a way that was ridiculous, unworthy. I had sustained a blow, both a general one and one to the head as well. I weathered the general one, but my head was aching. The absurdity of it: A man suffers a misfortune, whether through his own fault or someone else's, in such a way that he can no longer stand upright. These things happen, but you should keep them to yourself. But rather than make the effort to get back on my feet again like someone knocked down before the count, I toss a rope up to heaven and try to pull myself up on it while at the same time it's falling back down again. That's modern urban intelligence for you, and I was totally in its grip. So I raged against myself.

If the French academic whom I mentioned before does not notice that the French army has been defeated by an enemy that is superior to it in number and supplies and wants to make a religion of it, I react with amazement. But if I find myself beneath the wheel for a short while . . . no, I don't want to think about it. Let it rest. It could drive me mad.

And once again I find myself standing before a church! I enter, look around. My eyes fall on the crucifix.

In Mende I sat on a bench in an almost empty church and my

eyes strayed over to that figure hanging there horribly, questioned it, then returned empty. I remember. And now—the crucifix and I have come to an understanding. It is a secret we share. The one hanging on the cross doesn't speak to me, but I speak to him. I don't ask questions. I feel: You there . . . I am pursued, hunted, I feel horror. But what is my horror in comparison to what you had to endure on this earth, among us humans?

And behold, I decide that what I felt in Mende is not completely lost, forsaken. I still carry something of it in me. I changed my clothing in Beziers, but I didn't cast off everything.

I don't need to go to a church. Just the sight of a church cheers me. For, inside, I know that he is hanging on the cross.

I often have an intolerable longing for him, for you. But—I can't come any closer. That lies beyond my powers. Yes, I am afraid of myself. Someone must come and take me by the hand and pull me in.

## The Telegram from America

During this period a newspaper publishes a lead article, which appears to be medical, on the climate in Toulouse, signed by a "Doctor Toulouse." The climate in Toulouse is subject, it says, to abrupt fluctuations, not everyone is suited to it, particularly those unaccustomed to it—so that one must advise the many immigrants to pack their bags and be off. And who knows who is spreading the rumors that the Germans will arrive tomorrow or the day after? It is whispered that Germans have already been spotted, a small number of them are already here on surveillance. There are details. . . .

We had no idea what was going on in America, the consternation with which America was following the events in France, and with what dismay the French defeat was received. We, those of us here, don't know that they are thinking of us over there, that there are people holding meetings over there, conferring on how they can help us, without our appeals even having reached them yet. We—the refugees of this city—are obsessed by the idea that we are caught in a mousetrap.

A week later, as we are returning home from a walk, we find a letter from America signed by a friend from Berlin: we could probably get an American visa in Marseille, it said, in the meantime they would do what they could for us from that end.

At that point there was nothing that could have cheered us up, we were too afraid, too worried about our sons in the army; we existed, but we weren't really there, or anywhere. When we looked at it more closely, this latest news was promising but vague. For what did it mean, we could "probably" get a visa? That it was possible things would simply drag on?

Notices appear in the papers of a revision of the naturalization laws: so it was possible that they could confiscate our passports.

And then we happen to look at our passports and see that they have expired! Now we have to renew our passports! We cursed ourselves for our carelessness. All the time we have wasted in Toulouse! We go to the prefecture the next day. There are many bad things that can happen at a prefecture, but in the passport office here we encountered a secretary, a woman who performed her job efficiently and quietly, who was continually issuing, renewing, and extending passports. Our case fell within her jurisdiction; she asked pertinent questions and gave straight answers. But she told us something that depressed us: it would take a week, we had to make an application first. She gave us the forms. We had to fill them out and then take them to the police station. And then we would need new photographs, and that would take a day. And what will happen when we hand in the application?

People are milling around at the police station; there was a line. Gas coupons were to be issued here. The clerk sits at his desk, people file past him, but he wasn't issuing coupons, of course he isn't—there is no gasoline. We had to wait for our clerk, which was fortunate. For in waiting we chatted with others, and it turned out that to get passports, even to extend them, you needed a sponsor, two sponsors. Two sponsors? From where? And on such short notice? From the other line, the line for the nonexistent gasoline, we were greeted by acquaintances from Paris. We told them our difficulties and in the process were relieved of them. They would be our sponsors! When the clerk appeared and looked at our papers he was very kind, we got the piece of paper, a certification that there were no charges against us, and half a day later at the prefecture the efficient woman there handed us our passports, they had been extended.

And now I faced a different set of circumstances. The wind had changed. The fact that I had met the gentleman from Mende at a café, the one with the two suitcases around his shoulders, was the last sign from that dark period. And he too had changed: he looked happy and elegant, strolling about with his young wife.

Just how the spiritual aspect of things, the climate in which I moved, had changed was demonstrated by our efforts to get exit visas.

## A Dramatic Scene

You could not cross a border with a civilian passport, you needed military approval, but we were in the midst of a war. And so one morning we had to go to the office of the military command and present our request. Several officers seated at a table listened as we said we wished to leave France and go to America. They looked at our papers, pointed to sections of them, and whispered to each other until one of the men picked up a printed sheet and read something aloud from it. It turned out that this sheet of paper, which contained instructions pertaining to certain conditions of the armistice agreement, was directed at us. The gentleman admitted to us that the conditions had only just been ratified, but said that they were applicable to us and, according to them, it would be impossible that we, being of German heritage, would be able to leave the country. Yes, they had not overlooked us poor exiles; the victors, deeply concerned about us, had decided that we were to remain at their disposal, doubtless so that we could help celebrate their splendid victory. The paragraph was read to us a second time. It was incontestable.

My reaction? I listened, I read it, I shook my head and lowered it. That was all I could do with my head. Nothing else could be done. The officer explained that he had to comply with the stipulations. He suggested that we appeal to the government in Vichy—which was obviously a broad, broad domain.

Had I been alone at the time I would have stood there for a while, musing, and would have empathized with the officer who expressed his regrets to us, and would have pushed far from my mind the thought of hindering him in carrying out his appointed duty. For the thing was settled and had the law behind it. I even would have congratulated him on doing his duty, despite his obvious reluctance.

But my wife was standing beside me. At first she was dumb-founded by the information that had hardly come as a surprise to me. Then she was furious, beside herself that we were to be held here by order of the Nazis—that there was precious little that would prevent us from being locked up and then delivered into their hands. She simply couldn't believe it. She couldn't have cared less about the officer's sense of duty. But I saw the facts: the vanquished had to accept these conditions. The officers had nothing to do with it, no one here had anything to do with it.

But that, too, was of no interest to my wife, it didn't even occur to her. She was in a rage and didn't try to conceal it. Rather than accept things stoically, rather than congratulate the officer on his sense of duty, she explained our situation to them: two of our sons were in the army, one was a decorated soldier, I was connected with a French ministry. She didn't refrain from articulating everything she felt, as well as what she thought of this "procedure." She called it unheard of, incomprehensible. It was shameful, she couldn't believe that they were serious about detaining us, defenseless as we were, we who had found asylum here and who had supported this country. She wept. She protested, she appealed to them, they didn't say a word.

I kept still; she was absolutely right, of course, but of what help was it being "right" under these circumstances? Her thinking was understandable, but this was not an understandable situation—it was a bureaucratic one.

She stood by me in those weeks, but she also stood on other ground than I—on real, solid ground. She was realistic, she brought her authority to bear on the situation. She lashed out, she asserted herself. There was not only war and the written, published law, but also human beings who carried it out.

The officers whispered among themselves until one of them rose and stated that he would present our case to the general. He took our papers and disappeared. When he returned a few minutes later, he said, "You'll get the authorization."

France had lost a battle, but it was not defeated. Standing in Toulouse in the commandant's office, I realized this. A military disaster was not the same as self-betrayal.

If I search my memory of this period I can recall only a sudden strong feeling of rebellion against Mende. (But such moments were rare.) A great number of bells pealed in that town. At first I couldn't stand the racket—who could bear that constant summons to horror? And then I perceived it as a statement. I thought: They have understood that it is necessary to try to make more tolerable that which is sad and frightening. Frightening? Again and again I search for the connecting link between what was horrible, what lay beyond us, and what was human. Once again I stand like an Old Testament worshiper before an appalling image one is not permitted to approach, or if so, then with a veil over one's face and with one's eyes covered. I often was overcome by feelings of fear, of being judged. Damnation. I was plagued by thoughts of death, vivid fantasies of death.

When my friend, whom I had last seen in Cahors, returned to me at that time, the thick manuscript of my novel in the black, torn briefcase, I couldn't even look at it. What ancient, dead things it held. . . .

We have our passports in hand, have the train schedule, are permitted to leave—we will go to Marseille. Problems crop up, everything is magnified, we live on the brink of catastrophe. We are still the hunted.

We often hear singing coming from the long dormitory room next to our room at the school. Others are also preparing to leave, young people, two Alsatians among them who have been summoned home by their parents.

I can see the three of us leaving the school one evening, loaded down with luggage, walking down the street and then waiting on a street corner for the tram. It is ten o'clock on a beautiful summer evening, our train is scheduled to leave at midnight. We pass through an unfamiliar part of town. Once more we take in the sight of a large, bustling southern city.

A mob of soldiers and civilians is climbing the stairs to the train station. And as we walk onto the platform we are once again confronted with the image of war and of the end of the war: the platform is black with people sitting and lying there. And even more are arriving, families, individuals, who ask questions, crowd along the platform, settle here or there, then suddenly move again, running toward a train they assume to be theirs.

We wait. Not for long, not for as long as we thought it would be. Suddenly people are saying that the train now entering the station is going to Marseille. And then we act like everyone else, we scramble over each other, push forward, struggle up the steps of the car and fight for seats. We sat in the dark car, dripping with sweat. We oriented ourselves, arranged our luggage. A man who turned out to be a Russian émigré roughly shoved my wife away from the window seat she was in the process of occupying. The ruffian later proved to be quite personable; he was mostly personable and only infrequently a ruffian. During those first hours of travel we were not at all sure that the train was going to Marseille. For, after all, everyone had piled into the car at a mere rumor and no one actually knew where the train was headed. But after a while the general consensus was: it's going to Marseille. I would not have been at all surprised had it pulled into Lyon.

We arrived in Marseille, recalling the telegram: we will "probably" get American visas in Marseille.

# 12

# Marseille, or,
# the Pursuit of Visas

*I* have said that I would not have recorded these insignificant details had I not had the foreboding that this was no ordinary journey. I was not the usual passenger with his ticket, this journey was my own creation, it occurred both to and with me. It was a journey into my destiny.

But was it still a journey of destiny? I dreamed: No. No longer. That time has passed, I am safely in harbor now, and what happens next will happen within the framework of the normal. Yes, I definitely planned to get back to normal as soon as possible.

But things didn't turn out that way.

Again and again I realize that I am trapped in a state of baffling passivity. The things that I saw and felt and thought in Mende are still with me. They have settled in me like something unfinished.

What memories do I now have of Toulouse? Streets filled with people, it is an invigorating sight, but not always, it was actually fatal for me to be caught up in urban chaos when what I needed was solitude.

Marseille is a magnificent city. When we saw it for the first time in 1926, we liked it better than Paris. We left our luggage at the train station and went down the broad steps onto the street.

Early morning; we couldn't miss the way into the city, to the Canebière.

We arrived at the Canebière, and we sat down on the terrace of a corner café.

It was sunny and hot. We asked where the American Consulate was and slowly set off for it. Shops were opening, elegant shops. There was more food available than what we had had in Toulouse. It must be the harbor or more fertile soil, or fewer refugees. . . .

We came to a large *place*, half of which lay in the shadows of magnificent trees. The sun was scorching now. There were tables and chairs set up on the square with a pleasant view to the south: a café bordered the public space. It gradually filled with people who sat down, read papers, smoked. The square was the last stop of a tram line. People divided into two groups near the little station house. One group crowded onto the tram, the other was on its way over to a building that boasted a small brass plate with the words AMERICAN CONSULATE. Yes, all of these people were going to the consulate. The simply and the well-dressed, men and women. They were speaking German, French, Dutch, Slavic languages, and Yiddish.

When the doors opened, a few people sitting at the café stood up and joined the line. A woman sat at an information desk in the corridor on the second floor. Before we had a chance to explain our situation fully she gave us a slip of paper that had already been typed up: the address of the vice-consul. It also included directions; the tram stopped out front. We thought it would only be around the corner. But we rode and rode and still weren't there. The trip was not uninteresting, we saw fully half of the city. But our pleasure diminished after a while. We were obviously leaving the city.

And there—the steel-blue sea, an unexpected, magnificent sight. My wife and I reminisced about what it was like here in 1926. The son who was now sitting beside us hadn't yet been born then. The jetty, the bright colors, the surf, the blustery wind were wonderful; we had later traveled along the coast to Trajas.

There was a beach here, people were sitting on the sand, some were running into the water. We rode between small houses and villas, the ground rose to our left and was covered in woods. We kept thinking we had to get out, but the conductor reassured us—and not only us, for there were others going to the consulate. We arrived.

[ *191* ]

The American Consulate was located far from the city, in this splendid landscape.

We walked through a wrought-iron gate into a park and followed a wide roadway, trotting along one behind the other, a good dozen of us. We tried to stay in the shade. Finally, to our left, appeared an imposing building. But the people in the lead seemed to know where they were going and passed by it. We were perspiring and getting tired. Several cars sped by us.

This must be the building. Men and women had gathered on a broad section of the path that formed a kind of common. They were pacing up and down, or sitting on benches, reading. They were sitting on the lawn in the shade. They were waiting, waiting to be admitted. To the right, a short flight of steps led up to a lovely, medium-sized villa. The front door was open. People strolled back and forth, leaned on the balustrade, and looked out over the scene.

The sky was a bright blue, the sun gave off a blinding light no one was safe from.

Like the others who had arrived before us, we too wished to mount the steps. But then we spotted acquaintances from Berlin and Paris. They were standing with their hands in their pockets as we approached and they nodded to us casually, for they knew: it hadn't begun yet. We spoke to one another as if it had been only yesterday.

You had to take a number. People stood talking in groups up in the large waiting room. They sat on benches and read. They spoke with a woman who was giving out information in French and English. We got our number, there were a dozen people ahead of us, we had arrived late. We didn't even know if we would be received that day; the consulate was closed in the afternoon.

We took our number and went outside to join the people sitting on benches in the garden and walking about on the lawn. We spoke with a number of our fellow sufferers whom we had not seen since Paris. They had come from camps and told us about others who were on their way. Everyone was in a solemn mood: we would try, but there wasn't a great deal of hope. We talked about the political situation, a depressing topic. Strange how anxiety and fear made everyone suspect that the Nazis had it in for him personally, and each of us tried to figure out what it was he had said or written that was so suspicious and dangerous. Alone or together, we reviewed our catalog of guilt and considered ourselves to be doomed.

Alfred Döblin

And there was something else: there exists among us exiles no solidarity. We had always led very private lives; now we were particularly isolated from one another. We saw each other at the consulate and nodded: "Ah ha, you're here, too," but no one revealed his plans or the names of those on whom he depended. We guarded secrets. We were distrustful and feared that others would turn to them also, and steal our place. . . .

We avoided each other in the magnificent park of the consulate. In the end we all were admitted, the great moment arrived, the vice-consul appeared. We observed him at the table in the waiting room, a tall young man with a serious face, polite American manners, a man of few words, an attentive listener.

We went to his desk, one after the other. Some were overcome by impatience and tried to listen to and observe the vice-consul in order to divine what he expected of them. They were shown out. The three of us approached the table. The official glanced up at us; mostly he looked at the tabletop and played with his pencil.

We presented our telegram, which he studied carefully. We thought he would have a file on us, but he had nothing. We were amazed. They had telegraphed us that we would "probably" get our visas here; surely that meant that something must already have been initiated! Nothing. He didn't seem to notice our surprise.

I explained our predicament, my wife filled in the details. I told him we were requesting asylum. He wanted to know what connections we had in America. We mentioned the name of the man who had signed the telegram, we mentioned our son, and a well-known publisher who had published one of my books. I also presented my correspondence with another publisher. And there was more: the stamp in my passport that I had been to America the year before. The PEN Club had been invited to the White House at the time and my wife accidentally (accidentally?) had my invitation with her, and then there were the many French letters of recommendation that had been written on other past occasions.

This made a visible impression on the official. He stood up and invited us to follow him into his office in the next room. We stood there with him for a few minutes in front of a heater by the wall and finished giving him our information. The vice-consul comprehended our situation, he only wanted to fill in his general impression of us. He was a quiet, sympathetic man. Our conversation was

[ *193* ]

interrupted. He wrote something on a piece of paper and gave it to us: we were to return with the paper early the day after next. The piece of paper contained his signature and our names, with the note: "2 (3) visas."

We were dismissed.

What did the note mean? He hadn't said we should pick up the visas, only that we were to return. We had already reached the park when my wife returned to ask whether we should cable New York for support of our application. The vice-consul said it wasn't necessary. He was monosyllabic and noncommittal; he couldn't just give us a simple yes. So we left. We were sure only of the fact that we had not received a no.

There were difficult or even hopeless cases, like that of an elderly gentleman I knew whom we encountered in the park. He had no one in America, he said, and considered himself in jeopardy.

We went back to the city, and the longer we traveled and the more often we went over the whole thing, the more positive it seemed to us. When we got out of the tram at the large square that lay in the heat and shade of the hot midday sun—it was the square in front of the prefecture—and located a small restaurant nearby, we decided that Marseille was a fine place in general, and that we were better off here than in Toulouse. The waiter pointed out a hotel to us across the street. We were fortunate, we found a pleasant room there.

Yes, it was better in Marseille than in Toulouse. We weren't as depressed as we had been; there were cheerful terrace cafés here. We, too, sat under the trees on the large, shady square; the war raged in the distance, misery stalked the land. Millions of men had been taken prisoner—and, O God, Father in heaven, where were our two sons, our two soldiers, how were they faring? But we sat at a table and let the light and shadows play over us. We slowly calmed down. Things lost their edge. We became one with our surroundings.

## The Sword of Damocles

In addition to dealing with America, we had yet to cope with Spain and Portugal. Lisbon was our port of departure. We had to get through Spain. We checked with the consulates and ascertained that we would next need to obtain a Portuguese visa.

We went to that consulate. We entered a plain-looking building and found a crowd at the foot of the stairs on the ground floor. The door to the left led to the consulate, but it was closed. I didn't go in the first time. It was my wife who joined the crowd, and when the door opened and a woman showed a visitor out, my wife addressed her. The woman made it clear that an American visa was the first prerequisite, but that boat tickets were also imperative. That's right, we had to show our tickets to get a Portuguese visa. For God's sake, how will we get them? The woman assured us, however, that it was enough to show proof that the tickets had been ordered and that a deposit had been made. She mentioned the name Cook's Travel to us. And then she shut the door. People outside shoved against it, complaining that they had been standing there for a long time and that this was not their first visit. It never happened that everyone was admitted, and the consulate closed at twelve, they said.

We left the building depressed, a building we had entered only to ask if the consulate were open. What to do? The Spanish Consulate, the Portuguese, the American, boat tickets. . . . It was horrible. We had our telegram that said they would take care of our trip from their side, order our tickets for us, that is. Now we were supposed to pay for them here, at least in part—but how? And how would we pay for the trip to Lisbon? We were desperate now.

The travel agent had its offices on the Canebière. The wonderful Canebière—how it suddenly had lost its charm. It was now swarming with people who didn't want to let us through. On top of which it was a very long walk. We located Cook's. They were closed, come back tomorrow, they said.

But we had to be at the American Consulate the next day. Once again we went there, within sight of the sea. Swimmers clad in white were already on the beach. The gods had arranged a long journey on a difficult path to the American Consulate. We perspire, we wait, and finally the vice-consul appears at the desk in the anteroom to begin the process. He didn't recognize us. He looks in amazement at the slip of paper he himself had written, looks at us, and asks us the same questions again. Finally he nods and requests us to take a seat in his office. We are to wait there for his secretary.

We sat in the office. My son had gone out to play in the park.

We would call him when it was necessary. He stayed away instinctively; he understood that these things were scary and sad.

At first we thought it was wonderful to have been invited in to sit down. Then we just sat, and when we thought about it we didn't even know why we were here. Was it to go over the facts again for the record? And what then? Only then would we get an answer.

In the same room, statements were being made and recorded. An English-speaking woman with a child received an entry visa, a large and lengthy document. Even the child had to sign it. They took no chances. We became restless when an hour passed and nothing had happened. My wife got up and boldly asked the vice-consul himself, as he was passing through the room: When will we be received? He said that it depended on his secretary, who unfortunately had a great deal to do, each case took time. And then the secretary appeared and led us into another room. Our son was called in also. When she sat down and set up her typewriter we saw that she was issuing our visas.

The vice-consul entered the room as she was typing and asking us questions and typing our descriptions. She asked him the length of the visa. When he said six months I interrupted to say that we would like a visa for the duration of the war. He rejected this with a wave of his hand; this was a residence permit and it was valid for six months. At the end of that time we would have to leave the country. But because we were French citizens, we could go to the French colonies.

We listened to this with amazement and mixed feelings. We didn't argue, we didn't agree. At that moment it was important only to find a country of asylum. Six months, that was a long time.

When everything was completed, the vice-consul again appeared, reminded us once more of the six-month time period, and had us swear to it.

In the rush of all this we had forgotten to get passport photos taken. We went back to the city to get this taken care of and that evening we had the precious visas in our hands. We had taken a big step. It had gone amazingly quickly and smoothly. We should have been delighted but we weren't. We simply weren't capable of feeling much of anything.

We then paid 3,000 francs as a deposit on the steamer tickets, and used the occasion to inquire about the cost of going to the

Spanish border and to Lisbon. The amount quoted was devastating, outrageous. It far exceeded what we had.

We hurried to the post office and cabled America, pleading for help. What could we do but cable and cable?

In order for you to understand our haste, our anxiety, and the pressure we were under, you must realize that the sword of Damocles hung over our heads. We had received a permit allowing us to leave the country following that dramatic scene at the military office, it is true, but there was a time limit. The exit visa expired after seven days. We still had five days left, but there was no possibility of an extension. If we missed the deadline, we would have to repeat the whole monstrous, nerve-racking process. But we wouldn't have had the strength for that. We couldn't go through this again. How, in five days, would we be able to get Portuguese and Spanish visas, and the money from America so that we could leave?

In retrospect, anyone would call this whole thing an unproblematic journey, considering the circumstances. But to us it seemed just the opposite.

We finally figured out what we wanted. But how were we to get it? Each time we accomplished something it was only one small step along the way, and the path was made up of a terribly large number of steps.

## Miraculous Aid

We put down a deposit on our tickets and went to the Portuguese Consulate the next morning. First we were in a crowd with others, then at the door, and finally at a desk. And then it went smoothly, practically without a word.

There was a poster hanging on the wall that revealed how small Portugal was, but counting its colony of Angola it was of a respectable size. We weren't required to dole out a large sum here. It was midday. We had four days left. That afternoon my wife went to the Spanish consulate, but to no avail. The doors were locked. People desperate for visas hung around for hours there on the street and in the building's corridor. We got to know a few of them. We asked the security guards when was the best chance of being let in. They smiled: early, very early, best between five and six in the morning!

So I got up the next morning at five and traversed the quiet streets of the city to the Spanish Consulate. I stood outside the door. I was the first.

At six o'clock the security people arrived and greeted me. A line was already forming. We talked to each other and I saw some of the strange-looking passports and visas that the people arriving here were carrying. Around seven-thirty my wife appeared to relieve me. I went home and lay down. When I returned at ten-thirty she was just being let in. First they called the Spaniards who wanted return visas. It took a long time. When my wife then showed our passports to the less-than-friendly official, the man said that someone from the Portuguese Consulate had just called about us: there was something wrong with our passports. We had to go there and present them once again.

We had started the day at five for this. We had lost the entire day. We hurried to the Portuguese Consulate—it wasn't far—and asked what they wanted. But the Portuguese gentleman just shook his head, it was nothing, really. He had only forgotten to affix a stamp in one of our passports. There was no hurry, but he would take care of it right away.

That was it! And when it had been done we hurried back to the Spanish Consulate. As a precautionary measure we had notified the guard at the door that we were being sent over to another consulate and would return shortly, so he readmitted us immediately. The Spanish official looked at us in amazement. "But I just sent you to the Portuguese Consulate! There was something wrong with your passports." Yes, we had been there. It was only a missing stamp. He didn't want to believe us and right away telephoned the Portuguese Consulate. He satisfied himself that everything was in order. There was nothing of goodwill about this man. He sniffed suspiciously at our passports. I know what this type of probing means. He will find something—I know what he will find. And sure enough, he growls: "Hmm, hmm, French passports. Born in Stettin, born in Berlin. A nice state of affairs." A nice state of affairs, he says, in order to avoid using a more pointed expression.

But there was nothing he could do, our "nice state of affairs" was in order. He issued us the visas. He didn't want to do it—to issue visas, to help those people to escape whom his Fascist ally wished to capture. I am sure that he felt he was committing treason. It was an experience exactly opposite that at the military command in Toulouse. It was the other end of the rope. At one end tugged

legality, benevolence, and sympathy, while at this end tugged political narrowmindedness and hatred. Once in Spain, I soon learned
that Fascism and Spain are two different things. We had spent a
great deal of time at this consulate, a terribly long time. But it
was done.

We counted it up: we had left Toulouse on Monday evening,
on Thursday we had gotten our American visas, on Friday our
Portuguese, and on Saturday our Spanish.

And now we needed travel money.

We had an account at a large bank in Paris. With great effort my
wife was able to get an appointment to see the director of its
Marseille branch. He was disinclined to give us a cent. He needed
authorization. He advised us to telegraph Paris, it was still possible
to send a telegram. But when we went to the post office to telegraph
Paris, it wasn't possible. When we told the director this he could not
find enough words to express his sympathy. But he remained un-
moved. Then came Sunday morning, a bitter Sunday on which my
wife set out to visit people in the city whom we didn't even know
personally. I sent a telegram to my friend who had left Cahors to go
to relatives in southern France, and begged him to lend me money.
The answer came amazingly quickly: he didn't have it himself.

Who didn't my wife visit that hot, anxious morning? She went
to the editorial offices of the newspapers and to the Red Cross. We
visited a woman whose address my friend had given us. The woman
was in the country "at the moment." After the editorial offices and
the Red Cross, my wife went to a Jewish refugee organization. It
was a kind of soup kitchen and she spoke with a rabbi, a well-
nourished, well-dressed man who said, "Please, if it's a bowl of soup
you want . . ." But no, she said, we were in a difficult and dangerous
situation. He heard her out and smiled superciliously: what was
difficult, what was dangerous about it? First of all, the Germans
hadn't arrived yet, and second, they weren't in the least concerned
with us. My wife wouldn't relent; if neither he nor his organization
had the money, couldn't he give us the names of some well-to-do
people in the city to whom we could turn? She mentioned my name.
He repeated it and shrugged his shoulders. "Never heard of him."
When she became even more upset, it wasn't long before he showed
her the door.

There was little more we could do. The battle had been fought and lost. We sat in a trap: no money. The next day was Monday, our last day. If we didn't leave that very day, we would miss our deadline and all our efforts would have been for nothing.

I myself had no hope. I spent that Monday morning in a deep depression, I remember it well. We stayed at home. We had laid down our weapons and surrendered. It was already afternoon, between four and five, our final hours, when we came to. My wife recalled that the school director in Toulouse had given us the address of a colleague of his here who was supposed to help us find quarters. We had not used the address. Perhaps we could now.

The man was there. He received us in his office and listened to us sympathetically. He couldn't help us with money, he said, but perhaps one of his superiors could, he was also at his office in Marseille. He wrote something down on a piece of paper and wished us luck.

It would soon be six. We took a cab to the prefecture, for that was where the man had his office. We believed there was no chance at all we would find him in at that hour. But we went anyway.

He was there.

He didn't keep us waiting for long. An elegant, elderly man with a grave but friendly expression walked up to us and began asking us questions. He listened quietly to what we had to say. He held in his hand the piece of paper that the school director had given us. We told him of our plight. We had to leave that very night in order to cross the border in time. We showed him our passports and the date that we had to leave the country. The money we were waiting for from America would reach us in Lisbon if not here, but we needed money to travel today, right now, in order to reach the border and from there get to Lisbon. He read the piece of paper over and over again. On the paper, as a referral, was the name of that extraordinary man, the high official who had stood by us in France, whom my wife had encountered in Bordeaux. The official here did not know us, and he knew that the director who had sent us to him didn't know us either. We asked him nevertheless to give us the name of someone in the city to whom we could turn. He said he would like to learn more about us from the high ministry official whom we had given as a reference. He knew the man. He knew that the entire ministry, and this official, had left Bordeaux for Vichy; he was in contact with the man in an official capacity. The gentleman at

Alfred Döblin

the Marseille prefecture went into the next room to make a telephone call.

We waited. Our meeting with this elegant gentleman had calmed us down. But what was happening in there? Calling another city at this time? It was a miracle that we had found him here.

It wasn't long before he reappeared. We looked at his face: ah, a friendly expression. He told us in his soft voice that he had spoken with the man in Vichy. Our friend had told him that we were absolutely trustworthy. And now he invited us into his office. We breathed a sigh of relief. It was unbelievable.

We stood in front of his desk. We named the sum we needed for the trip to Spain and to Portugal, as far as Lisbon. We calculated it to be around 4,000 francs. He said that he did not ordinarily have that kind of money. But it happened that he had come into possession of a certain sum that very day, and he of course wished to do what was within his power to help us.

Then he reached into his breast pocket, took out his wallet, and handed us the money. No receipt. We promised to pay him back as soon as possible. He declined our thanks, we were in a perilous situation, he said, he was sorry not to be able to do more, he wished us luck, we shook hands.

The building closed for the evening behind us. It was seven, the last possible minute.

Our dilemma was similar to that of sailors in an ancient Greek saga. They had to navigate between two rocky cliffs that opened and closed like immense jaws. Most of the sailors were caught and crushed, hardly anyone escaped. This polite, unassuming man who saved our lives at the last minute took on the appearance of a miracle.

I forgot. I didn't want to know anything about him. He kept me within his view. He didn't let go. He gave no sign this time. He became involved.

I was shaken, and still am, when I think of it. How our son rejoiced: we're leaving tonight!

We had our baggage carried to the station for us, for there was no cab to be had at night. Our train was to depart early the next morning. The hotel clerk who was supposed to waken us was still asleep when we left.

We walked through the dark night streets to the station. The train was going to Perpignan. We were familiar with Perpignan. We felt a little more relaxed there, and spent the day exploring the town. We telegraphed New York that we were now going to Lisbon. Everything was progressing in giant steps. And it was at this moment that it became absolutely clear to us, and it left us with a slightly bitter feeling: we are leaving Europe, we must leave.

At the station they told us that the train, the last one we could take, would not leave that night. But it did.

We have crossed the border. There were many unforeseeable problems ahead.

When our group had left Paris from the Porte d'Ivry station on June 10, it had been an inconspicuous departure; the haste and confusion had enabled us to forget that we were leaving Paris. But now each step we took was glaringly apparent.

How hard it was for us to go. And to leave people whom we were attached to. To be forced to quit a land that had protected us. To flee while France was in its darkest hour.

Once again I experienced the shame of a deserter.

# 13

# Charming Spain

Port-Bou, the border station, Spanish soil. Dozens of people got off with us. How sad to be rescued this way.

We were searched. We were also subjected to a highly embarrassing interrogation. We had the francs we had borrowed. We could change only a small sum into pesetas, and were told that we would not be allowed to buy any more pesetas than these. My wife complained that it would not be enough for three people to travel through Spain. The official turned a deaf ear to her. He wrote down in our passports how much money we had, and in which currency. After we had paid for our tickets to Barcelona we calculated what we would have left for the trip to the Portuguese border. It was a pittance—Spain would be a new and very interesting adventure. We sat in an ancient wooden rail car in third class. We had the sea in view for a long time. Spaniards got on and off and carried on unbelievably loud conversations. There were farmers with live chickens in baskets. The poor creatures were trussed up in a pitiful manner and could barely raise their heads. The farmers shoved the baskets out of sight under the seats. This maltreatment was not owing to cruelty, but to an official decree according to which chickens, eggs, and certain other commodities could not be transported from one district to another without paying an additional duty.

We were French refugees, our fellow passengers engaged us in conversation and revealed themselves to be doubly concerned with our affairs. First of all, they had a natural sympathy for France; second, they pitied a neighboring country that had been defeated and was in agony. No one mentioned Nazi Germany. I had the impression that this wasn't out of consideration for our feelings. Germany was a long way away and didn't concern them. We avoided political conversation; we stuck to the war and the deplorable conditions that went with it.

They told us that their own country had been at war for a long time, and pointed out ruins to us during the course of the trip. They asked us about the food situation in France, it was a burning issue for them. The people traveling with us, for the long stretch as well as for shorter distances, were not undernourished, they ate well from containers they had brought with them, their fare seemed to consist mostly of sauce, and they swallowed a lot of bread with it. But it was very dark bread, not very good, and on top of that, they said, it was rationed and wasn't available every day. A young man sat across from me for a while. He was smoking, and he offered me a cigarette. I took it and gave him one of my rationed French cigarettes in exchange. He threw his away and smoked mine with great relish. At first I suspected I was sitting across from a police informer, but that wasn't the case. He traveled with us for a few stations, listened to the problems France was having, and spoke of the economic distress in his own country, which was magnified by France's misfortune. Would there be war here too? he asked.

At one point he saw my pocketknife with a name engraved on it, he studied the name carefully (it was not my own), and then, by way of introducing himself, he pulled a little book out of his breast pocket. It looked like a union membership book. I read his name and also *Association of the Brotherhood Against Marxism.*

So this amiable, unpretentious man was one of the notorious "Whites." This was what a Spanish Fascist looked like. I saw that his beliefs had not made a new type of human being out of him. Not as he sat there alone, at any rate, next to me. I do not know what he is like when marching alongside his "brothers."

## Barcelona

Barcelona, midnight. A vast, brightly lit station. How the glare startled us: in France we had undergone months of blackout.

Alfred Döblin

We planned to spend the night at the station in order to proceed on to Madrid early the next morning—to get Spain behind us as quickly as possible in order to avoid contact with officialdom. And we wanted to save money. No one was permitted to stay overnight in the train station. While still on the train we were offered advice by two ladies we traveled with for the last hour of the journey, one Belgian, and one Frenchwoman who was married to a Spaniard and living in Barcelona. The topic of conversation: our financial woes and where we would spend the night. The Spanish-Frenchwoman wanted to help us, but how?

Later, as we were walking with her past a café—bright, wide streets—someone greets her from a terrace. A man comes up to her and she asks him to lend her some money. He is happy to be able to do so. And the lady comes over to us and compensates for what the customs official wouldn't permit: she changes our francs into enough money for the night. We are overjoyed. But in our passports is a stamp that tells exactly how many francs we possess. "Then just say you lost the money!" We laugh at this solution. The lady says goodbye to us.

We approach two women in a charming little café, they are in the process of closing it for the night. One of them listens to our requests. She doesn't have a room for us but says, "You're coming directly from France? Oh, God, I'll go with you, we'll find something."

She says a few words to her friend in the café and without further ado comes with us.

She leads us through narrow streets that are full of life, festive — oh, our sad, faraway France. We stop in front of a nondescript building. There is a bar on the second floor watched over by a strong-looking woman bartender, our companion speaks with her. We can pass the night there.

The bartender leads us up a stone spiral staircase. There are several tiny rooms upstairs, "furnished" with a bed and a chair. We are shown a tiny washroom. We accept at once. I have the impression that this hotel is shady. Our new companion says goodnight to us, we thank her and prepare for bed—it is one in the morning. But our bartender is standing there, and when she hears that we plan to leave early that same morning for Madrid, she tells us regretfully that she has no other choice but to accompany us to the police station— immediately, tonight. The regulations concerning aliens are quite strict, she says, it is not enough for us to show her our papers, we must present them to the police ourselves. (She says this in broken French.)

She goes down the stairs, we follow. We are not surprised. We are by no means angry. We spend the next half hour, between one and two in the morning, taking an unscheduled walk through Barcelona.

On the way to the police station the bartender—in mixed French-Spanish—tells us about the bombardment of the city. We stop in front of a huge building and climb the stone steps. We trail wearily along behind our guide through several corridors, to end up in a large office. There are desks with files standing behind wooden cabinets, but at the middle table there sits a lone, elderly, bald man in a dark uniform. A table with a typewriter sits next to him.

"It's the vice-prefect himself," the bartender whispers respectfully. I feign happiness at having located such a high personage in the middle of night. The sprightly gentleman, prefect or vice-prefect, takes our passports. The bartender explains that we are passing through the country from France, we want to go on to Madrid, to the border. He glances at our passports, leafs through them, comprehends, already he is raising his hand: "*Partir, partir.*" That's it: leave, go.

He gives us a wave. We smile in thanks and take our passports. We can go. A hospitable land, Spain.


## Across the Scorching Countryside

An early departure for Madrid. There are young beggars at the station, they chase after cars. There are also hordes of young soldiers; some of them get on the train. We receive a pleasant surprise when they take our tickets: our son, who is thirteen, need only pay half fare. My wife is surprised: in Port-Bou he had to pay full fare. She decides to get to the bottom of this as soon as possible. We later find out the reason.

We rode the entire day in a car with open compartments. An armed guard paced up and down in the corridor. The young soldiers made a lot of noise, they played instruments and sang and shouted. The Spanish civilians (there weren't many) took no notice of them. There is a careful check on passports on the train.

## Alfred Döblin

The day had begun warm in Barcelona. By noon the temperature had climbed to an unbearable degree in the car. We passed through the brutal Spanish highlands, one long, scorched wasteland. There were infrequent patches of green, for hours we saw only crumbling mountain walls, bare yellow and brown masses of rock, extensive heaps of ruins. It became clear why this huge country was so sparsely populated: its center was one big crater. Whatever wished to survive clung to its edges. Life in such a landscape is hard, hard in a way different from that of the north German marches; knights and robbers dwell here in the stone fortresses of this wasteland. Aristocrats and warriors are bred here. Courage, romanticism, and misanthropy live in opposition here to the kind of development that flat and fertile lands experience. The heat in the train is unbearable. If you stick your head out the window the air is like the blast of a furnace. We keep the windows closed, but what good is closing them when they are broken? Our discomfort becomes even more intense when we go through tunnels, for the tracks run through the middle of a mountain range. Without the firsthand experience gained on this trip I would have thought it nice to go through tunnels in order to escape the heat from time to time. But these long, dark conduits offered an even worse, numbing and blistering heat. And the smoke, the thick, billowing smoke of the locomotive, filled the cars, pushing through the broken windows. At first our throats got scratchy, then we coughed and ducked down to press handkerchiefs over our noses and we kept our mouths closed until we were almost suffocating. It was a blessing when the tunnels stopped; we were feeling faint.

We could get water and drinks at all of the stations, so we drank and drank and perspired. We bought delicious apricots and finished the rest of our French white bread.

By afternoon it occurred to us to go to the dining car to have a cup of coffee, even if we weren't going to eat lunch. It was a long way to the dining car. We had passed through several cars when the controller appeared before us. We know we haven't done anything wrong and hand him our tickets. At the same time we ask where the dining car is, hungry and thirsty as we are. But the controller merely looks at our tickets and says something. He is speaking Spanish and we can't understand him. It has to do with our son's children's ticket. The ticket was issued to us according to regulations, we purchased it in Barcelona. We tell him this. We had asked what a ticket for him would cost and had paid the required sum.

The controller looks at the ticket and then at our son, who is standing beside us. The man shakes his head. He talks with people who have gathered around us in the corridor. My wife, with a look at our son, repeats "*treize ans*," which in French means thirteen years old—and the Spanish crowd laughs delightedly. "*Treize*," they echo, and laugh. We don't understand. What is there to laugh about? We are prepared to produce papers that prove their laughter to be totally unjustified: the boy really is *treize ans*. But the controller takes us in tow, as we are blocking the corridor, and leads us into a compartment and there is a woman sitting there who steps in when she hears us speaking French. And now we understand why the controller and the others had laughed so. *Treize*, pronounced "trez," means "three" in Spanish. Yes, it's true, our son was too big for three. The desk clerk in Barcelona had mistakenly issued him a children's ticket and we now had to pay the difference. Which we did.

And then we turn around. We don't go on to the dining car. We can't afford a cup of coffee now.

The young soldiers sang and made a racket. It was evening. The scorched region of Spain lay behind us. In the conversations around us we heard the word "Ma-drid."

## Madrid

And then we were in Madrid. We didn't need to look for a hotel room here. It found us. At the train station, offers flew at us from all sides in French. One man had an assistant with him who would carry the baggage. We went with him. He was a hotel employee, but he also rented rooms on the side. He advised us to go to the National Bank the next day and exchange what money we needed. We had the right to exchange money in any city we stopped in, not only at the border. The man at the border station had been a character, playing the big shot, frightening us, telling us we couldn't change any more French money. Our guide laughed. A cheerful reception.

After a fifteen-minute walk through this large, modern city, we

Alfred Döblin

arrived at his house—the three of us and two women, refugees we had met on the train. The rooms were plain and clean.

Our day in Madrid passed without incident. We weren't dragged to the police station as in Barcelona. We were ordinary travelers.

That morning we went to the magnificent National Bank, where we really did change our francs into pesetas with no problem, once having shown our passports and registered the amount. So we once again could eat lunch—our last had been three days before in Perpignan. We bought provisions for the coming trip. We had enough Spanish money, and it was advisable not to keep too much of it. We walked the streets, up and down. There were huge posters of General Franco plastered on wooden fences. We looked at the bombed-out houses and hotels. There were a great number of soldiers and young—very young—men in uniforms. Many of them wore little red caps. We bought our tickets at a travel agency (we had been told to do this once we reached the city).

That evening we once again packed our things and took a cab to another train station. It was in the working-class part of town and looked it. But our train was already there, with the wooden cars we knew so well. Some Spaniards were making a commotion in the next car, it went on for half an hour and seemed to be a goodbye party. It calmed down when we departed. The train set off into the night and the raucous people nearby began eating; then they went to sleep.

It was a pleasant night. I remember the beautiful moon and the brightly lit clouds. At the tiny stations people got on and off the train. The landscape changed, was mountainous, then flat. At dawn I noticed strange-looking trees outside. The bark had been partially stripped from them. At first I couldn't comprehend this act of cruelty, this crime against trees, until I spotted stacks of wood in the villages. Bundles of square, yellowish slabs. They were slabs of cork. The stripped trees were cork oaks. They peel the trees like they shear sheep. The sheep will run away if they are not held down, but trees are rooted and can do nothing.

We collected ourselves that morning and got up. Having spent long periods on benches over the last months, my personal observation is that they don't get softer.

The border station was called Valencia, not the famous Valen-

[ *209* ]

cia, but a more modest town, as was befitting the destination of persons in our circumstances.

Spain closed its doors behind us with the same vehemence it had opened them in Port-Bou. And it ended as it began, with money. They hadn't wanted to accept our francs in Port-Bou, and in Valencia they wanted to take them away. In the splendid gold-and-marble bank in Madrid we had proudly changed our francs into pesetas, despite the man in Port-Bou. Now we had too many pesetas. They began haggling with us. We had 200 pesetas; they wanted us to have only 120. We were embarrassed, then we spit fire. But customs agents are icebergs, they don't melt. We had to leave 80 pesetas in Spain.

The official divided them into three piles: we should take the first pile and have a good time with it in Valencia, with the second we should travel first class to the Portuguese border station. And as for the third, we should give it to him for the (let us say) Red Cross. We hesitated. The Red Cross is a very vague concept. "Couldn't you send the money to the French Consulate in Madrid?" The man considered it and boldly said: Yes. He gave us a receipt to the effect that he had received of us a sum to be delivered to the French Consulate—and that was the last we ever heard of it.

As it was morning, we had a "good time" with the allotted pesetas in Valencia by having a cup of coffee. And then to first class: we rode for twenty minutes and spent the whole time trying to store our luggage in the luggage rack—until the train stopped. It had arrived. That was the end of our good time. We now had to take down our luggage one last time, the luggage that had pigheadedly fallen down on us over and over again (it was smart, it knew this stretch), and carry it down the aisle and, as there was no one to help us, throw it down from the train onto the platform. We did this vindictively. Our bags had annoyed us greatly on the train and had spoiled the whole second part of our good time.

Spain, Spain, barely encountered, lay behind us.

A new chapter of the story began: Portugal.

# *14*

# Portugal

*A* new chapter. At the beginning I wrote, "As I now set pen to paper and begin to describe this part of my journey—a journey out of defeated France in mid-June, 1940, shortly before the signing of the cease-fire—I ask myself, after a brief overview: What is it all about? Is it worth writing down my journey from here to there, the difficulties that arose, other things that happened? Is that really of interest to anyone? To put it precisely, bluntly: it was not a trip from one French town to some other place, but a journey between heaven and earth.

"From beginning to end this journey had a—I almost said fantastic, dreamlike quality—but what I really mean is a quality that was not only real.

"It was 'I' who made this trip from beginning to end (has it ended?). But as a traveler I was not your typical passenger with his ticket.

"The journey happened to me, with me, and over me, all at the same time. Only because it happened that way do I undertake to describe it and its events."

And later I wrote, "I was filled with the urge to travel. I acted as if under orders. The orders were not only on the paper I carried, they had been put there as an order at my request. At 'my request'? I always stumble over the words 'I' and 'my.'"

And still later: "It is possible that I was rushing into the jaws of the enemy. I was prepared for this, as were others I had spoken to in Paris and during the journey. Some of them carried a revolver with them to put an end to it if they fell into the hands of the Nazis. I was also prepared, but in a different way. Death towered over me and behind me as well, I looked into its jaws. But I refused to act, or to consider acting. I felt bound hand and foot. My will was being held captive in a way that often infuriated me, my conscious self was thwarted, forced into a corner. But it wasn't destroyed; I was committed somehow. But behind my urge to go there was a dull resistance, an abysmal seriousness, a sorrow.

"I had suffered a defeat. A defeat, a major defeat, pushed its way into me. I went to meet it."

And what was it like now? How had it gone? It was as if the last weeks had drained my ability to feel. I didn't want to think about those first few weeks; only occasionally did I remember them, less and less often and with a deep sadness mixed with a feeling of guilt. It became a kind of encapsulation. And I preserved my experiences in a similar way, dehydrated, as spores. I couldn't cultivate them. I didn't know how to. I hid them from myself as if they were something evil, something forbidden.

That first period, from the time of my departure from Paris to Mende and Toulouse, was transparent, filled with coincidences and signs and pointers. After that everything subsided, my nervousness, my susceptibility, my perceptiveness. Things closed in around me, they became dense and abstruse. They passed into normal reality. And so I was led into Portugal, into a hot, bright, southern, peaceful world.

Right away we said to ourselves: Portugal is a wonderful country.

We had no difficulties with customs, luggage, or money. We could exchange as much as we wanted, though here too we had to swallow the bitter pill of the exchange rate; the value of French money had dropped drastically.

As we were looking around the platform in search of a baggage room—the train to Lisbon was leaving late that afternoon—the helpful official who had checked our passports took us to a little house on a street across from the village station, where we were received by several friendly women.

The house was incredibly clean, little girls were sitting in a room to the left, learning to knit and sew. We were served a big, delicious lunch and afterward we were shown to the bedroom for a siesta before our train departed.

I will never forget the wonder and delight one of the Portuguese women showed on hearing that we were from Paris. She clapped her hands in joy. She marveled at everything my wife was wearing, she praised our son. I was the only one in which she found nothing to adore, I am sorry to say.

The last leg of the European journey: from the border to Lisbon. We had been under way for long enough.

We spend the afternoon and evening traveling, and continue into the night. The Portuguese rail cars proved inferior to their Spanish counterparts as far as comfort was concerned. You had to climb over open rows of benches to get from one car to the next. There was no space at all for luggage. Our car was filled with a noisy crowd. There were many station stops; we got the impression we were traveling through a quiet countryside in a very heavy traffic jam.

As in Spain we were soon engaged in conversation and sniffed at as interesting specimens. Even more people got involved with us here than in Spain. And they acted quickly. Not only were we offered food and drink—neither was lacking as had been the case in Spain—they also made room in the crowded compartment for our son, who was exhausted. They cleared off a whole bench for him to lie down on. Those who had been seated there stood at the window or in the corridor.

Many of the passengers knew each other and conversed loudly and emotionally. Their mood made an immediate impression on us—being from northern Germany as we were. It seemed excessive, phenomenal to us. The phenomenon would be revealed in its purely natural state when we reached Lisbon. Everyone was exuberant and laughed a lot. One man, who wore his little hat down on his forehead like Charlie Chaplin, gave us his visiting card. We had not exchanged a word with him, he spoke only Portuguese, but he had been filled in by the others. He let us know that he had connections, he didn't live in Lisbon, it was true, but if we needed assistance with any kind of identification papers, etc., we were to get in touch with him.

We had a longer conversation with a man who spoke French. He asked, among other things, where we were going to spend the night on our arrival in Lisbon. When the train stopped at a large station the man got out for a few minutes, to inform us on his return that he had taken care of our lodging: he had telephoned a reputable, affordable pension that he knew and reserved two rooms for us. He would take us there personally. It seemed almost impossible to us that someone would take such an interest in us for no practical reason. But that was the case. There was nothing behind it other than philanthropy and goodwill. Having experienced the war and the chaos of retreat and escape, we were to learn that all of that was only one side of humanity. Human misfortune can act as a plea for help, it sets people in motion. We had seen this in Toulouse, in Marseille, on the trip through Spain, and here. And we were to see more of it.

The rumors we had heard about Portugal were less than pleasant: we would be held at the train station on arrival, we would not be allowed to go into Lisbon, in Lisbon there were already thousands of refugees waiting, the police shunted new arrivals into camps in the provinces. Steeped in these rumors, we now set out courageously from the train. We joined the throng crowding the gate. We handed over our tickets like ordinary passengers. No passports were required of us. No one detained us. Lisbon accepted us as naturally as it later disappointed us.

## Lisbon

It was two in the morning. We rode into the city, traveled through brightly lit streets full of happy people. Lisbon welcomed us with light, music, and laughter.

We will never forget the jolt it gave us. Not far from here, France was in agony, its cities engulfed in the shadows of war, the northern part of the country overrun by its conquerors. People were suffering and hungry, were waiting to see what conditions the victors would dictate. Millions of men had been taken prisoner, millions lived in terror, tens of thousands had been killed—and here the lights were burning brightly. People were enjoying peacetime.

We couldn't enjoy it. We could think only of what we had left behind.

[ *214* ]

Alfred Döblin

We clattered down into the bright city, hellishly bright (so it seemed to us). We stopped in front of a building closed up for the evening. The driver knocked and rang. The building appeared to be a private residence. The man said something to us, but Portuguese remained Portuguese to us, even when it was accompanied by vehement gestures. He wanted to tell us that they weren't opening the door, and that he didn't know why. Then, after he had once again banged at the door, a man appeared from one side of the house, he was probably a guard. He had keys and opened the door. A woman was descending the stairs at that same moment, and behind us the second car arrived with our female traveling companions and the Portuguese assistant from the station. Now the language problem was solved, our driver could be paid, and the discussion with the woman on the stairs could begin. They talked for a long time, we had no idea about what. We later discovered that the man often was a guest here himself. They discussed rooms and the price. We were given two connecting rooms, one with a window onto the street and a big bed that almost filled it (but there was also a cupboard, chairs, a mirror, all orderly and neat)—the other room was tiny, with no window, it was a storeroom, really. But there were two beds, one to the right, one to the left, and the price was reasonable. We were satisfied. We had arrived and could stretch out.

But dance music blared in the street for hours. The tram screeched by ringing its bell, cars honked lustily, people sang.

We listened to this lying in our beds, amazed.

The next morning at ten, when we went down to the dining room, a cheerful boy served us a weak—unconscious, really—cup of coffee, but there was also a white pastry that we quickly identified as rolls and gulped down whole with butter. This first encounter with the Lisbon cuisine was not bad. Lunch and dinner surpassed our expectations. There was a fantastic amount of food: thick, nutritious soup, fish, meat, and fruit, three times the quantity of a French meal. Quantity seemed to be the main thing here; and we were so hungry that in the beginning that was all we cared about.

We took our first foray into the city that same day.

The pension we were staying in, we now discovered, was called the Gloria. That gave me a jolt. What? The same mockery I had encountered before and during my stay in Mende? Gloria. The

[ *215* ]

lodging of the vanquished is called glory. I thought I had left all that far behind me—but it is good that I am being reminded.

"Glory" was a benevolent pension. (The last street I had lived on in Paris, incidentally, was the Rue de la Paix, and walking along it I often had muttered: But where is the peace? And in the last house I had lived there was a studio with the name "Pax"; but the Pax studio was, significantly, empty.)

When we went downstairs that morning the Gloria revealed itself to be a lively place of business, this entire area of town was a business section. We were living in the loudest traffic center in the city. A furrier occupied the other half of the third floor we were staying on, there were dining rooms downstairs and a doctor's consultation rooms. At the foot of the stairs was the parterre, and a clothing and lingerie merchant had spread out his wares in the wide hallway. We had to wend our way past his display table and his customers to get to the street.

We assumed that the long, narrow street led to the sea. It wasn't the sea it led to, however, but the mouth of the Tagus River. Trams, their bells ringing wildly, rattled up and down this small street. Cars and trucks rolled by. People crowded the narrow sidewalks, shoving each other along. Most of the shops offered clothing and lingerie fabric for sale. Merchants not only filled their shops and display windows with the rolls of fabric, they wheeled them out in front of their shops and draped them over the doors. They offered their wares for sale each morning, and each evening they rolled it all up and put it away. The entire area shrunk on Saturdays. And on Sundays it was only the gray private houses that faced each other on the now totally silent street, their eyes cast down as if they had been caught in a transgression. But even then they were secretly thinking about their raucous wickedness, of course, and were waiting only for Monday morning to arrive so that they could resume their old activity once again.

Just as our street was the dry goods street, other streets represented other branches. The street of banks, for example, was appropriately broad and grand. It was called Rua Aurea, Gold Street. But everything that is paper is not gold. Our bright dry-goods street was happier, and its noise, its laughter, its screeching and yelling, had character.

There appeared occasionally from a side street a group that looked as if they had stepped out of the Bible. These robust, straight-backed women marched into the city in single file, one behind the other, carrying jugs and baskets on their heads. The baskets were filled with fish or fruit. There was a large market hall on the side street with an abundance of fruit, vegetables, meat, and fish—an unbelievable sight. We also discovered the office of an American shipping line nearby. We were to become very familiar with it. And finally there were the immense, impressive buildings and columned halls, and it was here that we turned right, and were in the government sector and at the water.

There was a broad square located there. A stone balustrade protected it from the wide body of shimmering water that we at first took to be the sea, as fog hid its opposite shore from us. The water glistened. On it floated large and small boats. The large ones, painted gray, were recognizable from their shape as warships. As we approached the shore we saw their flags, and waving among them was the Stars and Stripes, the flag of the United States.

The government buildings, limewashed yellow, were long and flat and all of equal height. The square was circled by colonnades which acted as the hubs of the broad city streets that radiated from them. An ostentatious portal had been built here, a triumphal portal. Its pediment was covered with symbols and inscriptions. And in the center of this broad, sun-splashed square there was the statue of a bronze horse standing on a flat base, a stage that could be seen from far and wide. The horse was rearing up, it seemed to me, against the terrible heat of the sun, and it carried its master. Its movements were wild, its form violent, but nothing ensued. Horse and rider remained frozen in frantic grandeur. I encountered them whenever I went to the square.

And so it must have been with the Greek virgin—it was Daphne, I believe—who was hunted down by a god. She fled, stretching out her arms to heaven, and her arms turned to wood and she herself into a tree.

And over there in the same glare of the sun lay the building we were to visit daily, and around which our thoughts continually revolved: the central post office.


## The Tragic Poste Restante

Lisbon's main post office was a flat, long, yellow building surrounded by a hall of columns, like all the other buildings here. It had an open, modern interior with numerous counters and clerks. We were interested only in the poste restante counters.

They lay to the rear of the building in a little side corridor, pressed to the wall as we ourselves were. But we located it easily because many people were looking for it. Legions of them were standing in lines there, refugees, the shipwrecked, inquiring after letters and telegrams. Most of them were well-dressed men and women who wore the signs of their fate on their faces and in their gestures; the sad disquiet and anxiety. Many of them asked their questions numbly and then numbly left. They had been asking them for a long time; no one was answering. When someone received a letter, others rushed over to discuss it with them. People came here morning or evening, many came both morning and evening.

This poste restante corner in Lisbon, in Portugal, in this outermost corner of Europe, was the tragic meeting place for many in the unhappy year of 1940, a year that had exposed the frivolity and thoughtlessness of the false calm of the past. Entire nations were being enslaved, families scattered. Europe was doing penance for its sins and omissions. And we refugees, subjects of this Europe, were standing here in Lisbon and waiting for the life buoy to be tossed to us from the other side of the ocean. Some were also waiting for news from family members in France or Spain.

The clerks, mostly women, sat quietly behind their counters as people flooded past them. We followed their every move anxiously: the way they reached into the boxes arranged by alphabet, the way they placed the letters in front of them and began sorting through them. They sorted carefully—postcards, letters, telegrams. . . .

We soon received news and carried it like booty from this corner of destiny. It was a telegram that announced a transfer of money. The money was here, at a bank. We also received word from our son Peter. We knew how hard he was trying on our behalf. He gave us encouragement and repeated that we should have patience, our trip was being set up for us. We understood: it wasn't easy to get together the large sum needed for three people.

At least we now had enough money to wait. We waited for a long time. Now that we were out of danger it became a period of fitful leisure, often interspersed by irritability and outbreaks of anger.

As we didn't know how long we would have to wait, we weren't

Alfred Döblin

inclined to spend our money freely. We spent a lot of time in our hot, crowded, noisy pension. Our son's shoes were coming apart but we didn't dare pay to have them resoled. We had no clothes. We were still wearing our wools from France that were unsuited to the climate. A movie or any other type of entertainment was out of the question.

It was a relief from the last awful weeks, it is true, but it was a sluggish and brooding existence.

## Confusion Concerning the Boat Tickets

One hot and noisy Thursday afternoon when we went to the post office—after days of no mail—there were three telegrams and a letter for us.

Two of the telegrams had been forwarded from Marseille. They were the ones we had awaited so anxiously, and that were now irrelevant. The third was from Peter, and we shouted with joy on reading it. He had been able to purchase our tickets. The last part of the sum that was needed, he telegraphed, had been given him by friends in Westport.

Yes, there was an American married couple in Westport, near New York, who in the preceding year had received Peter and me with great warmth. My meeting with this family had given me a new impression of American graciousness and culture, a completely different impression from that portrayed by European literature, and following my return to Europe Peter had remained in contact with this family; nor had I forgotten them. Our son Peter, with his hard-saved money, and our old friends from Berlin and this American family in Westport had managed to get together the relatively large sum of money we needed for the voyage.

The letter was from a Jewish-American organization, it was an invitation to come to their Lisbon office to receive an important piece of information. Strangely enough, they knew our address, apparently from New York. We went that very same day to the office, it was in a hotel on the city's main square. The director was a young American. He told us that another American had already written to us, but had not yet received an answer. We had not received the letter. What did the man want? we asked.

[ *219* ]

The director of the American office here assumed that the other American had our tickets. We were amazed. "And where are the tickets?" "The man has gone to France. I assume he left the tickets at the American Consulate."

Things are moving all right, we thought, they're moving of late—but not smoothly. There's always a mountain in between, or a hill at the very least. The director tells us he will inquire about our tickets; we should come back in two days.

We're in no hurry, for the telegram listed August 30 as our departure date. But we are confused. Are these the tickets that Peter mentioned? The day arrives. The man informs us that the gentleman who left did not leave any tickets behind. But it was out of the question that he had taken the tickets with him to France. So where are the tickets the telegram mentioned, the ones that were cabled to Lisbon? We read the telegram together: SAILING AUGUST 30TH. GREEK LINE TICKETS CABLED LISBON FRIEND WESTPORT PRE-SENTED WITH COMPLIMENTS HALF OF IT. We study the text. We had thought that the tickets had been cabled to a friend in Lisbon as yet unknown to us. We then figure out that there is a comma missing after "Lisbon" and that the tickets are at the offices of the Greek Line here. The American Aid Committee has nothing to do with it; the man who has disappeared is no longer relevant.

How difficult everything is, right down to the details.

Where is this Greek Line located? It's eleven-thirty. We make our way there as the midday heat commences, it's not far, we ask for directions over and over again on the street. The building is a small, one-story structure, the cigar seller downstairs has never heard of a shipping line at this address. They've given us the wrong address. My wife returns after half an hour, she had gotten the address from the Jewish-American bureau; now she has found out that it wasn't the address of a shipping line, but of a branch of the Jewish-American organization, which, they assumed, would have the address of the Greek Line. However, in the meantime it was determined by telephone that the branch didn't have the address either. My God . . . But we found an ad for the Greek Line in a Lisbon paper. Its office was on our street, right at the harbor. It was noon.

Everything ruled against our being able to pick up the tickets then. I had no hope of it at all: the effort of finding the address, the confusion, the misunderstandings, the late noon hour; and it was Saturday. But who was listening to reason? It was a building on our street that we passed by daily, of course, the last house on the long street, we went up the steps, the office was closed. We go home, perspiring, our minds a blank. We were given a head to think with, but also to bang against walls with.

But when we go to the post office that afternoon we are handed a letter from the very Greek Line that we had been looking for so rashly and in vain: tickets had been ordered for us in New York, we should contact the office there.

They want to drive us mad. We also receive a telegram signed by our friend H. K., the writer, who is on a relief committee in New York, working energetically for his colleagues who are in peril. He himself, this wise man, had had the foresight to leave France at the last hour before the outbreak of war, and had crossed the stormy sea to New York, first of all to save himself, and second, to be there when fate dealt a blow to the rest of us, those of us who had not been far-sighted enough to see what was coming. By telegram this savant whispered in our ear: forget about the Greek Line tickets, they've been exchanged for American ones—and we would travel on Thursday. On the coming Thursday—in four days! The confusion had already taken on a comic character. How many people were involved in this ticket business? A happy afternoon followed the anguished morning.

We had nothing but praise for the estimable H. K., the wise man, the clairvoyant. And what did we do that afternoon to celebrate the event? Instead of our usual small cup of coffee we drank a large one, and as we sat on the cool bank of the Tagus around six that evening, we had our shoes polished! It was an inspiring moment. We were sure that H. K., the clairvoyant, could see our shoes gleaming on the other side of the ocean, and would know from them that his message had arrived and how grateful we were to him.

We would have preferred to go to the American line right away that Sunday, to announce the good news that we were taking one of their ships. But the powers that be had reserved this news for the coming week—they weren't open on Sunday. So we kept our joy to ourselves. But we didn't pass that Sunday inactive. We went to the post office as usual—actually for no reason at all, for we were leaving on Thursday and that was settled. We merely wanted to put in an appearance.

We smile at the woman clerk. To our total amazement she hands us two telegrams. Following our initial surprise we begin to tremble. Two telegrams, what can be in them? A retraction of the retraction? Or, since there are two of them, perhaps the second would cancel out the first. Then what we would have would be a retraction of the retraction of the retraction. We are totally perplexed. We weren't expecting any more news. We had all the telegrams we needed, more than enough. We had telegrams coming out of our ears. Before long we'll be boycotting the post office. We'll lock ourselves in our pension. . . .

Nevertheless, nevertheless, the new telegrams crackle in our hands, we haven't opened them yet. Finally we take them to a corner and summon our courage.

As we have no other choice, we grab the telegrams by the throat and tear off their heads. We have to read them. What are the clairvoyants up to now?

It was as we had imagined. In one telegram our prophetic friend retracted what he had retracted the day before. The ancient prophets were more consistent. When they erred, they erred for a couple of centuries or so. But those who err today do so for the short term. The other telegram was from our son Peter. He, too, obviously could no longer tell what was going on. He wanted to reassure us. He telegraphed only that we would receive further information on Monday.

So there we stood, on Sunday. And we had had our shoes polished for this.

Étienne, good son that he was, wept when he heard the news and ran home. He was having a hard time. The waiting, the back and forth, the excitement and tension were not good for him. He had nothing to do, no friends, his only contact was with the two of us, morose grown-ups.

Late that afternoon, when we decided to spite fate and go to a café, our boy sulkily announced that he wasn't going and that was that. We would be here until October and so we had to save money, and if we adults weren't going to do so, then he would. He wasn't going to any café in the afternoons anymore. In the end, he accompanied us there but stood outside the door, on strike. But he wanted to buy an issue of *Paris-Soir*. The boy was frightfully preoccupied with France, he wanted to know what was going on there. When-

Alfred Döblin

ever he saw a French automobile in Lisbon he clapped his hands in joy. But there was no *Paris-Soir* that day, they were sold out.

## Heat and Noise in Lisbon

And sure enough, following this tumultuous beginning our stay in this hot city stretched out over weeks.

The heat was unbelievable. It forced us to stay home for hours, and go out only in the evening. Sometimes we spent the afternoon in a cool café. Each time we went out we quickly crossed the large, sunny main square where the pigeons sat in the shade of a monument. There was a little man with long white hair who fed them, they sat on his shoulders and ate out of his hands. We gawked at him and hurried on to the café with the sign that promised a temperature inside of 68 degrees, a promise that was kept, and we gasped for air and marveled dumbly at the white-headed man who was feeding the pigeons outside.

This heat was unusual even for Lisbon, they said. "Unusual" was the word they used. But it is strange what all was "unusual" that year. Humankind and nature, both had their problems with the unusual—did anything that was usual still exist? While we were pining for normality, the world was entering a stage of experimentation.

For four weeks we sat in Lisbon in our pension that mocked us with its name, "Gloria," across from the market hall in the street of dry goods, on a corner where the tram made a turn. It is important to know that the trams run from six in the morning until two the next morning. They take a rest in the middle of the night. That's when the vegetable and fruit carts rumble to market. Around that hour certain guests in our pension have had enough of the cool night air and they stagger back after midnight to bring their noise and yelling home to us. Every room in the place has at least two doors, but the storeroom I'm staying in with our son has yet a third door, to make up for the window it lacks. Two of the doors lead to adjacent rooms, the third to the corridor. And for some reason I cannot ascertain, all of the rooms have glass windows high up on the wall, through which light from the neighboring rooms pours into our room at night.

The heat in the city subsides late in the evening—so it would seem. It's one of heat's old tricks. It creeps from the streets into the houses and rooms. We wake in the morning dripping with sweat. While we were staying here the temperature once climbed to over 98 degrees, but in the evenings it took pity on us and dropped to only 88. We therefore go to bed as late as possible. Then begins the exhausting night, we stay in our rooms until nine in the morning, then hit the street after breakfast, at eleven-thirty we were back at home. By four we'd had enough and set off for the comfort of the cool café. There we read the *Paris-Soir* or *France*, a newspaper of "free France" that was published in London. After nine we would take a walk, usually along the Boulevard da Liberdade, a magnificently broad and long avenue with movie houses, music, and benches for us. We spent our first days in Lisbon relatively alone, then day by day more of those who shared our fate appeared.

Lisbon is a city I had known only two things about up to that point: first, it is the capital of Portugal and second, in the middle of the 18th century there had been a huge earthquake here, in connection with which Voltaire made his biting comments on optimism and ours being the best of all possible worlds. During our stay we added a bit to our knowledge. First: It is a splendid city with a large number of interesting monuments, exquisite shops, and a brisk commercial life. The city is built on hills at the broad mouth of the Tagus. The harbor is deep enough to accommodate large ships. As the city is close both to the sea and to a major river, an amazing amount of fish is sold and eaten here. We often went walking in the area around the harbor. There were always hundreds of men and women waiting there with their baskets for the fishing boats to arrive. They transported the fish into the city and to the market halls. It was an incredible sight each time to see the women balancing the flat baskets on their heads, their heads held high as they walked along with a steady, elastic gait, their bodies bent slightly forward. Many of them were carrying figs that lay on a bed of broad green leaves in their woven baskets.

If there is one fundamental thing I should mention about Lisbon, other than the monstrous heat and the sweltering air, it is the noise. The tormenters of this earth thought up various forms of punishment for their fellow human beings. Their poets, weary of love, spoke of the hells of fire and ice. Others were particularly clever in describing diverse methods of torture, stretching, decapitation.

Strange that the torturers and their poets overlooked the sense of hearing.

The city of Lisbon is no torturer. Nor is it the poet of the torturer. But it is a southern city rich in naiveté and passionate temperaments, and it also enjoys a subtropical lack of ceremony. In introducing itself to us, and when it wanted to torment us, it rarely availed itself of the familiar, banal sounds of nature. For example, in Lisbon I heard neither thunder nor the splash of rain that composers and lyricists have put to such frequent use. No birds sang here. The large number of mute fish that were transported through the streets were a sign of something else. The fish were obviously put on display to intimate that people here were familiar with silence, at least in this form, that they recognized it and honored it, and ate it grilled.

Lisbon is a modern, large-scale factory for the production of noise. First there are the electric trams. They run close together, with or without passengers. They jolt along on the rails, they clatter along the tracks, they cause the glass in the windows to rattle. The conductor has at least one bell at his disposal, and probably two. A Portuguese conductor can make them sound like three bells when he rings them—and he rings them incessantly, he gets great enjoyment from it. He conducts bells.

At the front of the tram is a sturdy safety device shaped like a shovel. When the car turns a corner, you get the impression that the thing wants to mow down pedestrians. The tram cars in Lisbon like to turn corners, they actually prefer corners, and it is for this reason that Lisbon is equipped with so many corners, because turning corners makes possible a rich variety of sounds.

The Lisbon electric trams have a trolley pole above them which probably supplies them with power. But to the eye, or rather to the ear, they serve a different function: the trolley pole rolls, jumps, rattles, crackles. The electricity does its part with sparks and explosions. The people of Lisbon are accustomed to it, they aren't afraid. Street youths jump onto the car while it's in motion, they're barefoot, wearing torn jackets and pants, they're newsboys. On one hill you can see the original monument to such a boy. They deserve a monument—perhaps one day someone will also buy them jackets and pants. The boys shout as they leap onto the car. It's in their nature, and it's also part of their profession. They shout the news. Once I saw a boy running after a tram car with a cigarette in his hand, he had seen a man in the car who was smoking. With one leap the boy was hanging on to the outside of the car, the man lit his cigarette, the boy thanked him, shouted, jumped off, and kept shouting. Smoking agreed with him. A great number of automobiles travel the streets, not one of them without its own music. We all recognize the make of cars, but in the city of Lisbon cars manifest their characters in ways unknown elsewhere. For one thing, they move in an indescribably intricate fashion. The idea of starting up, the mere plan, the intention to move puts these cars, which apparently doze off very quickly, in a dangerous state of excitement, so that they begin to hiss like snakes. This is the way they express their intention to get going. Then they purr and growl. I avoided cars in Lisbon, for I didn't understand their language and who knew what they were capable of? I didn't learn their language. There seemed to be several automobile languages. Some cars, if left to their own devices while under way, begin to snore contentedly. Some start honking with no warning. Some of them snort like a rhinoceros with a stuffy nose. At night, we often heard cars in the distance that were fighting with one another. They must have been married. They were trying to outshout each other. They also have horses in Lisbon. Many rulers and generals have been put on horses in this city. But even to this day the people of Lisbon have not succeeded in getting even one bronze horse to neigh. The bronze horse apparently represents the outer limit of Portuguese inventiveness. Horses, in terms of the diversity of sounds they can emit, cannot compete with cars; a horse can really only whinny and clomp with its hooves. Nevertheless—when there are a large number of live horses around, all sorts of things can happen. For this reason there are a number of streets in Lisbon reserved for the horse-drawn wagons that seem to exist to transport vegetables and hay. Yet not one of these Lisbon horses is a normal horse; each is a clever fellow, a schemer. The ordinary street horse here advances step by step, pulling behind it the wagon that justifies its existence, and carefully counting the stones in the street. It pulls its wagon slowly, its head down. It raises a leg and whacks the stone it has counted with its hoof, turning it over. No horse conceals its learning. They whack from morning to evening, they're used to it, this happy science.

And the people? When it comes to their city the people of Lisbon joyfully do their part. They do what they can, and it's no small achievement. While the cars are racing around and the trams are wailing and rumbling to such new heights that the conductor feels moved to accompany the event with a resounding ringing of bells—the people take refuge in song, in yelling, in musical instruments. Day after day we encountered merry musicians and singers of both sexes. For one entire week we heard frantic dance music coming from the market hall. And if you haven't experienced the shouting of the newsboys here at seven in the morning, you don't know what the human voice is capable of.

People spit in Lisbon. One of the things I think of when I recall Lisbon is spitting. It's a fact of nature. They all do it, young and old, men and women, civilians and soldiers. They spit without chewing gum, free-handed, so to speak. They do it off the cuff.

Anyone who has traveled in this world knows there is more than one way to spit. You can spit cheekily, shooting it between your teeth. That has an amazing effect, it's over so quickly. Then there's forest and meadow spitting. Everyone is familiar with it. It's done to the side, casually. Usually there's something evil behind it, a bad tooth or a Nazi slogan.

Lisbon practices the worst kind of spitting: the anatomical spit. It starts with a throat-clearing sound, a hawking that gathers in the top part of the nasal cavity, and then the real work begins, a deep activity like coal mining, a careful, first-class excavation, a pumping action, a sucking up of discharge from all corners of the palate, the throat, the lower nasal cavity, from all nooks of the nose. Depending on the point of contact, there is a groaning or rattling or choking sound. Then there is an explosion, an expectoration of the matter so meticulously gathered. You have to protect yourself when it comes to the actual spitting. It can spritz by your face or land on your feet. The whole thing is horrifying, but, as I said, is common here.

And what is the significance of this spitting? Portugal is a neutral country. If it had been invaded and found itself in the same situation as Holland or Norway, then I would suspect spitting was a political activity, a way of venting anger. But fortunately for us Portugal is independent. There has to be another explanation. And it is: the noise. Spitting goes together with the noise. Because people can't always scream, and not everyone carries a cowbell on them, they spit, to at least show their good intentions.

The language of this country is a romance one, but with its

many sibilants and rolling *r*'s it sounds Slavic, it has a peasant hardness. Can one whisper it? I never heard whispering in Portugal.

At the end of one broad avenue a dramatic, elaborately allegorical, excessively baroque monument stands near a lovely park that is still being landscaped. The man they've put so high up there on a pedestal is the Marquis of Pombal, Portugal's tyrannical statesman from the end of the 18th century.

Several years ago, when I was writing about the rise and fall of the Jesuit republic of Paraguay, I too came across Pombal. The marquis was granted power by his mother, the queen, during the reign of a puppet king, and proceeded through his own sheer strength to force the entire royal family, including the queen mother, to the wall. He fabricated intrigues to get rid of the noblemen who opposed him and then he took on the Jesuits. He banished one group of them, locked another in subterranean cellars by the sea for the remainder of their lives, and he had one Jesuit priest ceremoniously burned alive because he had supposedly been involved in an assassination attempt on the king. This unfortunate was an ancient, feebleminded missionary who had returned home from the tropics suffering from a fever, and whom the Inquisition, under Pombal's brother, sentenced to death. Pombal was an enlightened despot of the sort that the period produced. He had promoted industry, and for that reason, and because he had gotten rid of the Jesuits, they had built a monument to him here.

A monument worthy of the times. The despots of that era were indeed enlightened. Those of today hold to mystical ideas; they preach race and nation. Whatever twists and turns history takes, tyrants quickly learn the tricks of oppression. The Marquis of Pombal was able to maintain power only for as long as the puppet king stood behind him. After that, he himself was banished. But he was prepared for this, had already transferred his fortune abroad, and lived well on it for a long time thereafter.

All of these Pombals, whether seated on the throne or standing before it—it's more exciting to be out in front, you get your legitimation gratis and then have the fun of keeping a king on a leash— merely carry into execution ideas that are in vogue at the time, and later take credit for being reformers. The Marquis of Pombal, therefore, was a progressive, a Voltairean, a patron of industry.

But his people and the troubled times he lived in knew him as a man as well. They were familiar with his "judicial method." The people knew, despite the banished Jesuits and a prosperous industry, that they were oppressed and without rights. And when finally they could, they banished the tyrant. To them he was a tyrant.

Now, two hundred years later, you go walking in Lisbon, you've got a tyrant on your back as well, and there in the lush greenness of the city, you come across a marble pedestal with an inscription praising a certain Marquis of Pombal, that same Marquis of Pombal they despised and banished during his own lifetime, Pombal, once again benefactor of humanity!

If this surprises you, and you want to know where the statue stands, you'll be in for an even greater shock: on the Avenue of Freedom. Such is history, which some wits refer to as the Last Judgment.

## From the French Newspapers

*Paris-Soir* has sometimes two, sometimes four pages. In one issue there is a discussion about the food situation. The minister of labor declares his intention to create jobs, but the economic situation in France is *particulièrement difficile*. Another article: Will King Carol stay on the throne if Rumania is divided? It is said that the war between England and the Third Reich is becoming a race to destruction. But, it is added, whereas England's targets are dispersed, the Nazis' target is crowded into a small space.

And again and again the question of the responsibility for the military defeat arises. At least they haven't forgotten that it was impossible that war with the Nazis could have been avoided, war had been waiting on France's doorstep. But why was it lost and lost the way that it was? They grimly report that the special political court called to convene in Riom would begin its work the following week. "The hour of justice has arrived. What have they done to France?"

A note in the August 10 issue of the *Paris-Soir*: "A reader quotes the Book of Luke, Chapter 14: "Or what king, going to encounter another king in war, will not sit down first and take counsel whether he is able with ten thousand to meet him who comes against him with twenty thousand? And if not, while the other is yet a great way off, he sends an embassy and asks terms of peace." This (writes *Paris-Soir* on August 10) is the way a rational leader acts. And didn't our leaders do just the opposite? Now if the French had sent such an embassy to the Nazis, he would have been treated in the well-known fashion: it had been tried by the Czechs, after all. France would have been occupied and the Maginot line would have been broken through without a fight. Was that the idea?

On top of which, who was to know that the enemy was twice as strong? Part of its superiority had been gained, after all, by the elimination, the loss, of France's allies.

You could also buy the newspaper *Free France* in Lisbon, it was called simply *France* here. In one issue I find three pictures. One shows Nazi pilots at the airport at Bourget, a second shows German soldiers on a terrace of the Champs-Élysées.

But the third is a drawing. A Nazi, standing on a ladder, is painting out the inscription "Liberty, Equality, Fraternity" on a wall of the mayor's office. But behold: a citizen smoking his pipe below says to him: "You can paint it out. But it will always reappear."

In Mende I was preoccupied with churches, in Toulouse less so, and in Marseille not at all. In Lisbon I doubtlessly passed by many churches, but didn't recognize them as such. One day it occurred to me to ask where they were. They had been camouflaged, anyone not seeking them would miss them. That's not a bad idea. There are some buildings that, from the outside and at a distance, you would think are gyms. They don't have a church tower with a steeple, they have no majestic stained-glass windows. They could just as well be administrative buildings. In creating the world, of course, the power that one turns to in these buildings made itself so easy to locate that it does not need this particular representation in stone. It is eternal, he is eternal, after all. It is God the omnipresent that we are talking about here. Surely he also is pleased by the magnificent buildings that people choose to worship him in, as is their wont. There are splendid works of art exhibited there, they proudly praise him in pictures and statuary. He is gratified by it. He knows that they are very often aware of the fact that they cannot create even one single blade of grass.

I didn't attend a service.

There's something horrible about my brooding that won't leave me in peace. It's often as if some fiend were thwarting my plans. Things never calm down because I never come to any conclusions. One time I sit there and scribble out all kinds of notes on paper. I want to write: "Who God is and what he has in store for us." And later, when I look at it, it reads: "Who God is and what he has in store for himself."

I sit looking at it in confusion.

I am always leading two lives.

One life struggles with things, wants to change them here, change them there. It fantasizes, is tormented, gets nowhere. It's like a fire of damp wood, full of smoke and giving off no light.

The other is barely visible. I seldom give in to it, though I know it is my true life. It's strange: I know this and want to devote myself to it, to stir its flames and build it up. But I'm always prevented from doing so. The smoke envelops me.

What is this feeble flame I carry within me that is always flickering and that I must tend, and do not tend?

It appears before me as a thought, a hopeful, pleading thought. I cannot follow it as I would wish to do, as I should do.

It's worse than my anxiety concerning all those trains I missed. I could get on this train, it pulls up inside me, it waits for me—but I don't get on.

When I feel "the thought" in me it works as a magic wand, changing the world. The world becomes profound and true. It stands there steadfastly, happily—and I am in it.

My misery and pain subside. What will help me to see? I have broken through dark illusion. I have escaped my helplessness. I feel, and am, power. I am one with all the powers of heaven and earth. Whether I speak or not: there is only one single, joyful You and We. I am afraid of nothing, neither tomorrow nor death.

It is difficult to know what Jesus would say today were he to see us—say about "his" church, "his" priests. Our pain is as intense as it was in his time. We don't know how to save ourselves, there is no one speaking to us clearly, they talk over our heads. Where are we?

They won't let us live—it is the nations, the organizations and conventions that act, that take the stage, our stage, and we have to be content with our part as the silent, passive audience.

Jesus wanted to set people straight, to return them to their original relationship with the divine ground of their existence. The natural relationship is that of children to father. It is not that of creature to creator. Even in the Old Testament mankind was not simply a lump of clay; it was breathed upon by the divine breath.

The massive churches, the pomp, the monstrous apparatus, the theology. What Jesus wanted was most simple, namely: to pray to God, to thank him for existence, to submit to human fate, to acknowledge responsibility, to see in all people brothers and sisters; to live courageously and honorably and to accept and welcome even death, our death, belonging to us.

How we have gone astray.

## A Letter from France

A long letter from our son Claude now reaches us in Lisbon. It is a long, touchingly simple, factual report. I have translated from the French the last part of it, where he writes about what happened to him in those same last weeks of June that already have been mentioned here.

And one last time before we leave everything behind there comes a whisper from those ill-fated days, a whisper from that country of such lovely and wonderful people whose fate is bound up with ours.

The letter:

"We think we can rest now. But that is illusory, the Germans are said to be in the area, and on the afternoon of the 21st we make our way to P, the first 10 kilometers on foot and the rest of the way by truck. In C, I receive a letter from Mama that makes me very happy. We are cooped up in trucks, but it's better than walking. I found a canteen and can now carry water with me. We survive an air raid in L. Our convoy is bombed and hit by machine gun fire: no losses. We get back on the trucks and go to P, where we arrive at five o'clock. We stop on the outskirts, sit down by the side of the road and wait for the others. The people here will be happy to see us leave: they are

Alfred Döblin

afraid of being bombed if the Germans see soldiers in the vicinity of town. We stay in the streets and take up battle positions, set up machine guns at an intersection. The rest of the group hides in a side street. It gets dark, we lie down on the asphalt and wait until it is time for our watch.

"On the morning of the 22nd, there is a change of position, we are now a kilometer away from town, near the crossroads of the *routes nationales*. Trucks pass by endlessly. We spend the whole day lying in the grass. That evening they finally feed us something: a little bread, some wine and 20 grams of cheese: we are hungry and never get enough to eat. Our section changes position again, and at 10 o'clock that night the word comes down: retreat.

"We travel through the night. I stand in the little truck, my head banging against its low ceiling, we are caged in, it's impossible to sleep.

"On June 23rd, there are many military convoys, tanks, cannons. Around nine in the morning we take up a group position one and a half kilometers from M. The day passes without incident, the Germans are always right behind us, that evening they are two kilometers away. The battalion retreats five kilometers from our position, our section stays where we are. Around nine that night German vehicles pass by within 10 minutes of our group and occupy M. They haven't seen us, otherwise we would have been taken prisoner. At ten o'clock we get the order to retreat. We assemble in silence and set off in the dark, without the others. Then we go through a forest. An hour later we are picked up and our convoy sets off, still pursued by the Germans. Our section transfers to a bus. On the 24th we are on the road the whole day. We get something to eat that morning. In A we were almost cut off from our column by the advancing German forces. Fifteen minutes after we pass through A, the town is taken. Our overloaded bus rolls slowly along, part of a never-ending line of trucks and cannons.

"That night we stop in B, and there, on the morning of June 25, 1940, we receive news of the cease-fire.

"I feel like crying.

"We have tried so hard, only to arrive at defeat. We are all so sad, and that evening in St. F, where we have been quartered, we get the news of the harsh conditions of the cease-fire. I am worried about the future; many of my comrades don't seem to know what the occupation of their provinces will mean. Only slowly do they begin to realize that their lives will change radically. I impatiently await news from Mama, Papa, and Vincent. I am very afraid for Papa, I only hope that he has not stayed in Paris.

"Then we go to P, where we remain for several days. The occupation troops are 500 meters away. We travel to D, a tiny place of 20 houses; then on to D, a hamlet. We stop there to rest. And it is there that I later receive a letter from Mama, and still later her first card. I am happy to find out that everyone is together in Toulouse. I hope that we will soon have news of Vincent as well; I'm only afraid that he has been taken prisoner.

"We receive our pay, and I get the 100 francs from Mama that have been under way for weeks. We are now in the Gironde, close to a little town about 10 kilometers away where our field postal service has dug in. We spend the first few days looking around. It is very hot. We rest, we bathe. But soon—with nothing to do—boredom sets in. We walk about a little and sleep a lot. I play cards and in the afternoons, I hang around the office to see if there are any letters for me. We are disappointed to return from the post office empty-handed, but how happy we are when we hear our names called out when mail arrives, and then everyone withdraws into a quiet corner to read it.

"I'm waiting for the demobilization of my class. I hope they will send my civilian clothes from St. Germain. I have nothing else to put on. I want to be free again, to rejoin my parents and find work. I want to work again after this period of almost three years of doing nothing. My head is full of ideas for window displays—when will I be able to realize them?

"I think a lot about my parents and what they will do now. Soon the day of freedom will arrive, and a new life will begin. I hope that it will be a life without incident, happy and productive.

"I have faith in the future. It will be a better one than the sorrowful past.

"Let us await the day we will be discharged, and then to work."

## On the Ship

We have registered for the American line and are supposed to depart at the beginning of October, in about six weeks. We are not happy about this, of course. We've gotten an additional monetary advance and are buying provisions.

The rumor is spreading that tensions between Greece and Italy are not so bad, and that we could risk taking the Greek ship. It's on its way here. We decide we want to take it, and inquire about transferring our tickets to the Greek line.

We are sent to be vaccinated. The ship, the *Nea Hellas*, has arrived. We treat ourselves to a Sunday outing at a popular resort on the Tagus, and on our way there we pass the centennial exhibition and our ship, anchored out on the water. A fresh breeze is blowing. Soon it will be over. The horror of the last months will be put to rest.

The friendly Portuguese gentleman who had found us a room in Lisbon visited us often, and offered us his advice. He appeared on the morning of our departure from the Gloria as well, and I again made jokes about the name. We said goodbye to him and to our hostess and to the robust and droll housemaid. We went to the harbor—and then it was over an hour before we could board the ship. Dozens of people stood waiting on the dock. And when the signal to board finally was given there was so much crowding that a clerk called down to appease us: "No pushing, ladies and gentlemen, no crowding. The Nazis aren't after you here." Before being allowed on board we had to show where we had been vaccinated, a certificate wasn't sufficient. Then we sat around for a long time. It got to be noon. Only late in the afternoon did the elegant first-class passengers arrive. We ate our first Greek meal in the steamer's dining room and received a visit from the director of the emigration office that had assisted many of us. The ship got under way in darkness. It was slowly turned and towed down the Tagus.

The centennial exhibition across the water glittered as in a fairy tale. Its magical light was the last we saw of a Europe sunk in sorrow.

## The Crossing

The ship was packed with people like ourselves. For the first few days, until we reached the Azores, anxiety ruled: would the trip go smoothly? We worried about submarines. The English patrolled the Azores nightly. But the only sign of this was that the ship stopped and stood still for an hour. Then we traveled on smoothly and quietly—to America.

The previous year, when I had boarded the American ship, the *President Harding* (it had been sunk in the meantime, and the lovely French ship I traveled back on, the *Champlain*, had been destroyed as well, sunk in harbor by a mine), it had carried a large number of German emigrants, mostly Jews, many of them from Berlin. I spoke with a few of them during the voyage. It was a strange journey. People talked about Nazi Germany only when asked. They didn't want to have anything to do with it. One man was so much like a Nazi himself that I wanted to change my table assignment at our first encounter. It turned out that he was a Jew and had been in a concentration camp. I heard how people who wanted to leave Germany were robbed and mistreated. How could this journey be anything but tragic for them? A journey following a shipwreck.

For, after all, they had been persecuted without having done anything wrong. Would they reflect on their fate now? Would they consider the fact that they had not been persecuted as individuals but as Jews, something they could do nothing about? And they weren't even religious. What, then, did they think and feel? I encountered individuals only, private individuals. Many were embittered, women cried when they told how they had been humiliated. But that was all, it never went beyond that. And what were they concerned about? Business. They worried about how they would earn money in New York. They shrugged their shoulders as if to say: I'm a Jew, people treat you any way they please.

They dressed well. The ladies dressed elegantly at table, particularly for dinner. At the point that their cash was about to be confiscated, they invested a lot of it in clothing. And so it was that in the afternoons and evenings the refugee ship was transformed into a deluxe hotel. Handsomely attired men and women appeared—the persecuted. They strolled to the bar and danced to jazz music. (Life goes on, they said. No, apathy goes on. They weren't aware of anything at all, they had comprehended nothing. They were and remained ordinary citizens, merchants, clerks, and didn't perceive that they could no longer exist as such. After arrival in New York they scattered in all directions. They heard no clarion call, nothing awakened them.)

This time, on the Greek ship, many of the passengers belonged to intellectual, political, or artistic circles, that is to say, for the most part they were aware of things. They had fought as well as they could for their socialist convictions, for democracy, for a humanitarian ideal. Defeated, they left and were "saved," so to speak. They were depressed and sad, though they livened up in conversation. Many were from Germany, Austria, Czechoslovakia, many had come from Eastern Europe through Germany and France. Many spoke Yiddish. All had had their means of livelihood taken from them. But that was only one side of the story. The other was as bad, and they knew it: it was the spiritual side. They had suffered a defeat. What should they do now? Keep on going as before? They knew only that they were going to America. I knew that they would continue their old way of life in the New World.

I chatted with several of them. I talked about Jewish matters with Yiddish acquaintances, about politics and the general state of affairs with those who spoke German. They ransacked the past. They discussed things only superficially, always stayed on the surface. They were crushed. And they wanted only to go to America. I couldn't discuss what I was thinking about. I couldn't articulate it. I was amazed how alien they had become to me. Was it that the thoughts that preoccupied me had reached such an advanced stage, had taken root so deeply without my having remarked it, were so convoluted and many-branched under the surface that they had pre-empted my entire inner being?

We arrived in New York. As our ship entered the harbor, it hit another ship and its side was split open.

Before we docked, we saw our son Peter standing on the dock, waving, and Mrs. R, dressed in black. On the way into the city she told us that her father had died. I had met him the first time I had come to New York, he had been an ebullient man (I now hear that he was in his late seventies): he was a splendid person, a gentleman of the old school. It had been a joy to share his company. He had died totally unexpectedly, was gone, over in Europe.

What happened then? We were "saved."

While still in Lisbon we had received a telegram that a major film company in Hollywood had prepared a contract for a dozen of us writers who had escaped. Skeptical as we were, we hadn't believed it. But it was true. In Hollywood, W. D., a successful actor and director, a magnificent man, had had the idea of getting the film industry interested in us, stranded as we were in France. The idea was taken up by his energetic wife, and by Mrs. L. F., the wife of our colleague B. F., and they had set up the contracts that now fell into our laps. After a few weeks in New York we traveled to California, straight across the continent. So we live on the other side of the continent now, on the Pacific, enjoying American protection.

I have begun to write again, it is the beginning of 1941 and this is the first work I have done of my own.

Once, on opening a suitcase in search of a book, I came upon the manuscript I had completed on May 16, back in St. Germain, on the day I was sitting at my desk with the sound of the radio coming from the next room, when the announcer said that they weren't able to close the "pocket" on the northern front. I leaf through the notebooks and see that there is much talk of—Jesus. Already then, long before the capitulation, before the whole debacle. The central character of the novel is grappling with him. A defeat, a breakdown follows, the question of Jesus emerges, and absolute devotion follows.

What I had then experienced, the approaching crisis, I had pre-experienced intellectually. It was written down, foreseen—pre-experienced but not resolved.

It was not to be "resolved" in my imagination. There was only one way to continue: to go through the experience. But my hero, Friedrich Becker, is much further along than I.

I consider what the year 1940 has brought us. I have forgotten nothing. I don't want to forget. That is why I am writing this book. And my wife and I will least forget our loved ones, our two sons whom we had to leave behind.

# BOOK II

# America

# 15

# What Hollywood Was Like

*I* was fifty-five years old when I left Germany in 1933. I left Paris at
sixty-two, fled through France, and arrived in America with my
wife and youngest son, having come through Spain and Portugal.

It is now 1948, and I am seventy and not young and no longer
totally healthy, and once again I take out the manuscript in which I
reported on my journey of destiny, having arrived in Hollywood in
1940. Having laid this manuscript aside for seven years, I now wish
to bring it to a close.

We were in Hollywood. Far away, Europe was at war. The
three of us, my wife, my youngest son, and I, sat here among other
refugees on the beautiful—but not always beautiful—Pacific coast.
We were among the first to arrive. I remember the reception I was
given by a group of resident immigrants in Hollywood. We gathered in a church, and I was greeted by an old and good friend from
Berlin, L.J., the former director of the theater there. We drove to
the church in a downpour, in the car of a famous actor. Both of
them are dead now, in 1948: the director who lived next to us at
the hotel and who would read to me from the memoirs he was then
writing, and the charismatic actor A. G. as well, who was in his
prime and had recently published a wonderful account of his life.
He had done reasonably well in Hollywood films, he had even

managed to overcome the miserable language barrier tolerably, and then he was called to New York for a Broadway show, he was moving up. Soon after he got there he had his appendix removed, the operation went well, but an embolism killed him, putting an end to all his ambitions.

They welcomed me then in the Downtown Church in Los Angeles. Several people gave speeches. Finally I myself spoke, and the only thing I remember of what I said is the word "demonic." I had brought that word with me from my weeks of flight. They spoke of the political situation that had forced us to cross the ocean, I spoke about what had happened in the last months and how I had experienced it. I had to talk about it, and labeled the events I recounted "demonic"—horrible, frightening. I did not call any individual person demonic, but rather the entire situation that had befallen Europe, and in which we were entangled. And it affected them, too, those who were apparently safe here.

That's what I said in October of 1940. And that's what I said again in 1943, at a celebration of my sixty-fifth birthday, held in a small theater. I don't know if they understood what I said in the church. I had become much clearer about it all by the time I spoke in the theater. I did not except myself, or any of us, from the grim judgment that was being passed on the world. What I said was received in silence. It was not the speech to deliver at a birthday party.

We lived at first in a hotel, then in a furnished apartment. I worked for a year as a screenwriter, drew up scenarios like the others, created stories. But none of it found favor with the powers that be. Others who had been rescued from Europe drifted in. It was no different for them. Some stayed in New York and tried to make it there. We in the film studios soon noted that the companies had only wanted to do something for us; they didn't take our work seriously. We could write what we wished. It was an industry. The mediocre tastes of the producers and the barrier created by the established professionals made all of our efforts illusive. The contract expired after one year and then things changed. We gave up our furnished apartment and took two unfurnished rooms and a small additional space in a "flat." We bought a little furniture, mostly second-hand, our friends contributed some things. For a few months I collected unemployment. Then a charity stepped in on our behalf, and in the years following we were watched over by a relief organization. And in New York our loyal son Peter didn't forget us.

We had settled in magnificent surroundings. Los Angeles, which Hollywood is part of, was spread out over the hills, and was as big as a European province. Night and day cars rolled by on endless highways. There were over a million automobiles, no one went anywhere by foot, you only walked as far as the nearest neighborhood or to the market or a bus stop.

You drove; the streets were to a large extent undeveloped, then a few houses would appear somewhere, then the houses would group themselves around a shopping center with stores, movies, drugstores. Downtown Los Angeles had been aggressively developed as such a center, with huge department stores, shops of every kind, movie houses, restaurants, theaters, cafeterias. There were churches and libraries. I saw a Mexican district. Pershing Square was at its center.

We took a trip to Santa Monica; a beautiful garden city on the ocean, several of our friends lived there. We often spent Sundays on the beach in the hot sand, thousands of people came, not only on Sundays, to go swimming, play water sports, sit in the cafés and refreshment centers. Merchants sold hot dogs and doughnuts on the beach. Pacific Palisades was not far away.

For five years I experienced Hollywood, in peace, in war, and finally during the armistice. The great political and military events of our time washed only gently over our faraway beach. There were only onlookers here, or readers or listeners. What did I do, what could I do, what did I want to do? I watched people on the streets, in restaurants, in public, as I always had. I read newspapers and magazines and studied the books that were available to me. I listened to a lot of radio. I collected newspaper articles and pictures from magazines during these years. The presidential race between Roosevelt and Wendell Wilkie took place at the end of 1940. In 1944 came the one between Roosevelt and Dewey. Then came Roosevelt's sudden death, preceded by his celebrated trips abroad during which, as film and photographs of him showed, he could stand upright only with effort. There was the San Francisco Conference and the formation of the United Nations. They prayed for its success in the churches.

There were sensational trials: Charlie Chaplin's paternity suit—

a young actress employed by his film company named him as the father of her child. He didn't deny the relationship, the press printed all the details, a blood test ruled out Chaplin as the father but the jury sentenced him anyway—women made up the majority. There was the suicide of the Mexican dancer Lupe Vegas, a film star, a volatile woman in her thirties; she was pregnant and took sleeping pills, she loved the father of the child, a young French actor who had left her. Other strange criminal cases: a rich man's young daughter who lived alone in the city was found dead, naked in her bathtub, after having attended a military ball. The murderer was never found. And along with these there are cuttings in my file of photographs of military cemeteries, one cross after another. One picture shows a recruit being drafted; he is calling out: "It will be fun!"

# 16

# I Feel Nothing

During this long period I felt nothing. I thought of the journey from Cahors to Mende and felt that this trip had not yet ended. That became clearer to me every month.

Our youngest son was attending a junior high school. He liked it, he adapted to it quickly, I once visited one of his classes and could only commend it, particularly the group spirit, the camaraderie, the lack of any kind of domineering authority. But there was one thing I did not like about this type of instruction and education. My wife and I discussed it. It turned out that we agreed.

It was not right for the boy to grow up without learning about the world and human existence, without knowledge of our fate, without direction or support. And classes in languages and math and science would not teach him that, nor would camaraderie. What was a young vine to cling to on its way up? We had grown up in the same way ourselves. We had swallowed languages, math, and sciences whole, and to what end? How had that shaped us? The boy should receive better guidance. We talked about Christianity. What made me think of it? It was this: as was my custom, I had let things happen without coercing them. But when I looked at my boy it seemed to me that while it was all right to treat myself that way, to let things drag on, it wasn't fair to do that to him.

I had not consciously pursued the topic of Christianity in the interval. I let it work within me. I was waiting until the time was ripe, until something occurred to me consciously.

We—my wife and I—were now of the opinion that it was time for us to change our passive attitude. We couldn't just hand our son over to the school, the state, to everyday life in the same way that we had been handed over to, thrown at, them to see if we could manage them before they managed us. Life had to have its coordinates, it was not merely a framework.

The present, politics, war and peace should not be the beginning and end of existence. I had long since acknowledged a truth I called "original meaning," it was a vague feeling in me that I affirmed visibly in the major and minor details of nature—but this truth influenced neither my actions nor the course of my daily life. It remained a silent truth and passive knowledge. It was not something a child would follow, and I myself could not carry it into my everyday life. It was now time for me to reveal what I carried within me. It was necessary. It had reached that point. My heart was full.

The catastrophe I had been pulled into was to be kept alive, was to escape being buried in time. A memorial was to be built to it. One that was not merely a token of memory.

Christianity—had I come that far? How? Why? I had barely progressed in my thought, in what I could formulate. But the profound inclination, the affinity that I felt, my will, had become dominant. Though I didn't know why, I was certain that it was Christianity, it was Jesus on the cross that I wanted. I had not made a move toward him, I hadn't buried myself in the topic. I had barely even taken a look at the Gospels. I didn't want to. I didn't want to do anything that was a move toward myself—out of fear that any move I took in that direction could be the false one, dangerous. I had a feeling in me that was like a little flickering candle that I held inside and protected, it had been burning for a long time. It burned all alone, like a single altar candle in a dark cathedral.

But when it came to the matter of my son's education, I opened my mouth. I discussed it with my wife, broaching the topic of Christianity. Even if Christianity yet had no power over my thought, something in me sought this course and would not be deterred. I felt a great warmth, an absolute certainty in myself when these things emerged in me. I was now to treat them more concretely, more consciously, these things that I had kept inside up until now as something without language or form.

I turned to the libraries to help me with my decision, and found that there was not only the ancient schism into two orthodox churches, and not only the more recent split into an orthodox and a reformed Protestant church, there were also within the Protestant church hundreds of choices, diverse confessions and sects. So many churches and divisions of churches, and all of them were assembled around the cross.

Where was the truth, where should I turn? How should I familiarize myself with what distinguished the various confessions? For I had to move toward one confession, I couldn't remain isolated in empty spiritual space. Into what skin should I slip?

I had to consider this; it was difficult to the point of despair. What is it to "choose" a religion, to quasi select it from an array! And in truth, after I had combed the libraries for weeks, reading, I had not found my path. The effort exhausted me and was pointless. I was afraid I was extinguishing the candle within me with all of this.

I lived in a foreign country indeed. I understood and spoke the language inadequately, and knew very few people. We occasionally got together with a Unitarian, a friend of a mutual acquaintance in Europe. The Unitarian was a practical man. So I read what the Unitarians believed, what their goals were, what they had accomplished. It wasn't bad, like so many other things I heard of weren't bad; but it didn't move me, it didn't hold the key to myself.

But just as God often had given me a sign during my journey, my flight, he did so once again. And subsequently I am of the opinion that it was in fact self-evident to expect that the deity would intervene here, when it had to do with finding my way to him. We were friends with an art historian, a German scholar who had only recently left Germany with his family. He came from Westphalia, from a devoutly Catholic family. We told him our worries in the course of conversation, and he told us that we lived near a church where there were beneficent, educated, open-minded priests, it was a Jesuit church. The priests would surely be willing to talk to us.

We made an appointment with them. The priests knew what we had come for. We went to them often. We considered it an opportunity to inform ourselves. It quickly became more than that.

They gave us catechisms. And that's how we spent our time

with them: the priest would read one or several paragraphs and explicate them. This suited us, in this way we could form our opinions and also learn more than just what the paragraph was about. We asked questions and received answers. It went beyond information; it became instruction in which we played an active role.

I participated, as I said, in order to learn something about the Christian faith directly from a Catholic. I wanted to know what the Catholic faith understood and preserved under the concept of Christianity, under the teachings of God, crucified on the cross. I was attentive, increasingly more so. But what does attentive mean in this context?

And then there were the priests. We met with three of them over the months, for our instruction lasted for months. One of them left for San Francisco. The one who spent the most time with us and taught us the most was the priest of this church, a serious and resolute man, and then there was a younger priest, all from the Jesuit order. It was strange that I stumbled on this order, for I had been occupied with it and its believers for years in Paris, in writing my novel that was set in South America and that related the story of the founding of a Christian republic in Paraguay. So we sat across from these men from this very active Christian order, highly educated men who, despite the fact they were called Jesuits, did not worry me. They had truly devoted themselves to their faith and what they said, and their knowledge lacked any hint of aggressivity. They were people whose character and outlook obviously had been formed by Christianity. They were Christians and priests in the way that people are capable of being Christians and priests. It did me good to sit with them and listen to them and to hear what they had to say on subjects sacred and profane. They conveyed to us the treasures of the Christian faith as the ancient, and now the Catholic, church preserved and defended them.

We had heard such dreadful things in the past about the Jesuit way. It was said to be a perversion, a foul misrepresentation of Christianity, tomfoolery, a jumble of superstition. It was accused of lies and even crimes. But here before us sat representatives of this church, priests who were as rational as we were, who had been trained scientifically. We would have made it difficult for them had they tried to mislead us. But they tried nothing of the sort. To the contrary.

Alfred Döblin

In the past, I had taken an aesthetic interest in the opulent, ostentatious exteriors of many Catholic churches, it belonged to being an educated person. Church and religion reduced to art. But we weren't concerned now with art, nor with a grand façade. We went inside and found religion.

The priests set forth paragraph after paragraph of the catechism. I didn't understand it all, not all of it was transparent or plausible. But that wasn't important. There were things that could remain unclear without being false. The building I had entered was ancient and spacious. I was taken from room to room, through many rooms, up broad steps, through echoing corridors. This or that door was opened to me. I looked into the new additions, brightly lit rooms and dark ones. It wasn't necessary to see the whole building, to enter each and every room. There is plenty of time. The opportunity will arise.

It became clear to us that when we visited the priests we were no longer going there for information, but as preparation and for instruction. We were increasingly willing, we even greatly desired, to belong to this spiritual community whose members saw the world, and our existence and fate, in this way and whose representatives acted and expressed themselves like these Jesuit priests.

We had no doubt that we wanted to join them or that we already belonged to them, for we were filled with joy by our meetings and talks with them, by the contemplation of, and understanding and connection with, what we learned. It was a blessing we had never before known.

The hand of God! The sign! The sign took this form, a feeling of happiness. How could we doubt that we were on the right path? We did not hesitate to take it.

Our son entered the church's school, which was run by nuns. At first he didn't understand why we had transferred him to another school. But that soon changed. The nuns' devout benevolence had its effect on him. His soul received the sound sustenance that it deserved, and accepted it.

# 17

# Church and Religion
# from the Inside

*A*nd now we received what the Church had accomplished, what
humankind—people who were struggling, suffering, feeling—
had attained and left behind for us over the centuries. It formed the
invisible community of the devout and the wise, the pious and
the holy. It was the mystical body of Christ, the Church.

The teachings of the Church were celebrated throughout the
year. Our discovery of these celebrations, our participation in them,
proved to be informative, stimulating, and exciting to us in the
period that followed our introduction to and acceptance into the
Church.

Christmas had been a children's holiday when presents were
exchanged and received. Two days when you didn't have to work.
Now its history became clear: the incredible, inconceivable fact of
God's entrance into the world—combined with the wonderfully
enchanting, no, the wonderfully glorious, account of a human
being—the fulfillment of mankind, "full of grace"—who lived a
reclusive life, but who towers over all of those who preceded and
who followed her: Mary, chosen to envelop God in human flesh on
this earth and to deliver him into nature, to humanity.

Alfred Döblin

\*   \*   \*

But where am I headed here? What I wanted to do was to speak of the discoveries I made following our introduction to and acceptance into the Church, how I approached its festivities, and how I was slowly affected by their meaning. The meaning of Advent, pregnant with the future, the four weeks before the appearance of the Messiah, imbued with a reality that endures. Jesus in the manger, the songs of the heavenly hosts, the wise men from the East—what it is like, what happens at that moment when it is no longer merely picture, tale, story, but a reality and truth of increasing profundity.

And it is something even superficially. Advent commences with the thunder of the apocalyptic judgment. And simultaneously the darkness is penetrated by a new light, a light that becomes clearer and clearer. The child is lying in the manger. It is a tender scene that edifies and strengthens the soul.

# 18

# Afterward

$A$fterward, after being admitted and accepted. There is an afterward.

You don't start from the beginning. You are something already formed. You become more set year by year, more resolute, which is not to say that in this way you become ever more what you truly are. You become more set, but never thoroughly set, reset, as a saline solution recrystallizes. Throughout whatever happens, throughout all the stages of your life, you retain a bit of mother liquid. It is an oscillating, nebulous, germinating mass that assumes the battle with time, a mass that time feeds on voraciously. It gives to time as much as it can, but never exhausts itself, it always maintains itself. This mass need not fear time, it never flees from it. It gives to time ever new resolutions and forms.

This mass, this star cloud, repeatedly hurls things into time, into nature and death, and each thing that it hurls has a name—new organisms, plants, animals, crystals, and they all are individuated and all are set and can consider themselves to be irrefutable. The huge, inchoate cloud mass endures because it has within it the turbulent force of the words of the creator. It happily triumphs over what it has delivered, what it was capable of surrendering to darkness, to a thriving nature, to frailty, to death—even to death—but it continues on its way, it is about life.

Alfred Döblin

What is religion? What does it achieve, where does it belong, what does it do to the person who surrenders to it? It has something, but not much, to do with whether we are speaking of an impressionable young person or of an adult. For in both cases it has to do with creation's effect on something that is already extant, set, on something that has already adapted itself to nature.

Religion affects us—but how? Like one mechanical body affects another? Like heat and cold affect the flesh? Does it change the body like a nutriment? The active center of religion extends far back in time, it cannot be spoken of at all in terms of our own associations and experience. It is there—the world, the framework of the world, the form and synchronization of things, it is there, and affects humankind from the point of religion: the force that makes the history of the world, that makes the *world* history. It is there: the original fact of creation and God's entry into the world and how he, God himself, sinks like a seed into this crusty earth as a dying mortal and then explodes this crust with the force of his growth. From that point on, religion divides itself: the seed germinates and touches the true core of man. It touches his person. The person becomes the carrier of destiny and the true passenger of the journey that stands before him.

I now had to revise everything I thought. This was newly conquered territory and the conqueror newly assessed his possessions—I read a great deal. It was a strange learning process, for it was not about assimilating something new and adding it to my store of knowledge, but rather about assigning a central position to the new and allowing it to function. Only in this way could I achieve a devaluation of my old ideas.

I didn't force the process. Gradually there would have to be a spiritual change. For the first time in years I reread the *Confessions* of St. Augustine, and his *On the Trinity*. In his books this former Manichaean shows how thoroughly saturated he was in the pagan knowledge of his time, and how, having become a Christian, he combats the pagan world. He searches deep within himself and arrives at a synthesis. The new Church did not develop in a vacuum. Christianity set upon humanity as a higher state of well-being, the true well-being of humankind. It seemed to me that the same held true for the individual who is approaching faith.

And so, after my youthful discoveries of Hölderlin, Kleist, Dostoyevsky, and Nietzsche, I began a second, discrete period of discovery. Whatever happens or doesn't happen to a person (I know this from experience) depends on "coincidence," and I have given my opinion of "coincidence" here already, of how I see it. So now it was libraries I sought out to nourish me, mostly the city library in Los Angeles, and I took what I could find there, whatever I happened to come across. I came across St. Thomas Aquinas' *Summa contra Gentiles*.

It's strange, at the mention of the name Thomas Aquinas it occurs to me that in listing my earlier gods and heroes I forgot Karl Marx and Sigmund Freud. How remote they have become to me, how far away that is, it is hard for me to even remember. After the First World War, I read and studied Marx's *Das Kapital* and other writings, particularly his early writings. And I discovered Freud at almost the same time. I took from them what I could and, as the physician and empiricist I was then, found them to be relevant. I had read Hegel as a student. From there it was easy to find the path to Marx. And as I had worked in insane asylums for years as a doctor, I was drawn to Sigmund Freud. But no matter how much they engaged me, these two men did not become gods or heroes to me, or even inspirations, though I agreed with them in many things and took some of their ideas for my own. Neither of them moved me deeply, neither changed my view of the world. I turned to their writings often after that, but they eluded me.

Then, when I encountered Aquinas' *Summa*, my hunger for sustenance was satisfied for a long time to come. I can remember how strange and astonishing this work was to me in the beginning, for example, the doctrine of the angels, those higher, invisible creatures. My views then were still those of the malingerers and cranks of today, the so-called objective natural scientists. The Middle Ages recognized two kinds of light—the natural light of reason that leads to knowledge of nature, and supernatural light. Knowledge of the highest Being does not derive from our sense organs, at least not from what can be inferred from them alone. The individual plays a role.

I discovered that in reading, and in the process of assimilating, I slowly lost a certain resistance that stemmed from my old way of thinking.

Alfred Döblin

\* \* \*

After a while I assessed where I stood, what I had accepted and incorporated, that is to say, of what had become "mine." And so that I might possess it completely, I had to look at it and translate it into my own language. Could I talk about it? I asked myself. The test would be how I put it into sentences, into my language, and to the degree that these ideas penetrated my sentences, they would penetrate me more strongly and steadfastly. So these new ideas were to perpetuate and prove themselves flying themselves under my flag.

All this was to become a talk on religion entitled: "The Immortal Man." It was designed to accomplish this function. But in writing it I assigned it a second task. The path I took was not to be mine alone. It was surely also the path many others took. I was not a writer merely to enlighten myself, I also had a responsibility to speak out. But at this point I did not know when I actually would speak and be heard. It was clear to me that I had taken a positive but very dangerous position. I could foresee the arguments against me, against my ideas and my stance.

The transcendental will hits a person like fire. Transcendental energy is not received as alien, nor is it alien. It appears as a blessing, as mercy. It brings security with it, so that we accept it without proof or question. Our epoch, the epoch of natural science, forces a terrible practicality and anonymity upon us. It isolates human beings just as it isolates everything at first, in order to look for correlations, occasionally to find them. Over there is nature, the world—and here am I. Over there is the past and history, and here I am, the present and future. But it isn't that way. That's to lay the world on the dissecting table and to imagine that you have something there on the table; but it's a phantom you're dissecting.

What is remarkable about religion, remarkable for our consciousness and our understanding, is that it opens up the human being, it leads him into the world and unites him with the course of the world. The world is history and deed—and the human being is implicated in a marvelous way.

There is no death. Suicide is impossible.

# 19

# The End of the War, and News

On December 7, 1941, Japan attacked Pearl Harbor, and America went to war. There was a blackout for a while on the West Coast and the occasional air raid alert. The face of the city changed, everything adapted to war, factories went up, there was a great migration from the East Coast and also from the interior of the country to our coast, where ships and planes were being built. Our son Peter was drafted into the army and went to a training camp.

We had tried very hard immediately after our arrival to bring our son Claude, who had been demobilized in France, over to the States. Once again it was a question of money. I could not raise the sum myself, and everyone we turned to refused us. And finally, when the same woman in Westport who had contributed to our voyage from Lisbon said yes, it was too late. He had to stay in France. But we remained in contact with him for a long time, until the south of France was occupied, that is. The armament of the Western powers, a huge undertaking, extended over years. England and America fought a major defensive war in Asia. The Japanese pushed ahead. And then came those suspenseful, decisive days of earthly judgment against the aggressors. There was the invasion of North Africa, the major battles that carried the adversary all the way to Egypt. And there its might was broken and it was driven from Africa and there

Alfred Döblin

then followed the occupation of Sicily and southern Italy, and finally the fall of the Fascist regime.

In the movie theaters of Hollywood at that time they showed gruesome pictures of the executions of leading Fascists; once we saw a large square, I think it was in Milan, where Mussolini and his lover were displayed, both of them dead and hanging upside down, surrounded by a cheering crowd.

In the East, at Stalingrad, the death knell had sounded for the Nazis. The Allies landed in Normandy with an invincible force of men and military supplies. The bloody march into Europe began. France was liberated. Then the final curtain: Germany, fanatical in its resistance, endured the destruction of its cities, the Western and Eastern fronts closed, and the head of the National Socialist state committed suicide. And then came the German capitulation. Not long afterward—the heavy fighting in the Pacific raged on, Australia appeared to be endangered—the first two atom bombs fell. Japan capitulated.

At the beginning of 1945, when the end of the war seemed near and its outcome no longer doubtful, our youngest son was to leave us, he was at the tempestuous age of eighteen, and had to serve in the army according to American law. He was a French citizen, as were we, but could also enlist in the American army if he so chose. We had endless debates on the subject. Finally he decided to join the French army, in which two of his brothers had served. The three of us made the trip together to San Francisco to take care of the formalities. He had to register at the French Consulate. Not long thereafter we accompanied him to the train station in Los Angeles. I can still see us sitting at the station in the overcrowded waiting room, and then his train was called, the one to Chicago. We went with him to the gate. He said goodbye to us, our youngest son. He went to New York, where he met his eldest brother, our good Peter, and others, European friends of ours. He was in a French training camp for a short time. Then he went to Europe.

Immediately following the liberation of France we received letters from our son Claude. He had conducted himself bravely during that difficult period and, as part of the organization ORT, had been able to save many people, until he was forced to flee the Gestapo, who were arriving in southern France, and cross the border

[ 257 ]

into Switzerland. Then he was in a labor camp, and now it would not be long before he returned to France.

And now finally, finally, we received news of our second-oldest son, Wolfgang, whom we called Vincent. We had heard nothing from him for years. We thought he had been taken prisoner. My wife was always contributing to the prisoners' aid fund with him in mind. Now France had been liberated and letters began arriving. They had looked for him in France. There was no trace of him. Then a letter arrived written by a girl, a student friend of his. The letter illuminated things.

It was the illumination of a lightning bolt striking a house. His grave was in the Vosges Mountains. He had fallen in battle with the enemy in June of 1940, the 21st of June. That was the "fatal" day my wife and I missed each other in Rodez, she on her way south to look for me, I continuing my dark and obstinate journey north.

And now, following the departure of our youngest child, my wife and I were alone in Hollywood. We took care of his little dog, the funny black cocker spaniel Zita, named for the sheep dog he admired so in St. Germain, our former residence. I had sat around Hollywood for five years in silence. I liked America very much, on the whole. It did me good, but it didn't accept me, it wasn't my country, or I wasn't the man for this country.

I liked America. It had big cities, New York, San Francisco, Los Angeles, and drugstores and the many comfortable libraries with their reading rooms, the people were open and related to each other in a friendly way with no sign of subservience, and with a great personal willingness to help. Atheism was not obligatory among the educated and the politicians of this country, as it was in Europe. There was an ancient Christian religiosity here, in a watered-down form, it is true, but it was a great moral force. But none of this changed the fact that I lived in America in a vacuum. My desk drawers were filled with new, ever newer manuscripts.

Then came the afternoon—I was taking a leisurely walk with Zita as usual along Hollywood Boulevard—when people began spilling out of the shops right and left, shouting. Others opened their windows and shouted down to the street with the same exuberance. They waved and laughed. Businesses were abandoned. The shops closed. They were yelling: Japan has surrendered. Armistice, armistice!

And then I experienced something new to me. People standing at their windows tore up newspapers, old books, notebooks, anything that was paper, and threw them out onto the street. Paper rained down onto the sidewalks and the pavement.

The horrible war had ended. This latest threat to humankind now belonged to history. The dragon lay slain on the ground. I had reason to feel relieved, but was I happy? After the storm had passed, after the roar of the bombers, the droning and whistling of the bombs, the raging waves of fire and the rat-a-tat of machine guns had faded, were we happy, did we forget the catastrophe and think blissfully of the future? Did I feel a victory? How many people were there who, even had they not been directly affected by the war, did not see before them the destruction of nations and the unprecedented disaster. And what we had witnessed here of what was horrifying and raw and ice-cold in mankind had made an impression: a human being is a unit, yes, something whole, a person, but on some natural plane he drags along with him a terrible mix of things. There is no future in this person, but mercy exists, mercy alone, even a blind man can see that.

During this time I talked to several friends who had shared our fate. They all comported themselves in the same quiet and subdued manner. The past weighed on them with no sign of new courage or hope. First we had fled and could believe that it was not the end, that everything would straighten itself out again. But over the years we became resigned, and now we saw the end: Europe was bled dry, its interior now partially a wasteland.

# 20

# The Departure Signal

*I* began corresponding with Europe again during this time and
received a letter from the friend I had left Paris with. He wrote
that a cultural office was being established on German soil in connection with the general plan to reeducate the Germans. Friends and
acquaintances from the agency I had been connected to earlier were
interested, and asked me if I wished to be a part of it. The discussion
went back and forth for a time. I hesitated. Why should I want to go
to Germany? My wife, following the loss of our son, trembled at the
thought of setting foot again on German soil—it seemed to her to be
a betrayal of our dead son.

But I could not remain forever in Hollywood's eternal summer,
nor did I wish to. I had led the life of a recluse in my room, working,
reading, writing. The spirit that dwells within me has no effect on
the outside world. I had been so accustomed to activity before, to
activity and excitement. I lived among people, got involved, discussed things. Writing represents only one side of my existence. I
was repelled by the purely aesthetic and literary. And then came the
call from abroad that enticed me. It meant that there was a way back
to the everyday life that I loved. I, or at least that part of me that was
left, could re-enter the everyday. And then came the sign that was no
surprise to me at all. I wanted to, I had to get away from the charity
of others. And my wife also wanted to return to Europe, to France,

Alfred Döblin

to our two sons who lived there and, above all, to the grave of our beloved second son.

When we had decided once and for all to return, all of our acquaintances who heard of it supported us and considered it natural for this reason or that. We began making plans for our departure. For one last time we needed help with the travel expenses to cross the ocean. It was a large amount, for we also had to cross the continent. But we pulled it together. We sold our furniture and dispensed with the books I had collected in the interim. We packed everything we wished to take with us in a few sturdy suitcases. We left with more baggage than we had arrived with. People gave us presents, visited us to say goodbye. We had made a few real friends here.

At the beginning of the year we had accompanied our son to the train station. We knew that he had served in Paris, after which he had been transferred to Marseille, from where he had visited Nice once, for his brother Claude's wedding. Now we, too, boarded the train. Our little dog Zita did not come with us, he had to remain behind, we couldn't take him on the ship. But our youngest son had given us strict instructions that were carried out: we found a home for him. Our son was sure that he would return for the dog one day. (Years have gone by, he too has married, he has a small son, Francis. He did not return for the dog.)

American trains are very comfortable. We traveled for days, the climate changed. We traveled to the east and north, often at considerable altitudes. In Chicago we got off the train and went to another station. We had gotten a view of the huge gray city on our arrival. There was a little intermezzo at the mammoth central station that I would like to report here.

We had a stopover there, and had to buy our tickets to Buffalo. My wife took over the latter task, buying the tickets, and I assumed the former, the waiting. It was, as I said, a huge station and the rooms were overflowing with civilians and soldiers traveling from east to west and west to east. The crowds got larger and larger. By the time the trains were to depart, the people had gathered in tight clusters. I knew that the ticket counters were somewhere off to one side and down a bit. That was where my wife was. I sat somewhere with my suitcase and performed my duty: I waited. Time passed. I am well aware that it passes without my doing anything at all. More and more time went by.

Where was my wife? I left my seat and went in search of her. I couldn't get through. On top of which, there were a great number of counters and people were standing around everywhere. I slunk around here and there and finally retreated again to my seat on the bench, my suitcase next to me. But I wasn't sure that I had found the same bench. The train to Buffalo was supposed to depart around four. There were ten minutes to go. The doors to the platform were already open. People are pushing and shoving. The great hall emptied. I sit there alone with my suitcase, feeling more and more alone, and then I once again go looking for my wife. An ominous memory of my journey through France arises in me, of the train stations where I stood waiting and waiting for trains that didn't come.

It became clear to me that we had missed each other. She was probably on the platform. The train would leave soon. I gave up. I wouldn't go to Buffalo after all. I would stay here and take the next train to New York. It was two minutes past departure. Then someone rushes up to me, beside herself. It is my wife, undone, in tears. She pulls me along behind her, furious. What did I think I was doing? What was I up to? She had been looking for me for an eternity. She had already notified the train officials. I had been paged over the loudspeakers, hadn't I heard anything? I hadn't heard anything. What could you hear in that racket? I had been looking for her, too.

She drags me through the gate at the last possible moment without a word. We get on the train and even find seats. The train sets off.

From the train I take one last look at the landscape we are leaving behind. One factory after another, as far as the eye can see. How industrialized this country is. What might, what technological will. What wealth, and potential.

We arrived late at night. Our nephew was waiting for us. We drove to Snyder, a town near Buffalo. His young wife worked there, we met her for the first time, she came here with him from Germany. She taught at a private school. He, my nephew, is a musician, a cellist like his father, my eldest brother, and also a conductor. They gave us a warm welcome, and in the few short days we were there we met other teachers from her institute, but no students, they were gone. It was vacation. And then we encountered Niagara Falls (I almost said: we encountered the Niagara Fall). It is not far from Buffalo. I remember the factories along the way, they were probably driven by hydroelectric power. Then we drove down lush green roads through a rolling countryside. There were roadhouses, hotels, restaurants. It's a popular place for honeymooners. And then we reached the Falls.

I didn't want to get too near the cataract, but I didn't want to miss it: it seemed to me that I had seen larger ones, in Switzerland, for example. This one had undoubtedly created an enormous drift. But it didn't have what one wanted in a falls, what one expects, namely something vertical. Niagara was lacking in that. I don't want to say it had nothing to offer in the vertical department. It was all right, respectable, but not up to its class. A harsh judgment, but that's how it is when something that is superb in itself is pumped up falsely by advertising.

So I freed myself of Niagara Falls propaganda during that first walk and could then take a second and a third quiet, unbiased walk. And the whole thing took on another perspective. It wasn't a question of horizontal and vertical. It was a matter of looking at the thing candidly and taking it for what it was. It is highly probable, though I am not the one to make the comparison, that it is the most colossal falls in the world. That's right. It is a titan, compared with which everything that other countries have to offer, Switzerland for example, seems doll-like and dull. It's not a matter, after all, of water spouting and spraying at a certain altitude. It's not a matter of a playful veil of spume. Those are poetic, European standards. That's how a proper, well-brought-up falls in Europe behaves, one that grew up in limited circumstances and dates from the pre-war era. And which, you have to admit, does what it can with what it has.

But Niagara, ladies and gentlemen, is as powerful and distinctive a part of earth as, in Asia, are the Himalayas, Tibet, and the landscapes of China and India.

America—impossible to describe—is not a stretch of land between two seas, like the Baltic and the Mediterranean, but rather stretches between two oceans, the Atlantic and the Pacific. And so this is not a Niagara Fall, it is Niagara Falls. They lie on the Canadian border, near the city of Buffalo. The hotel you can see in the distance is located in Canada. And the second stupendous thing about these falls is that words fail in the face of the colossal mass of water flowing here. The water lunges, streams, plunges, and rages with a driving, grinding power. Standing before it, the imagination is rendered deaf and dumb, paralyzed. It cannot be measured on an earthly scale, it is cosmic. Here the earth is still a child of the universe, a star. When you're crossing the ocean on a comfortable, large ship and smoking a cigarette in your cabin or on deck, you don't consider what a perilous, unearthly, or, rather, subterranean thing the sea is, water that goes miles deep with fish and plants and minerals and growing things that have never even been seen. You know a bit about it from botany or zoology. But what is it? It is the earth as star, the earth in cosmic space. Oh, it can be very educational to cross the ocean by ship, to turn off the radio and open your heart and your eyes. But we cross the ocean as if it were a kind of asphalt road traversed by specially built cars, steamers. You don't travel Niagara Falls, it won't stand still long enough for that. It isn't there. It comes at you from three sides at once. It ignores aesthetic demands. It knows nothing of education. This giant, this herd of giants, knows only how to create itself day after day. Night after night to create itself, to tumble and rage, roar and churn for hundreds of years, for thousands. The herd, the pack, is not concerned with purpose or meaning. It could not care less about results and performance. It is simply there.

And also: it is not the herd that acts, that roars and slams and rages and creates itself. Something else is expressing itself here. But who can speak of it without falling silent, dumb, falling to his knees to praise God and ask for mercy.

We took our leave, grateful for the warm reception we had been given. We said goodbye to our nephew the musician, a wonderful young man, and to our new niece, a clever, talented young woman, and steamed off to New York. We were greeted there by our loyal Peter. We found lodgings quickly. In the next few days we saw and spoke with many acquaintances and visited old friends. We were going to Europe. We were none of us young any longer, we did not know when we would see one another again, that is the nature of emigration, the back and forth, you remain torn. Many of those who shared our fate have acclimated themselves to life here. It seemed to me that they thought it quite laudable that I was returning to

Europe, they themselves resisted it, it was actually a premature and risky thing to do, we had many serious conversations about it. I thought it sad that all of them were sitting here on this side of the ocean, far from their roots, and were nevertheless ardent and true Europeans. Many of them will remain here in limbo, some will succeed in some calling or other, it is a bitter situation, a difficult one that will remain difficult. But they felt the same way about me.

The teeming streets, the huge department stores that I loved so. Masses of people everywhere, but not the mass man of the aristocracy's naive and vapid imagination. Our son Peter and our friends were very helpful to us. Everything went smoothly, in contrast to years before in Lisbon. The ship was ready to sail.

As the ship set off I went up to the deck, we were slowly passing by the spectacularly impressive wall of skyscrapers. It was still light, shortly before the sun went down. Soon ten thousand windows would be lit up. In the darkness, while we are floating across the ocean, ten thousand lights will flicker magically, under the surface.

This country has given us so much.

Farewell, America.

You were not very fond of me.

But I love you still.

# BOOK III

# Back Again

# 21

# Europe

A mighty ocean liner converted into a transport ship carried my wife and me from America back to Europe, from the new world to the old at the beginning of October 1945. Six of us had left Nazi Germany in 1933. One son, the eldest, had become an American and had remained there, one son hadn't been able to follow us when we came to America and was now in France, in Nice, newly married, and our youngest, the last to leave us, was now in Paris. And the other son who had not followed, and whom we thought of continually, not knowing for such a long time where he was and why he didn't write, lay in a soldier's grave in the Vosges Mountains—our Wolfgang, Vincent, his mother's darling, her heart's joy.

I had left Germany twelve years earlier. The country had become intolerable long before I left. The chaos, the hopelessness, the apathy. I had struggled against the stagnation. I had a strange vision in 1932, the meaning of which eluded me. An ancient and moldering god leaves his heavenly abode just prior to his own demise; he is ordered to descend to earth, he cannot refuse this order. He is to do penance there for all his past sins. And so he wanders through a sweltering land among the ruins of the temples in which he was worshiped. What was it all about? Only as I began writing about this Babylonian journey did it become clear to me: it was my own hopeless situation I was feeling. It was a feeling of guilt, a great deal of guilt, heavy guilt. It had become unbearable, and my desire to escape would not go away. It became a command to revolt. That was what the moldering Babylonian god meant. He was the foreshadowing of my exile, and much more.

But how did I consciously perceive this idea, how did I process it? Happily, cheerfully, arrogantly! My god, called Conrad, did not want to repent and he held fast until the end, he kept laughing and did not repent. I ended it with a lofty quote from Schiller's poem "The Diver": "But all was for his best, he was carried on high." I mocked the deeper experience I could have called on, and for a long time to come used the image that represented this deeper experience to no other purpose than ridicule.

Yes, I was free when I left. I soared, I thought I had escaped from a cage.

When I left, when I came back.

When I came back—I didn't come back. You are no longer who you were when you went away, and you will no longer find the home you once had. You don't know that when you leave. You are given a hint of it only on the way back, and you see it when you enter your home. Then you know everything, and behold: yet not everything.

We crossed the ocean to Europe. The last thing we had seen when we left in 1940 was the lights of Lisbon. We had left at night. We returned at night.

The powerful black ship docked at the man-made pier in Le Havre. The old pier had been blasted in the war.

And down below, in the darkness, the first thing I saw of Europe was a car driving by with a bright spotlight mounted on it. It threw a blinding light onto the lower section of our ship. A wide ladder was placed against the open door of the ship's hold. And now, in its cone of light, a horde of men who were all dressed alike climbed the rungs. From above they looked like gnomes. They disappeared into the belly of the ship and reappeared dragging crates and boxes, clambered down the ladder with them in pairs, two by two, set down their load, and started up the ladder again. It went as smoothly as if it were a theater production; you didn't hear a sound. These were German prisoners of war. That was my first sight of Germans again. I was fascinated.

When we disembarked they were standing there in a group. They watched us voyagers from the other side of the ocean silently, without expression. People passed by them as if they didn't exist. That was the first encounter, horrible and depressing.

I could not rid myself of this eerie impression of the vanquished, the condemned.

I saw Paris destitute and suffering, incapable of protecting itself from the darkness, and glad to be able to hide its pain under cover of night.

Then I left for the north. My wife remained in Paris with our youngest son.

I traveled alone, just as I had at my carefree departure in February of 1933. What did I think about? What did I feel as I traveled through the night and approached the border? I felt alert, I explored my feelings. No, it wasn't the feeling I knew from before on returning to Berlin and seeing the bright lights of the city blazing: I would take a deep breath then, it felt good to be home. I remembered my first trip to France twenty years ago; I had taken a manuscript with me and had wanted to do some writing under way. But I couldn't, and only at the end of our vacation, back in Cologne, could I go back to it and write as if I had put it aside only the day before; I was home. Now I questioned myself. But there was no feeling there. There were all kinds of things there, but not the feelings from before. I am no longer who I was when I went away.

In Strasbourg, at the square in front of the train station, I see the ruins that I will also see once I am in Germany: ruins, symbol of the times.

And there, now, is the Rhine. What occurs to me? In the past, "Rhine" had been a word pregnant with meaning. Now all I think of is "war" and "strategic border," bitter thoughts. All that remains of the iron railway bridge is lying in the water like a felled elephant. I think of Niagara Falls, that unparalleled flood of water back in the huge, vast country of America I left behind.

Calm, alone in the car, I cross the current.

So this is Germany. I pick up a newspaper lying next to me: When am I returning? My family crossed the border on March 3, 1933. What is today's date? The coincidences, the signs, the clues! (I thought I had left all that behind me.) I am shocked, I lower the paper and then look again at the date: the 9th of November! The day of the 1918 revolution, a disastrous date, the date of a failed revolution.

Will it be as bad now as it was then? Shouldn't there, mustn't there be a new beginning here, too?

I cross into the land I had spent my life in, that I left because I was suffocating, that I fled from with the feeling: it will be for the best.

This is the country I left and it seems to me that I am sinking back down into my past. The country has endured what I was able to escape. A Moloch arose here, he has left his traces, he straddled the country, he raged and devoured. They beat him to death with clubs.

You see the fields uniformly planted, an orderly land. They have cleared the meadows, the paths are smoothed down. The German forest, so often praised in song! The trees are bare, though some of them still display their bright autumn leaves. (Take a look at that, you Californians on the ocean, sitting under magnificent palms and dreaming of these beech and chestnut trees. There they are.)

Now it becomes clearer: rubble, cavities, craters made by shells and bombs. The ruins of houses stand behind them. And once again the bare fruit trees, staked up. An intact sawmill, the houses near it destroyed.

Children stand in the field and wave at the train. The sky is overcast. We pass by clusters of incinerated cars, their frames twisted and crushed. There is a dark line in the distance—mountains, the Black Forest, we are traveling along the foot of them, but they are far away.

Neat piles of bluish bulbs lie there, turnips that have been dug up. We are in Achern. There are factories with many chimneys, undamaged, but none are smoking. It all makes a grim, dead impression. Something happened here, but it is over now.

There are pretty little houses with red-shingled roofs. The steam of the locomotive gathers in white clumps outside my window and dissolves in tufts. We pass through Ottersweier, a sign reads KAISER'S COUGH CARAMELS from a time of peace when one fought a cough. Then come larger houses, the first groups of people, soldiers waving the French tricolor. I read signs, STEINBACH, BADEN, SINZ-HEIM, BADEN-OOS. That station is terribly crowded; people are changing trains there.

Baden-Baden. I have arrived at my destination. My destination—which destination?

I wander down a German street with my suitcase.

## Alfred Döblin

(Nightmares during exile: I have been spirited away to this place, I see Nazis, they are coming toward me, they are interrogating me.)

I shudder: Someone near me is speaking German! Someone is speaking German on the street! I don't see the streets and the people as I saw them before. A cloud covers everything that happened and everything I carry within me: the dismal pain of twelve years. One escape after another. I tremble, and look away in my bitterness.

Then I see their pain, and see that they have not yet experienced what it is they have experienced.

It is intolerable. I want to help.

# 22

# In Baden-Baden

The town where I now live, the spa of Baden-Baden, is full of people, but none is visiting the spa. There is a small permanent population, and the military and civilian administrative personnel of the French zone. Their offices occupy the large hotels, the luxury hotels as well, and their staffs fill the rooms of many of the villas and houses. Unlike the Americans, they have not occupied entire blocks. The street scene is not a happy one. It is the end of the war, the cease-fire, and war and defeat continue to be felt. Poverty is not quite yet visible. The shops are closed for the most part, and when they are open they have nothing on display and very little to sell.

What kind of spa is this? What is being cured here? I ask myself. It seems to me that you could get sick rather than well in Baden-Baden, there is so much fog and dampness and rain. I am told that the city lies in a valley encircled by mountains, which causes the clouds to form. That may be. It's an explanation, at least, but it doesn't help my rheumatism. It's better up in the hills—the city is quite spread out and offers a nice view—it is pleasant, even. Perhaps you could live up there and stay healthy. But who can find a place to live? I am housed in the center of town, in a little room in a family pension that is not exactly first-rate. There is a little ceiling lamp, I don't have a table lamp, but someone in town loans me one. Friedrichsbad, the large spa located nearby, is one of the few comforts I find here in the beginning. It has a hot springs and the spa itself has not been destroyed.

Alfred Döblin

A few months later my wife decides to join me from Paris, our son remains behind alone. We move farther from town, but are still in the valley, and I now have a long streetcar ride every day, and sometimes twice a day, to work. A streetcar ride is something to be experienced. You stand wedged in or cling to the running board outside. Once some people on the running board were mowed down by passing cars and badly injured. For a while they prohibited standing outside the car, but it was a habit that couldn't be broken. There are too many people in the city and not enough means of transportation.

As if I didn't have enough moisture to deal with in addition to the fog, the rain and the dampness, there is a small stream called the Oos near where I live. If you're taking a cure there in the spring, it is pleasant to stand on its lovely banks, particularly if the grounds are being kept up. The water flows quite briskly. But I can't help it; contrary to my nature I have an aversion to this body of water. I view the Oos with mistrust.

We are living in two rooms in a little house in a housing development, and have a very nice landlady. The walls are thin, we are living on the ground floor, the cold seeps up from below. No one could be envious enough of us to say: "That is where the victors live!" My office, however, is pleasantly warm and dry, it is there that I am the "victor." It is in a large hotel, I work there for most of my stay in Baden-Baden, I spend almost every morning and afternoon there, without writing a book—and in the evenings I toddle off to wait for the streetcar, tired and spent, in the quiet hope that not too many of my buttons will be ripped off or that I won't suffocate entirely.

I was not, as I soon read in the papers, occupying a "responsible" position here, nor was I serving as a "cultural adviser," as others reported. I had a limited task, namely to read works of fiction and poetry, epics and plays, and to give an extensive, or less extensive— the shorter the better—opinion on their aesthetic value and point of view. I was, that is to say, a reader of manuscripts. There were those similarly employed in other realms of literature. Those in other positions took our opinions and papers and used them to make certain decisions. For the next three years I read countless manuscripts and books, I had assistants to help me as well. I scanned many of the works, others had to be plowed through with patience. I knew how important this preliminary stage was.

This allowed me to orient myself to the spiritual condition of the country, within certain limits. And in retrospect I can say of that first encounter with what was left of literature after the war and what germinated in its aftermath that it drove me to despair. With time I gathered courage and got hold of myself. I was confronted with such helplessness. There was so much that was repressed and confused and, above all, obscure, that presented itself as "mystical." And mixed in with this was the work of hundreds of writers who could now write again without being afraid, and whose work screamed out in what was largely invective and rhetoric. They sit writing in their wretched rooms, pulled this way and that. They had read and learned very little, and then they had discovered writing, and this was the result. This soil yielded little more than grass and weeds.

I also had direct contact with the writers in this corner of Germany, and helped them organize an association. And then I founded a literary magazine, which many others were doing at the time—not that there were so many people clamoring for something on paper, but that there was so much on paper clamoring to be read. Newspapers, magazines, and brochures were among the few things that could be bought then. Actually, during the period when the Reichsmark was still being used as currency, it was merely a matter of exchanging one questionable piece of paper for another. Nevertheless, many of the magazines of this period served their purpose, as a substitute for books. In the immediate postwar period there were few books, and they appeared slowly, there were no presses or binding materials. What I wished to accomplish with my magazine was obvious: I wanted to promote a literature that had been suppressed—a new literature, I wanted to introduce it as soon as it was written and to contribute, insofar as a magazine can, to healthy and normal conditions in the country's literature.

It was important to replace the military mentality with something better, by returning to its rightful place the European, Christian, humanistic traits that had once existed in Germany. As I received more and more submissions—and it didn't take long for that to happen—it became clear that literary Germany had changed. The German mentality, no longer clothed in Nazi uniform, proved to be fundamentally heathen. It offered a great contrast to French literature that, despite Voltaire, Rousseau, and the Revolution, was suffused with Christianity. To me it seemed necessary that the message be given in this country that the bell tolled not for Christianity but for heathenism.

[ *276* ]

# 23

# What Germany
# Looks Like in 1946

When I left Germany in 1933, the Reich that now lies in ruins was at its height. It consisted of hundreds of large and small towns, many of which I was familiar with. I made my home in the largest city of all. I was aware of the growing tension. Millions of people were unemployed and you could see legions of them milling about the streets. You could also see companies of the SA marching in the streets, and hear their coarse, aggressive, shrill singing which they threw in the faces of passersby. They were already a menace and were consolidating their power. No one stopped them. You could see and feel that the country was decaying.

But as bad as things seemed then, no one could have foreseen what was coming. For better or for worse, the fact that Germany was in the hands of one individual—and what an individual—and was being transformed from a flourishing communal life into a grinding war machine was something no one reflected on. Nor on the fact that, in the end, Germany would be annihilated.

When I think back, I am certain that not even the darkest pessimist could have imagined then what has now become reality. There are German cities of which little more remains than their name. Others have been altered to such an extent that they have lost their character. What was once a productive land—one weakened by crises, it is true—has become a wasteland.

I read Jeremiah's lamentations on a city's destruction. The old prophet is grieving only for one city, though a particularly richly populated one that is holy to him. I am reminded of ancient events that still have not been forgotten today, of the volcanic destruction of the Roman cities of Pompeii and Herculaneum, devastation of mythological proportions. If people found this sudden destruction so monstrous that they have passed the story of it along from one generation to the next, then what name will be given to the leveling of the country that once was called Germany?

The Germans appear to have an odd, detached attitude toward it all. They listen, engrossed and shivering, to tales of ancient catastrophes such as the fall of the Roman and Babylonian empires. Jeremiah's lamentations on Jerusalem still move them. But they scarcely acknowledge the incredible ruin they are standing in the midst of. They treat this diluvian catastrophe as if it were some unfortunate accident, like a large fire. Occasionally, one of their poets or wordsmiths will undertake to describe this calamity that passes all understanding, and will call upon apocalyptic images to that purpose. It has an artificial, shallow ring to it.

A (supposed) central motif comes to mind, one of the strongest of all human passions and certainly one in this case, too: their drive for possessions and profit. They toiled and slaved to make their money. They'd take you to court for a few marks. They were envious of one another individually and as a class. And now I hear of cases in which former millionaires are living in squalid little rooms, and they are doing so quietly. They're having a worse time of it than those whose property was expropriated in the Bolshevik revolution, who were subjected to the rage of the mob. Now, one such person announces that he regrets having to receive his visitor in such squalid surroundings, but he has lost his house and his possessions, and what can you do?

You can shrug your shoulders. The war has been lost and everyone is in the same boat. Now the elegant daughters of the bourgeoisie, the professors, and the doormen's wives all peacefully stand in line next to each other to receive their meager weekly rations. I do not believe that people committed suicide due to the loss of fortunes, but there were many known suicides for political reasons. All of this reveals the strange fact of how little the person who allegedly clings so to possessions actually does—and also of the power of the collective mind.

Anyone entering Germany at the end of 1945 cannot avoid the impression that its citizens are running around in the ruins like overwrought, industrious ants on a crushed anthill, and their real problem is that they can't get to work right away, owing to a lack of materials and leadership.

The destruction doesn't seem to depress them, it seems to intensify their work incentive. I am convinced that if they had tomorrow the materials they lack today, they would rejoice in the fact that their old, ancient, poorly planned towns had been leveled, and that they now had the opportunity to replace them with something superior and modern.

The swarms of people in a heavily populated city like Stuttgart, their numbers increased by an influx of refugees from other cities and regions, move about the streets among the colossal ruins as if nothing at all had happened, as if the city had always looked like it does now. At any rate, the sight of gutted houses has no effect on them.

And if you believe, or previously believed, that misfortune in one's own land, and the sight of acres of ruins, would cause a person to reflect, to learn something politically—then you are wrong. People point out groups of houses to me and say: These were hit during this bombing, and those were hit during that bombing, and then they tell a few anecdotes. And that's it. No particular message follows, and there is certainly no further reflection on it.

There already are theaters here and there, and concerts and films that I hear are well attended. The streetcars are functioning, horribly crowded as they are everywhere. People are pragmatic, they help each other. They are concerned with the immediate present in a way that is disturbing to a contemplative person.

A bartering system (a clever example of mutual aid) has been set up. It consists of an association of the most important branches such as the shoe, furnishings, and clothing branches. You pay with an object you have and receive an object you want if it is available.

The countryside looks well-tended. Only the cities are destroyed. I saw pictures of these cities in movie theaters in America. You can walk through the streets of many cities—the streets and often the sidewalks have been cleared of debris. You see things to your right and left that you perceive were once buildings, but which now appear to be open boxes of stone without lids. These stone boxes have been split and opened up in various ways. Some still have all four walls but nothing in the center, a pile of rubble on the floor. Sometimes the whole box is leaning to one side or has caved in. Sometimes the front and back walls are standing but the side walls are missing. Most often, nothing resembling a building is left standing, and where there probably was once a solid structure there is now a pile of rocks with iron girders, window frames, and doors sticking out of it. Radiators, crushed buckets, and water pipes can be found buried there as well.

And the rubble conceals corpses. They lie there and cause the streets to be terribly silent. People were caught unaware in their apartments and were crushed to death or suffocated in the collapsing houses, in cellars that didn't offer enough protection. Many burned to death. Those the bombs missed were consumed by phosphorus fires. In some places the asphalt is ripped up as if the earth had suddenly buckled. But everywhere, reusable bricks have been salvaged and stacked against the walls of the buildings in neat piles. They are awaiting a new function. As I have already said, the industrious, orderly people who live here have not changed. They have always obeyed their government. They obeyed Hitler, and for the most part they do not grasp why their obedience turned out so poorly this time. It will be much easier to rebuild their cities than to get them to comprehend what it was they have experienced, and to understand how it all came to pass.

In a city like Pforzheim, you get a forceful impression of retribution. Pforzheim doesn't really exist anymore. It has been razed, wiped out. You see row after row of exposed foundations with twisted piles of rubble behind them. It looks like a movie set with backdrops, façades, foreground structures—a dead, deserted city. But if you look closer and linger a while, you will be amazed at the subterranean life that exists even here.

People carrying knapsacks and bags full of booty through the streets of a decimated city create a ghostly effect. I often saw them clambering up the ruins. What were they doing? Looking for something, digging? They carried flowers in their hands. They had set up crosses and plaques. These were graves. They lay the flowers there, they knelt and prayed.

There are a number of people in the streets who are dressed

Alfred Döblin

normally. They are wearing leather shoes while the streets and steps of Paris clatter under the sound of wooden clogs. And it was only a short time ago, in Paris in the fall of 1945, that I saw shabby, torn clothing everywhere I looked, clothing worn by the middle class, professors, university students. Here they are wearing the clothes they had before, they will last for a while. Of course, those who lost everything in the fires and bombings—what will they do?

And where do so many of these people live, following the bombing of their homes? For many, the comfortable life they led, not to mention bourgeois existence itself, no longer exists, nor will it for a long time to come. People occupy former bunkers, live in air raid shelters, barracks, in ruins, in basements.

They are alive and they want to live, they are already setting up apartments and stores in dilapidated buildings. There are countless tiny shops in the buildings that remain. Merchants put up posters outside to point the way through desolate corridors to their establishments. In one city, a department store had been destroyed but the entryway to the ground floor was left standing. Peddlers had set up outside it, and the department store continued doing business in the basement. The owner himself offered his wares on tables and shelves in a single room. A saleswoman stood at each table and people crowded in, looking for something to buy. There were only rationed articles and the sole items on sale without restrictions were useless objects like stuffed dolls and bookmarks. Up to the first half of 1946, I saw nothing in all of my travels that deserved the name of reconstruction. Foundations of houses are still waiting to be demolished, and the movie-prop streets have frozen in time.

That region once called Germany, which until recently was occupied by the Nazis, is now being run by the Allies, and although the word *Deutsch* appears everywhere—on newspapers, stamps, and on public buildings like the *Deutsche Post*, the word *Deutschland* does not. With one single exception: the Berlin organ of the Socialist Unity Party calls itself "Vorwärts: the People's Newspaper of Berlin, the Evening Edition of Germany's Capital," less a fact than a program for the future. The region once called Germany is now divided into four areas called zones. Anyone living and functioning here comprehends that "zone" is not just a word. Each zone has a military government and an economy, and while there is plenty of paper to print on, there is a lack of printers, whereas in the next zone there are printers enough for everyone because there is no paper. That is no different, in principle, from people in Europe starving while Americans have more than enough to eat.

There are barricades and passport controls. Anyone wishing to travel from one zone to another has to fill out intricate forms. Each zone puts anyone threatening to enter it to the acid test. This is due in part to the bureaucracy, in part to self-defense, we are in a country that is being closely watched. And that leads to outmoded forms of procedure. There is the question of food distribution, a common enough topic. Or let's take newspapers. Mainz and Frankfurt lie in the same area. But just try sometime to buy a Frankfurt newspaper in Mainz. Occasionally brochures and books appear in the American and British zones. You hear about them occasionally. Someone passing through will mention a title. You write for it. If you're lucky the opus isn't out of print yet. Everything disappears rapidly. Someone sends you a copy by mail, but it takes forever to arrive. Everyone reads with interest the paper, the book, that was published far away, far, far away—if not in Turkey, then at least a few dozen kilometers from here. We live in a time of jet planes and the Great Wall of China.

Anyone who has visited that region once known as Germany will have stories to tell about it. The distances are short and the experience is long. Everything moves reassuringly slowly. This is probably dictated by justice: the Germans, having penetrated deep into Russia and Africa, have satisfied their need to travel and can now stay home for a change. Most of them, if they have a home, are glad to do just that, of their own free will. They don't travel. Each departure and each arrival creates for the voyager a multitude of problems that require the skills of a detective to resolve and great tenacity in addition. Only someone who is at once crafty and unassuming can undertake such a trip.

Trains seldom go from where you are to where you want to go, most trains have plans other than your own and you have to deliver yourself over to the whim of the railroad. If the trains are in a good mood and are running, they are packed. They are loyal to their country and stop everywhere, in every village, and there are innumerable villages in each zone. These villages are not to be found in any atlas, and at the end of a short day of travel your knowledge of them has greatly increased. After six months' residence in this country and a little travel you can establish yourself as a professor of geography. The railway will also take care of your need for exercise: you have to get in and out quite often, very often in fact, for you have to constantly change trains. Which also serves to demonstrate that there are many rail lines and that the country wasn't so badly damaged after all. That's the railway's idea of propaganda.

Be warned about automobiles. This particular means of transportation, so widespread in America, is rare here, and as a rule, kaput. The chief word on German highways is *Panne*: breakdown. I've traveled a few times by car. And each time we had a breakdown I was glad, gratified, relieved. The suspense was over.

All of this, the division into zones, the broken-down cars, the bad gas, contributes to keeping the population at home. In addition to which you can starve during a major trip in this country. And that brings me to the topic of food.

I have said that you could starve on a trip. The average German would correct me by bringing my attention to the fact that you don't need to travel to accomplish that, you can starve at home. But that's an exaggeration. A great many Germans occupy themselves every day with the search of food. Whoever wishes to eat must not only be able to work, but also must be able to wait. And be able to hike as well. And be skilled and unafraid of physical exertion. A young German, the head of a family, sat across from me recently in a train and when the topic of food came up, which is to say almost immediately—it's like in America, when "How do you do?" is immediately followed by a discussion of the weather—he remarked that he thought it was truly amazing, a miracle, medically speaking, that hordes of people weren't dropping in the streets, considering the food shortage, for calorically speaking, things were totally inadequate. We contemplated this miracle together and came to the conclusion that any miracle that manifested itself daily in so many thousands of people cannot be a miracle. It must be something else entirely. And I offered my frank opinion that people were eating a great deal more than their rations allowed.

At which point a discreet grin appeared on the face of the man across from me and he hesitantly admitted that most people doubtlessly were finding a little something extra. I asked him to enlighten me on the topic, to tell me how people, himself included, managed to find a little something extra. Well, he confessed, that's why he was on this train. But he did not reveal his secrets to me, instead he veered toward generalizations: you had to know where, in the many places we were stopping, there was something to be had, you might even have to proceed there by foot. Ah ha, I thought, that's why the train is making so many stops. And then, he continued, you had to "organize." Organize is the key word here, as I quickly established. You "organize" potatoes. What does that mean? It means that you know where you might find some. Then you find out, directly or through two or three middlemen, what the person with the potatoes wants for them. Then you consider how you can acquire the desired object directly or indirectly, an object which then takes priority over other offers, and then you have to work to get it. So an entire plan of operations is called for. On top of which it's a risky business, for certain foodstuffs are restricted, it is forbidden to sell them. So if, having carried through your plan of operation, you find yourself in the possession of the "organized" object and are quietly and triumphantly transporting it down the road (for no one would chance onto the train with it, the control at the gate prevents that), when you're met by a police patrol that stops your little wagon and makes you open your knapsack and empty it out—then all your effort has been for nothing.

There are many thin, pale faces among the elderly, and the young people on the street are also thin. Hunger is a powerful force in this country. Hunger, in particular, makes people sullen and rebellious. It is a well-known fact that it is hard to bargain with someone whose stomach is growling, and if that person is already sick of politics he is not going to change his attitude if he believes that the people he particularly loathes are the ones taking his daily bread from him.

I have seen, incidentally, that one can fight hunger on paper as well. I have read a little pamphlet that gives tips on how to overcome hunger through thought, through the will. It's an idea that's easy to ridicule. It speaks volumes. In any case, hunger has a psychological and a physiological side—if the sufferer can't control the physiological side, he will try to appease the psychological.

These are the same people I left in 1933. But a great deal has happened to them. I see this in my daily contact with them. They have the same interests and forms of behavior they once had, the same appreciation of music, many of them are very learned. But on the whole they are less diverse, less individualistic than before. They appear more uniform, to me at least, coming as I do from the outside. Very few influences from the outside world reached them during those twelve years, and those that did were harshly controlled. They were subjected to systematic propaganda, an uninterrupted flood of official lies, and it leveled them, the educated and uneducated alike.

I got the impression, and I kept it throughout that entire initial period, that I had entered a house that was filled with smoke—but those living inside it noticed nothing at all.

New to me is a certain intellectual awkwardness, a heaviness. It's as though they have rusted somehow. A restricted repertory of ideas has been impressed upon them and they work with these ideas and it's hard to wean them away from them. That is the Nazi legacy. And that is why all the appeals made to them bounce off, and why the brochures written for their enlightenment have little effect and are read with disapproval and anger, as if Hitler were still running the country. And that is why you get nowhere with them on the topic of guilt. It is why they refuse to discuss politics with anyone of a different opinion. They are troubled, tormented, they want to be left in peace. That's understandable. But where do you go from there? Above all, you proceed rationally, without forcing it, by letting things happen, letting events run their course. The reports and the statistics on concentration camps and other horrors that are now being publicized can have an educational effect in themselves. But people are simply not inclined to believe them, for it is strangers, foreigners, as a rule, who are reporting this news. Seeing what happened to the cities might have the same effect. But they are under occupation now. To those adherents of the old regime, and there are many of them, of course, the occupation is a gift dropped right into their laps. It can be used as it was after 1918, after the First World War, as the Revolution and the events that followed it were used as an obstacle to enlightenment, as the basis of a new legend of having been stabbed in the back. Now, during the occupation, as the effects of the war unfold—what could be easier than to blame the occupation for everything? That's how difficult the situation is.

When I think of the aftermath of the First World War, the upheavals of those years appear as lucid as a fresco compared to the troubled picture of today.

# 24

# They Had Such
# an Opportunity . . .

*I* had a lengthy conversation with a young woman from a good family. I'll tell it in the third person. It was an attempt at conversation, an exploratory talk. She (early twenties, tall, lively, living at home) says: We were so worried then, at the beginning of '45. Father waited each day for the evening news reported in German from London. It was always the same question: When will the Allies finally arrive? We knew it was over. And then the constant air raids, and the fear. And then they said: They've already reached X. But we didn't believe it, we'd heard that too often. This time they were right.

We were so excited! One morning when I went into town to buy a few things they said German troops were there in the park. And they were—hundreds of them, in terrible shape, hungry and exhausted. They were given something to eat. They didn't stay long.

We knew then it was over. We could hardly sleep because of the excitement. And early the next morning, I had just managed to get a little sleep, I sat straight up in bed and said to myself: What is that? Our little house was shaking. There was a roaring sound that wouldn't stop. Bombers? I stood up and went to the window. It was cannons, they were firing over our heads from both sides, the Allies from over there and our troops from here. It went on for a long time.

That afternoon they said: The Allies are in X, and that evening:

They're in Y. And the next morning when I wanted to go shopping they said I shouldn't. The Allies had arrived, the military was everywhere. But I went anyway and it was true. We were all so happy. It had been a terrible time and now it was over.

He: Fräulein E, why were you all so happy?

She: Because it was over. I tell you, we greeted the Allies with joy, as our liberators. In those first weeks everyone was happy. The Allies had such a good opportunity with us. But then the requisitioning started—rooms, hotels, apartments. You couldn't keep anything. Then things deteriorated. . . .

(We walk up the mountain in silence.)

He: What did you expect, Fräulein E? They had arrived, where did you expect them to live?

She: Yes, but even so . . . I can't even repeat the things people say about it. Go ask them yourself.

He: But you yourself, as I recently discovered on my visit to your home, were quite comfortable, sitting there in your living room.

She: Yes . . . if they wanted to take away the living room . . .

He: You have your own room, and I was in your father's room; he has a large, bright study.

She: But he needs it.

He: Of course. I am happy that he has it.

She: We're doing all right at *our* house. But you should see the others.

He: I know. But there are many who have it much worse. You know how people in Berlin and Cologne and Saarbrücken are living.

She: Almost everything was destroyed there.

He: And in Paris and in Lyon, Le Havre, do you know what it's like there? You don't know—I can tell you. It's one of the Allied countries. People are living on top of each other. The housing situation is indescribable. People get by as best they can, they freeze in the winter. There is one essential word there, and it says it all: war. When they heard firing and saw the Germans withdrawing, they thought to themselves: *The war is over and peace has arrived.* They really thought that peace would arrive the next morning. The shooting was over, the air raid alerts, and now everything, everything will be all right.

She: And why shouldn't it be over?

He: First, the war wasn't yet over, and second, it still isn't over today, and third, it won't be over tomorrow. If a drunk stumbles around the house and breaks the furniture and knocks over the stove, and smashes the dishes and the windows and then is taken away—is everything all right? Someone has typhus for eight weeks. He pulls through. Now he's lying there. The typhus is gone. But he has neuritis, he is covered with sores; he is miserable. He feels weaker than before. He can't eat, he can't sit up, he has bedsores and he aches everywhere. He cries. You'd barely recognize him. But—he no longer has typhus!

She: When *I* had typhus my hair and even a few of my teeth fell out.

He: You see. That's called a subsequent illness and general debility. But it's the same with war. It begins with flags and parades. It ends with shooting and cannons, with drums and trumpets. The fever died. But the worst is yet to come. It slowly comes creeping along behind.

She: And when will it end?

He: When the ruins are gone, when the rubble has been cleared away, when new houses have been built and everyone has a place to live, so that they can leave the bunkers and barracks behind. When the economy improves and the political situation is stable. You're young, Fräulein E, you will experience peace. Later, when you look back on this time, you'll be amazed that you were so young then as to believe that this is peace.

She (becomes reflective and pauses often; then she shakes her head vehemently under her fur cap): But they could have been more considerate of the civilian population. I assure you that we really and truly were happy and excited and relieved. The Allies had a big opportunity with us.

He: Fräulein E, this is how it is: you were wrong, and now you are blaming others for it. Should I tell you what many people on the Allied side, who know how their people have suffered, would say to your attitude? Disgraceful.

She (defiantly): I am not alone in my opinion, at any rate. We are disappointed, and that's that. We thought the Allies were our liberators.

He: And weren't they? And aren't they? Just because the occupation brings certain inconveniences with it? Have you already forgotten Nazism, the whole system? Or do you approve of it?

She: Please. You know how—

He: Fine. You've been liberated from it. And the Allies were your liberators then and still are today.

(They stop near her house and look down into the valley.)

He: So enemy troops came from there and you stood here and were liberated, received them with open arms. You were willing and ready to greet those soldiers as your liberators—from the agony of war, from the burden of rationing, and from Nazism. . . .

But he wasn't interested in that. Can't you understand that? He had something else in mind. He would have been dumbfounded to hear that you were "giving him an opportunity," he would have responded to that with a roar of derisive laughter (not in your presence, of course). He was thinking of what France had endured during those years of occupation, of the mass deportations, of the struggles of the French Resistance, the appalling destruction. You knew nothing of that, but the soldiers did.

She (clears her throat, pulls up her collar, shakes his hand without looking at him and says sharply): I must say goodbye now.

He: Have I insulted you?

She: Not at all. We simply are of two different opinions.

He (confused): Two different opinions? Still two different opinions!

She (smiles at him, looks down at him from above, nods, and opens the garden door to her house): Of course. Father is of the same opinion as well. *Auf Wiedersehen!*

He (trotting down the hill alone): Two different opinions! She calls it opinion because that's as far as she gets. Two times two equals five—is that an opinion?

(Only when he reaches the bottom of the hill does he begin to consider it): She won't admit it. She probably sees it, but something, stubbornness, prevents her from admitting it. I'd like to try to think my way into the head of someone like that.

She (alone, taking off her hat, hanging up her coat): He accompanied me up here. That was quite an accomplishment for him. He tried hard to convince me. As if I didn't know all that already. He'd like to tell me even more. A man like him doesn't see that I'm sad, I have nothing, nothing to be happy about, just a roof over my head and my daily bread. Any child could figure out how that feels, and would say a kind word to me.

I'd like to scream in his face: *You're right, a thousand times over, I'll put it in writing. But you can take your being right and go straight to hell.*

(She sits down angrily and weeps.)

# 25

# A Little Trip to Mainz

*I* took a little trip to Mainz to attend the dedication ceremony of a new university. At five o'clock one afternoon I got into a car with three other people and we sped out of the city. The weather was nice.

There were women and girls walking along the highway under the green trees, they were going to Rastatt, were carrying baskets and pulling little wagons behind them: they were "organizing" food. Much of Rastatt had been destroyed, the major highway lay in ruins. Then our steel steed sped through the thick lowland. We reached the Rhine amazingly quickly, and then our steed didn't know what to do. It didn't see a bridge and we didn't either; there was none.

But what a body of water. It's good to stop so close to the Rhine and not be able to cross. It has a smooth surface, it's a running ribbon of fluidity, a flowing land. A ferry approaches, the men standing on it look ominous in their life jackets. They offered us life jackets too, but we refused them, laughing, we had no watery experiments in mind, we only wanted to get to the opening of the Gutenberg University in Mainz, nothing more. They agreed to take us.

When the car was on the ferry and the ferry floated off, the river demonstrated its immense strength to us. It was unimpressed with the burden of us, we barely scratched its surface, we made our way right across it, ferry, car and all, just as the current intended. We noted that, clever as humans are, they had studied this mighty creature and had learned how to behave on it. Accordingly, an iron cable was stretched over the river, it was connected to our ferry by an iron guidewire that wound around a spool the ferrymen turned. So while it was true that the mighty current drove us, we humans also had our way, and rode to the far shore on the back of this fluid creature, which paid no attention to us or to our resourcefulness.

The village on the far side was called Selz. We spotted its church right away, it was standing wide open like someone whose chest is split open. It had been cut in two by bombs, only the spire was left standing. There was grass growing where the other half had been, it was creeping into the church's interior, innocently making a pilgrimage inside, and the church, ever holy and conscious of its office, received the tender grass with a Franciscan benevolence.

There was a stork in a huge nest on the chimney of a nearby roof, standing guard on one leg, but not against us. We looked at him wondering: how will he and his family keep from getting smoked, roasted? An expert among us came up with an answer: he never nests on a smoking chimney. All of us marveled at the stork's intelligence.

We sat down in a nearby restaurant, thinking we would relax a bit. Actually, we had had a breakdown. Our car had announced that it didn't feel well and several doctors were attending to our lame steed outside. They consulted with it for an hour, and then for another half hour, and then it decided it could run again. But nothing happened, we waited until eight that evening. We had been on the road for three hours already and should have been arriving in Mainz to spend the night. We wanted to get a good night's sleep in the golden city of Mainz and rise early for the special services. We are finally able to leave, and head toward Lauterbach.

A toll bar is raised to allow us through; this is the Lower Palatinate. The side of the road is littered with crates and piles of something covered in straw, army property, munitions abandoned to the elements. We now are traveling in what was no-man's land in 1940–41; the fighting was fierce, the poor forest shows signs of it still. It's all scrub now, the trees have been broken and splintered. Gentle nature has been badly treated here! But when rulers do battle, it is the people who suffer.

To reveal its power to us, nature now makes a sovereign gesture, a sunset. It is one of its simplest gestures, but to us it has a dramatic majesty, it is a show of marvelous splendor. Plants, animals, and human beings all take part in it, from no-man's to everyman's-land. The blinding light of the sun pales to yellow, the great celestial body amasses a cluster of clouds, draping itself in them and pouring streams of golden light over them.

We're rolling, rolling along all the while and observe with pleasure the rows of undamaged houses and the long stretches of tidy streets. Dark forests receive us and the sky goes pink. To our left the sky is red as far as the eye can see. But to our right the bright blue is fading to gray. What lies to our right is being abandoned by the light, being surrendered to another power. Twilight and night approach—night, the other force, as magnificent as the sun. As if to present itself to its powerful sister in all its majesty, the sun, in taking its leave, pulls out all the stops and waves to the darkness and the earth. It throws out ten thousand colors in differing shades and that is only the beginning. Who can describe these magical subtleties: our words are merely banal, pedestrians who limp along behind a wedding coach. What can metaphor accomplish? The sky is on fire, the firs, even the mutilated ones, ignite with joy. The fire rages upward. The director is up to something new. He can change scenes without a curtain. Long, narrow strips of clouds—sheets stretched out across the sky—catch the sharply crackling cones of fire and carry them into the night.

A somber stillness reigns. This is the day's last hour. The light sinks deeper. Darkness sinks down silently to occupy the abandoned territory. The fiery light has caused no damage. I look in gratitude at what it has left behind.

We enter a large city, wind through the unscathed streets of Speyer, where we will spend the night. We haven't made it to Mainz. We want to be there by eight the next morning if our steed is willing.

All four of us are in the car by six, keeping the same seats we had the day before in Baden-Baden. There are four of us: two priests, a man from the theater, and a writer. One of the priests is driving.

Today everything is gray. Rain pours down. The sun should have appeared long ago, but it hasn't. Heavy clouds surround it instead. It surrenders the day to shadows.

But if it is not the sun that is to entertain us, then a no less powerful and splendid escort appears, it flows close to us here on earth. It is the Rhine, the same Rhine that the ferry carried us across so smoothly yesterday. Our road runs to its left, and if yesterday we were enraptured by the fire that danced overhead, today we have the water, that gushing, streaming, flowing element, rain all around us, the Rhine next to us. We roll through beautiful, fertile countryside among fields of grain. High, thin stalks, green from top to bottom, stand beside each other in bunches, in fellowship. They're conferring with each other, nodding their brown heads in conversation. They never go to bed, they have no problems with housing. They stand here always with their feet on the ground, they eat and drink and sleep here, bring children into the world and pass away. The rain, the sun, and the wind belong to them: what a healthy life they lead.

Frankenthal has been horribly bombed. A church exposes its pitted roof in the fog. An iron bridge to the right has fallen into the river, warehouses have been blown to bits. We glide over the shiny asphalt on our way to Worms. The Rhine is now a broad sea.

The landscape becomes hilly and we note with joy that we are entering the wine region. Green vines wind their way around the stakes. They stand farther apart from each other than do the stalks of grain, and they aren't speaking. Each stands alone, clinging to a stake and dreaming to itself. Later, we will taste in its juice just what it was thinking. We pass through Oppenheim and Nierstein, significant names. A blue-gray light has settled over the water and is attacking the hills. Inns and restaurants line the road along the riverbank; the war has left them untouched, to the joy of a connoisseur of good wines. But the earth has been seduced by the magnificent stream of water and has waded into it, the river receiving and joining it. Now there are long, narrow green islands lapped gently by the water's flow. We are now only a quarter hour from Mainz and hope to arrive soon. The extent of the devastation is growing, however, huge factories have been leveled as if by earthquake. So much hard work went into them, so many people were involved, they could have accomplished so much, and now all of that is gone, broken, finished, like someone who has had his neck broken.

And because our steed had made it this far, had achieved so much since leaving the church square in Baden-Baden, had seen so much of the sky above it and the earth around it along the way, it could do no more, and went on strike. It had already shown signs of acute exhaustion. It didn't even want to sound its horn anymore. We saw that this time it was serious. Out of sympathy for us, it dragged us along with its last strength to the end station of the Mainz streetcar—and then collapsed. We climbed out and the four of us pushed the exhausted creature into a side street—we could do with it what we wanted, it would not take another step. Two priests, a theater man, and a writer cut through the underbrush, got on the streetcar, then flagged a passing car and arrived at the university, formerly an antiaircraft barracks. It was nine-thirty in the morning. They had made it.

On the streetcar you could see what an important day it was for Mainz. The traffic moving toward the university was detoured. We were moving . . . but where was Mainz? There was merely rubble as far as the eye could see, faceless masses of it, foundations, iron girders, façades. This was Mainz.

We pass through a gate into the broad, square courtyard of a massive building that almost looks like a castle. It has survived somehow.

We enter the crowded foyer, push our way through a door, and find ourselves in a large room with red curtains, white walls, and a podium of light-colored wood, all of which had a cheerful effect. Cameras have been set up against the wall to the right. The room fills up. Students have arrived, only a few of them can find seats. At ten o'clock extra chairs are set up on each side of the room. Civilians and military leaf through translated copies of the speeches to be delivered. English and American uniforms among them. The temperature in the room is rising.

Soft, delicate music is heard coming from the foyer—Mozart's *Magic Flute*. We hear steps, the faculty makes its entrance. I am familiar with these ceremonious processions, the long strides of scholars walking two by two in their voluminous robes. The robes are usually black and they wear the black, flat caps of a past century on their heads, which are no longer dark, are often white, sometimes bald. Strange that our scholars, the bearers and disseminators of progress, dress like this. In America I saw high school students at their graduation strutting across the street in similar costumes. It seems that mankind doesn't place much trust in its own expertise, it seeks legitimation in its past. Many of the professors are wearing robes of other colors, one even appears in bright red. Who numbers the peoples, who names the names? The gentlemen look straight ahead as we stare at them. Three thousand students have shown up to hear these scholars speak, half of them are from the English and American zones. One thousand male and five hundred female students were allowed in, plus three hundred guests.

The procession of costumed men is followed by a conventionally dressed civilian group made up of prominent citizens, officials, and uniforms. A few of them are familiar. The strains of the *Magic Flute* can be heard occasionally. The rustling and shuffling and whispering of the crowd swallows up the music.

People have taken their seats up on the podium and the ceremony begins. We listen respectfully, for that is the reason we have come here from Baden-Baden.

The first to speak is the mayor, and the loudspeaker carries his voice to the hundreds of people outside in the foyer, on the steps, in the courtyard. The mayor admits that when he was asked to form a commission to study the founding of a new university, he didn't have much faith in tangible results. The city was too devastated; its population was broken. There were so many problems with getting enough food and clothing and shelter that everything else, it seemed, had to take a backseat. He could now happily confess, he said, that he had been mistaken.

The next speaker, the president of the state government, called the Gutenberg University the key to the material and cultural reconstruction of the region. A bishop used a lovely image to express his hopes for the new institution: just as the cathedral in Mainz incorporated all styles in its architecture, so might this intellectual center take all things of the mind unto itself, assimilate them, and crown them with eternal knowledge. The Evangelical community is contributing an organ to the assembly hall.

His Magnificence the Rector announced that universities were to be built on a new foundation, according to new principles. He quoted Count Sforza: "The European problem is a moral problem," and Thomas Carlyle: "It's a sad story, we have reached the apex of civilization and yet nine-tenths of humanity must wage a hard battle for its existence and a brutal, savage battle against hunger. The prosperity of the nations is reaching a new high, but the people of this earth are poor, poorer than ever in both internal and external properties, poor in money and in bread, poor in knowledge and in

[ 295 ]

faith." (And why is that?) "We must again become human beings to again become citizens, and become citizens to become nations."

A speaker wearing a uniform, a General Schmittlein, head of educational affairs—the founding of the university was done at his initiative—tells us about the men who have accomplished this task. At their head is General König, who served the cause of freedom four years before when he stemmed the "tremendous tide" that attempted to crush the Allies' position. The speaker does not include himself in this list; I have heard that his adventures took him from Norway to Russia to Africa.

Music is heard in the foyer, the procession reassembles, the podium empties. It is raining, and when it stops we wander the streets of the ravaged city. Street after street is eerily deserted, and I can't stand it for long. There is something going on in the ruins, a hatch opens in the ground, a head pokes up, people are living in a windowless cellar. The cathedral with its various styles is pointed out to us, it is hard for me to take it in at the moment. After a while a man drives up in our car, it has totally recovered, he tells us enticingly, and has been waiting for us. We congratulate him on its recovery but prefer to take a bus. He heckles us, calling us cowards. We accept the slur. He vows to get to Baden-Baden before us. We accept the challenge.

And then we settle onto the comfortable leather seats of the bus and again go by the places we saw yesterday and today. Nothing has changed; everything looks different. Our eyes sadly pass over the ruins, we mourn the fallen bridge, we greet the vineyards and ask the green vines their opinion of this agony. They say nothing, continuing to draw sweet fluid out of their dreams.

The Rhine is covered in fog. What a beautiful, fertile country this is! As if created to be the homeland one has always longed for, always loved—now crushed by the savagery of war.

It is night. We ride for a long, long time. We do not break down, no, not that; but it seems as if we are lost in the darkness. That can happen to a vehicle, too. We arrive around midnight to discover that our little car has already been there for an hour and a half.

# 26

# Rendezvous with Berlin

*I* had been gone for fourteen years. In 1947 I returned to Berlin again for the first time, the place I had lived since 1888. Berlin was already a big city then, the capital of Prussia and of Bismarck's Reich. But the period of the city's real development came later. There were no streetcars then, no automobiles, apartments were lit by gas, the incandescent bulb signified unheard-of progress. The telephone didn't yet exist. What blessed times those were. I remember seeing the Wright Brothers' first airplane on the Tempelhof field: behold, the crate actually rose up in the air and stayed there for a while. We came to view airplanes differently later. And department stores and the subway were yet to come.

When I left in 1933, Berlin was a rich and magnificent city, noisy, congested, and full of life. It had become a true capital, a center, a point of exchange for intellectual and political ideas, and for the economy as well, a tumultuous city to the outsider. But anyone who lived here knew that for all the many changes, the Berliner remained the same: as dry as the sand that the houses were built on, tending toward irony and wit, not at all coarse, though not necessarily highly cultured; sober, skeptical, and industrious, a quick and clever type, found at all levels of society. This personality type had already been described in the time of Frederick the Great.

But Berlin was not well loved in the rest of the country, to the west and to the south, or in the provinces. It had a swelled head, was ostentatious. That was the opinion when I left Berlin. It was my true home, I was happy to see it each time I returned from a brief trip, but in 1947 I returned to Berlin reluctantly. I had already been living on German soil for a year and a half. I knew, I had read and had heard that there was still a place called Berlin, but I shied away from it, I was almost afraid to go there. Why turn back the clock? I knew, after all, that the people there were not the ones I had left there, and I myself, was I the same?

I entered through a back door, in Frohnau. And then I saw it. I knew it all already. Having seen the shattered remains of dozens of cities, it didn't take much imagination to envision what this one would be like. Mutilation is mutilation, and here too I found the sad rows of skeletal foundations, the empty façades, the piles of rubble, everything that war had left behind. There were houses left intact, overcrowded streetcars, sad, heavily burdened people, rumbling trams and subways, total darkness on the streets at night, lifeless squares. Reality outdoes even the worst sort of fantasy.

I lived in Hermsdorf. It had been a place for Sunday outings in the past. Now I live here with my wife.

But it feels wonderful to be here. The buildings and trees emerged slowly from their apathy and touched something in me. I recognized the trees, I remembered them, and they reminded me of myself. It was nice living in Hermsdorf and it got nicer by the hour. Something hummed in me, a unique, strange feeling.

Many things contributed to this feeling. The air was cleaner, more pleasant, it suited me. And the trees: their trunks were festooned with scraps of paper advertising all kinds of things to buy, to sell, to barter. And I recognized this sight, it is an unforgettable one for me—it was seven years ago, in 1940, in my year of destiny, I was in Toulouse, fleeing, and there were refugees there who had lost contact with someone and were trying to find that person, and the refugees had stuck similar scraps of paper to the walls of the town's city hall on the main square. Search notices. I have mentioned them. It was a strange sight because the front of the building was covered with these bits of paper. When the wind blew, the papers fluttered and it looked like feathers ruffling, as if the building wanted to fluff itself up and fly away. . . .

The trees in Hermsdorf reminded me of those pieces of paper.

Alfred Döblin

Between then and now lies an abyss—I am amazed that I was saved and could crawl up out of it.

There is a train that runs from here to Berlin. It was a suburban line then, with a steam engine. Now it is run by electricity, like the subways. An incredible number of people can crowd into it. Who are these people? Shabby, dragging sacks and packages along with them, a despondent group getting by in hard times, you can see that right away. It wasn't like this before. There are many children. The adults wear unhappy, bleak expressions. How can they be happy?

We go to the Stettin station. It is strange for me after such a long absence to be entering the city at the same point I entered it sixty years ago, the first time I saw it. A childhood memory rises up in me as if in a dream, I'm taken so far back in time: we arrived from Stettin, my mother and we children, and changed to the municipal railroad, and in going from one train station to the next—they all looked exactly alike—I thought we were just shuttling back and forth between the same stations. And now I'm taking the same route.

The view along the way almost exceeds the limits of reality. It is an inconceivable nightmare in broad daylight.

The city must have experienced a terrible battle in the time of darkness and has emerged from it looking battered, cruelly wounded. What, what had happened here? It's the same from station to station. It's a good thing the train rushes through it all so quickly.

The last part of the trip is underground. We push our way up dark steps into the light.

Daylight We're in Berlin. We walk through a crumbling terminal out into the open air. This was always a gray, poor, dangerous area. Over there are the old familiar tenements. I see them once again from the square in front of the station. Yes, this is Berlin. Over there on the side streets is the red-light district. The same fist that smashed entire factories from top to bottom went to work on these filthy buildings as well. The ragged old hag has had her teeth knocked in. But she is still standing, her insides have collapsed inward, her guts are gone. But the skeleton still stands, still retains its form, has not capitulated. Long rows of streets are in this same deplorable condition, dead and yet not dead.

Many of the buildings still bear advertisements, announcements, posters—mementos from a time when the buildings were still alive—a corpse in a brightly colored apron, wearing a cheap

[ *299* ]

bracelet. As I look around outside the station I hear a loud voice coming from a loudspeaker set up somewhere nearby, at the streetcar stop where many of the wretched-looking people have gathered to wait for the streetcar that seldom comes. A shabby street entertainer is having a good time working this awful environment. His show is intended to cheer people up. After that someone sings Verdi. That's right, at the Stettin station someone is loudly singing Verdi to these empty windows in which, as the poem goes, fear and horror dwell. The singing is very bad. We move on.

The broad square in front of the former suburban station is deserted, surrounded by houses that are half caved in. We are approaching the Chausseestrasse. On the other side of it we see a strange sight. There, in a fairly intact building, is an elegant restaurant with chandeliers and sheer curtains, the signs outside are in Russian. It must be for officers. Chausseestrasse, a broad street, continues over the Weidendammer Bridge and runs into Friedrichstrasse. We continue on foot, the streetcar has yet to appear to take us to the Lehrter station. I have taken this route a thousand times to the hospital and then to the Institute of Science. We walk by the tunnel to the subway at Invalidenstrasse and take the overpass. We make our way carefully, the asphalt is ripped up and full of holes. The archeology section of the Museum of Natural History once housed the remains of prehistoric animals; it has now been transformed into a prehistoric animal itself. The buildings of the institute are charred, have fallen in. This is where I entered and left the building decades ago; only the façade is still standing, there are steps leading up to it, one wing appears to have survived—in the basement. Time has passed over what is left. It is early afternoon and an eerie silence reigns. Imagine, in a huge city like Berlin, a broad street with no traffic, few people, and no noise. To the left is Luisenplatz, once a patch of green; people sat on benches, children played there. Now I look down empty Luisenstrasse, which in the past was crowded with students and automobiles. Some Russian soldiers walk by. They have solemn, quiet expressions and avoid our eyes.

As we are coming to the Lehrter station a crowd streams toward us. They look like the same miserable procession we saw on our way here. Everyone is schlepping something, loaded down with bags and sacks. Many are in rags, a few look like cave dwellers.

At the Savignyplatz station things change. A few of the buildings have survived and people look cleaner here. But Bleibtreustrasse, where we are headed, is in terrible shape. We are searching for a certain house number, but how can we number the houses? Then the one we are looking for appears between two piles of rubble. When we enter the hall everything is clean and orderly and when we press the button the bell rings as it always did. And when we enter we walk across a carpet. Then a well-dressed woman opens a door for us into a large, well-furnished living room with a sofa, club chairs, with pictures on the walls and flowers and floor lamps and everything like it was in the old, old, days. Yes, the house is still standing. Why this house and not the others? Even the furniture is still intact.

And then we sit down and have something to drink, an amazing experience. We drink tea from dainty cups and smoke cigarettes as if nothing at all had happened in the meantime, as if outside were the Kurfürstendamm and the places we used to entertain ourselves, and we chat. We sit there as if we were on a ship on a stormy sea; but everything is watertight and not a sound reaches our ears from the outside.

There are five of us. My wife and I and S, the publisher, and the young owner of the house and his wife. Later, a chubby-cheeked two-year-old joins us, he shouts, and addresses the feather on my wife's hat as cluck-cluck. And we talk about how we stayed alive and how we have spent the last years. And outside is the wasteland, the desert, the silent battlefield that stretches for miles, once a city that bore the name Berlin.

I ask: What do people do here, how do they live? And am told that many people sell their possessions, if they have any left, and live from the proceeds, relinquishing one piece after another. Many deal on the black market, a great many.

Later we go to Kurfürstendamm. It was a broad avenue lined with trees, a boulevard that stretched to the Halensee, with magnificent, ostentatious buildings, with movie theaters and bars. Who frequents it now? The money has been driven away. There are shops in the ruins that sell perfume and flowers. One shop calls itself "Interior Design," its windows are full of boxes that are carefully and tastefully arranged, lampshades, even bracelets. We come across a bar now and then. We walk by the Café Vienna, it still exists. People are sitting outside at the tables, playing at prewar life. And why not? The weather is beautiful, the bombs couldn't change that. The customers are not elegant, are not drinking coffee, and what they call a *Schorle*, a wine spritzer, is not much more than tinted seltzer water. Many customers seem to be from another era, come back to haunt this one.

The sidewalk is torn up, the impact of the bombs shifted the slabs. Farther on we see a tower with a round black crown. These are the ruins of the Kaiser Wilhelm Memorial Church, totally consumed by fire. The Romanisches Café is open, enormously open; you can go in if you want. You can see clear through to the back rooms from the street, and into the second floor. There was a movie theater across the street. I can no longer locate it; it once premiered the film of my *Berlin Alexanderplatz*. Nor does the rotund actor who played the main role still exist, he died in the East. Only I am still here—to witness it all.

The huge restaurant at the zoo, the Wilhelmshallen, has been destroyed. The zoo: an incendiary bomb fell on an elephant here, the animal put up a terrible struggle trying to smother the fire. But the sun shines equally on the just and the unjust, the huge, unsuspecting animal was dragged into humanity's woes, and died horribly. The city raged, it's something you don't hear anything about today, the inorganic raging of the elements. An all-consuming heat caused a firestorm, it roared through the city, people were screaming, there was a roaring sound.

It could hardly be imagined; and now that everything is over it is harder still to imagine how—drowned out by the elements—the living screamed, or didn't scream. They were barely heard even then, the human screams of fear and pain. Man's own creations had gotten out of hand, and now this thing that was the elements, this thing that up until that point had been at man's service, raged overhead.

The alarm came too late, people rushed down dark steps into basements, and anyone who was knocked down stayed down, no one saw him and no one helped him up. Children and those who couldn't protect themselves were trampled to death by the herd— and then they were all entombed.

All of this took place in a prosperous city in Europe, a Europe in which music and literature were blossoming at the time, in which antiseptics and infection-fighting drugs were being developed.

## 27

# A Walk from the Friedrichstrasse Station to Unter den Linden

*W*e have made an appointment with a reporter who wants to ask me some questions and are to meet him at the clock at the station across from the Admiralty Building. But what remains of the Admiralty Building, where once there had been a theater and splendid public baths? Even the huge building across from it is gone, once a military school. Grass and weeds grow behind the fence there.

We set off on foot. We note what still exists and what doesn't, what we must expunge from our memory or transfer to another sphere, what has died out.

The Winter Garden no longer exists, nor the great vaudeville theater with its starry dome, nor the Zentral Hotel. At the corner of Unter den Linden once stood the Victoria Café. There are great pits in the earth there now, iron railings and bricks. It's the same everywhere. So why stumble around in it? But I want to see it, for I have to understand this, too. Something catches my attention at the corner of Friedrichstrasse and Unter den Linden.

Arcades? Arcades on Unter den Linden? Yes, I hear someone

say, the Swiss Travel Bureau was located there. I shake my head. Even now, after they have been shattered, these arcades annoy me.

Unter den Linden—such bad taste. . . .

This is what has become of one of Berlin's most elegant streets. The basic outline still exists—but the streets are gone. How empty and wide the Linden is, a huge square that extends into the distance. No trees. I look out over houses, through houses. Beyond them I recognize the Brandenburg Gate on Pariser Platz. It stands in empty space, there is nothing to the right or left of it. There is something lying or standing on its roof, where the Quadriga once stood, but it's different than it was before.

Friedrichstrasse is quiet and empty, as is the Linden, through which throngs of people and traffic once passed. It was once necessary for police to direct traffic at Kranzler-Ecke. Now, as we stand here, a young Russian soldier approaches us from Friedrichstrasse, he has a young woman on his arm. She wears a plain blue dress. They walk past us solemnly. A vision, a hallucination: across the devastated, empty streets of the Linden, among the ruins of this obliterated city, a young Russian soldier walks along, serious and quiet, with his wife. Could anyone have imagined this five years ago, not to mention fifteen years ago when I was still here?

I mention this to the young reporter walking with us. He shrugs his shoulders and concludes his political observations with the comment: "With the way things are going in Europe and in the world, anything is possible. Who knows, maybe in ten or twenty years Ivan will be walking with his wife across some boulevard in even more badly smashed-up cities of the West."

There is the memorial to Friedrich II, whom they call the Great. The memorial, which is walled up, sits on an ugly square stone box at the entrance to Unter den Linden, in front of the palace of Wilhelm I, the first German kaiser of modern times. His famous corner window is no longer there, nor is the Opera House across from it, what was once its stage is now a mass of iron sticking up in the air.

Why has the second Friedrich been so carefully walled up? I remember a radio report from 1933 on the occasion of Hitler's visit to Potsdam, to the grave of this flute-playing king. Potsdam was once again being played off against democratic Weimar. It was the prelude, the cue given to the Third Reich to rearm, make war, and destroy. Radio Potsdam played its signature tune, "Be Always True and Honest." They already saw that a coalition was being formed against them, but to the end they perhaps looked for a miracle like the one that saved the Prussian king. The ironic thing about the story is that it was a Russian, the Russian czarina, who rescued the Prussian. But the Russians have corrected their errors of the past. . . .

We go no farther. I have never liked this area. As schoolchildren we were made to stand here in the cold each January 27, the kaiser's birthday, on the doll-sized bridge called the Schlossbrücke. The second Wilhelm, walking between his sons and his generals, would come over from the palace at noon to the armory to give the watchword. On a hot August day in 1914, I was wedged into a crowd that stood here in front of the palace that now lies in ashes. The crowd sang one song after another. Then they marched up the magnificent Linden, drunk with war fever. Four years later I saw revolutionary workers marching up the same streets beneath red flags. A band played the "Internationale," the Weimar Republic appeared to have arrived. The workers assembled over there in the amusement park and on the square of the palace on the first of May, there was music and a sea of banners. Nothing of that is visible now, or audible, there are no people there, none of the buildings exist. This is a patch of earth through which the Spree flows. This is what history looks like.

# 28

# Alexanderplatz

The subway took us to Alexanderplatz that afternoon. Everything is still familiar, everything has been reduced to silence.

Looking at the square as I left the station, I once again experienced the bitterness I had felt two years before at crossing the border from France and seeing those first German villages. I feel that bitterness again now and ask myself what I am doing here. Shouldn't I get away, refuse to look? They disgraced themselves. I feel betrayed. This square is still familiar to me. I knew it even before the massive Tietz Palace was built here, which has been crushed along with its dome. (The palace resembles a man whose neck has been snapped with one blow, whose skull has been driven down onto his chest.) I knew this square from the time when it was a quiet place, when there was a small hill in its center covered with friendly green grass; there was shrubbery too, and benches where you could sit with others in peace, peaceful in the greenery in the middle of Berlin on Alexanderplatz.

We sat here often, my mother and I and one of my brothers as well, when we went to the big market hall, and would carry my mother's bags for her. We liked to go with her. We lived on Blumenstrasse, and on Grüner Weg, and later on Landsberger-strasse. From around 1888 to 1890, I attended the parish school at

Friedrichshain, at 1 Höchstestrasse. How long ago that is. There were horsedrawn streetcars and no electric lights. I remember how surprised I was when they put up the wires for the electric tram; I didn't like them, they looked like a grid over the city. There were no automobiles. I remember the huge motor vehicle that often stood at Unter den Linden and Friedrichstrasse, across from the Café Bauer, which took sightseers on a tour of the city. Such vehicles were called mail coaches. They were a kind of omnibus without horses and it seemed to me something was missing from the front section, namely the horses, and when this bus started up it made a great deal of racket, it seemed to us that there was something wrong with it somehow.

So Alexanderplatz had a hill then, and there was much to see at the market hall. We looked at the fish in the great marble basins, walked along the row of meat stands. I can still recall a ditty I read there. It was a justification for why the customer had to accept bones with the purchase of meat: all animals had bones as well as meat: "And that's why when the meat is weighed, everyone gets a bone inlaid!"

Time passed, and department stores, heatedly debated and considered ridiculous, entered the scene—in the beginning they were really only storage spaces for junk. On the north side of Alexanderplatz there was a large academy for tailors, it was torn down and Tietz, the first department store, took its place. It was also here that the huge bronze monument to Berolina, for whom the city was named, was erected, she gestured grandly with one arm, perhaps to invite people in or to greet them. She was positioned in front of the department store and dominated the square.

Just as in so many ancient European cities dark and dubious streets radiate from the cathedral, so do they from Alexanderplatz. The nearby "barn" district bore that name for a reason, I can still recall the wooden stalls; that pompous theater, the "Volksbühne," did not yet exist. And on the south side of the square stood the immense and ominous red box: police headquarters.

When as a physician I later settled in Frankfurter Allee, I took my daily walk to this point and sometimes a bit farther to Königstrasse, close to city hall. I would arrive between noon and one o'clock at the Café Gumpert, a large, lively place where businesspeople met. You could read newspapers from all over the world there, and drink coffee. Sometimes I brought a manuscript with me, and would listen to what was being said around me, and soon I would be writing. I enjoyed all the noise around me as I wrote.

I didn't witness the last stage of development to take place on Alexanderplatz. I do not regret that.

I exit Königstrasse, empty and silent. The Wertheim department store, which suffered heavy damage, is closed. The restaurant Zum Prälaten is still there, I stop and observe the people, the handful who are passing by or loitering about. I hear them talking about food. A Russian soldier stands next to me, watching them as I do. He continues on his way.

The square is not empty, there are a few trucks, and women are pushing baby carriages piled with wood. There are tables set up in front of the Tietz department store, the dome and globe of which have been damaged, and street merchants are peddling the same cheap wares that are for sale in all German cities.

I look down the larger streets that radiate from the square. I wander along Münzstrasse, there were many restaurants and bars here earlier, including some shady ones. And there was a great deal of criminal activity here as well. I can't find the old places. I am like Diogenes with his lantern, I seek, and find nothing. I return to Alexanderplatz and remember the Teachers' Association clubhouse, where so many gatherings were held, and the large café there. The building is still there, but it has been flattened. Gatherings are a thing of the past.

Yes, it's all history now, past. Here, as on Friedrichstrasse, on Lützowplatz, at the Stettin station, everything is destroyed, smashed to bits. Destroyed is the community that they labored on for centuries. An incredible amount of energy was expended on it. The people became prosperous, but they couldn't control the larger segments of reality. In the end everything fell apart.

But the destruction did not emanate from this square or its people. Life was peaceful here, as only human life can be with all its faults and burdens and corruption. All that is gone now, was sacrificed—the apartment buildings, the department stores, the shops and cafés and restaurants, the little half-concealed hotels, and with them all that made daily life enjoyable. Nothing about it was excessive or violent.

So if the ship went down with all hands on board, if everything

[ *308* ]

fell apart, then it was not from here that the U boats came and finished things off.

Frankfurter Allee, where I lived for so long.

The broad streets, what a place it was.

It was not the abyss.

It was not a place of pleasure and contentment. The farmer and his family worked hard, there were setbacks, disappointments, hard times—but what about those who lived in the poorer quarters or slums of a huge metropolis? Those who lived here in the dreary four- and five-story tenements that stretched along the streets for miles, whose rooms looked on gloomy back courtyards, they knew worse things than poverty and hard work. They were the factory workers and their families, the clerks, the shopkeepers and whoever else was barely surviving, whatever else that had sprung up in poverty. It was often a squalid, forsaken world, and the part of it that was best protested against it. Human existence, as fashioned by the Creator—he gave humans power over all life on earth, life in the air and water, that it might serve him—included comfort, sun, nature, friendship, and the repose and contemplation that make it possible for humans to have an inner life, to know where they stand in the world.

But where was the chance for that here? I passed through my old neighborhood in East Berlin. The sight was shattering. I realized then what terrible force was necessary to knock these houses down.

I passed through the area where I had lived for years, where my children had gone to school. Here and there a surviving façade signified where a house had once stood. It served as a reminder, but then it didn't, as well. It was far from what it had once been. It is no longer what I knew, or where I lived. But it was engaging in a new way. It has been struck and marked by a divine light. You had to sit here in the ruins and let them affect you, as I repeatedly said and felt.

But I was glad to speak to, to be greeted by, this person or that. Some avoided me in silence. But I can do nothing about the fact that I have changed. A person can change more easily than a city, a person can stay alive, a city falls apart.

Am I a prodigal son who doesn't want to return? How many of us are scattered around the world, how many have joined modernity while I'm still walking and living around here? I carry within me the image of the old city. It should have changed, it had to change. It couldn't. So it is we the living who remain, who are not lying in ruins, but who are no longer the same.

In 1947 I traveled to Berlin with trepidation. I dreaded it, I was almost afraid to go there. Why open all that up again? I knew, after all, that the people living there were not the people I had left, and that it wasn't the city it had been when I had left.

And now, in 1948, I've come to Berlin a second time, to participate in a panel discussion and lecture. I read before a group I had once been closely associated with. And then there was a discussion in a public hall, a disorganized public event of no consequence. After fifteen minutes I regretted having come. It was a difficult and subtle discussion, addressed to the audience. It involved art, poetry, reality; we were supposed to address the realistic value of art, or its remove from reality, and this against an obviously political background. It proceeded without plan or preparation. We said whatever occurred to us, or whatever the others provoked us to say.

Again, the image of the city. We see sad rows of architectural skeletons, façades, whatever fire and the furies of war have left standing. Yes, something happened here, I again saw it. This was the main stage of the nightmare. It was here that atrocities occurred, that the population allowed itself to become anesthetized, a place of singing, chanting youth and cheering onlookers. It surged through the streets and echoed from the walls of houses now lying facedown. Try to avoid thinking about retribution. . . . It is true that millions of people who lived here then did not take part. They merely watched as the witches' sabbath was celebrated. But then their houses collapsed and people were killed. That is the terrible voice of justice in history.

The streets. It's all very different from what it was. It is no longer that which I knew. But it engages me in a new way: it has been struck and marked by a divine light. During the panel discussion I said: You have to sit in the ruins for a long time and let them affect you, and feel the pain and the judgment. Yes, it very much affects me.

And once again I see that it is easier for a human being to change than for a city. A human being can transform himself. A city falls apart.

Alfred Döblin

# A Speech and a Reply

I had given a talk in Berlin. Though I had done so in other places
and though I had had several things published recently, it seemed
to me that they knew little about me, they weren't familiar with me.
I had made a name for myself, a name connected with the words
"Berlin Alexanderplatz." But that was scarcely more than words
now, for the book had long since disappeared, and they didn't
know where I stood now or what I had gone through. It was not I
they knew but a phantom from an earlier epoch, invented by
shallow critics. I had piled up so many big books and also had
taken part in this city's daily struggles against backwardness,
against an intractable military mentality, the coming Nazi wave, the
treachery of boss rule. I blasted the vain, pompous soft-soapers and
traditionalists as well as I could in my writing, the imitators, the
parasites who lived on others. Particularly despicable to me were
those literary figures and their widespread followers who did not
like the big city—though most of them lived there—they extolled
the provinces, the cow bells, while at the same time modern,
ultramodern science and technology and industry were dominating
the scene all over the country, in this Germany. The pall of a
pathetic German provincialism fell heavily upon the metropolis—
the metropolis, the only real force from which the country's wealth
and strength derived. But that other force, the spiritual backwardness of the past, proved stronger in literary, political, and social life.
It was difficult to fight against it, to help the present come into
its own.

How differently this race between past and present had been
run in America and in England and France. How proudly Walt
Whitman had spoken of democracy, and he meant all working men
and women, those in the country and in the city. What songs of
praise he penned for Manhattan; no one in America was to consider
country life superior to that of urban life. And I had never seen
evidence in England of the poisonous effect of antagonism between
city and country. The provinces of France had developed out of the
essential characteristics of both city and country. For centuries
the king and his court had set the tone in Paris without disturbing
the life and character of the provinces. A refined culture emanated

[ *311* ]

from Paris, and Paris proved itself as a capital, the uncontested capital, and everyone basked in its glory.

It had also not helped that I had written an epic account of the "truly weak," that had reflected the theme of *Alexanderplatz*, and followed that with the story of a king from the Thirty Years' War who couldn't deal with power, who was frightened by power and the terrible things that authority could do, and who therefore allowed himself to be ruled by his field marshal, Wallenstein, until he becomes trapped in his own passivity—he, too, was truly weak. And *Manas*: one man's journey through the world of the dead in India, repenting his acts of cruelty. None of that mattered. They had reduced me to a formula: a writer of the *milieu*, the underworld, the Berlin underworld, so that when I spoke in Berlin I was judged accordingly.

I spoke in Berlin on how the organization twists itself around the spirit and destroys it, and I gave all sorts of examples and expounded on the final one: how socialism was corrupted in the political sphere and how it deteriorated into boss rule. What was to be done now? I asked. We must transcend concepts like "socialism" and make a fresh attempt to determine basic values. We had to get back to the source. I told them that considering the brazen nationalistic and atheistic arrogance that Nazi Germany had demonstrated, what was now required of Germans was humility. I spoke openly— and also mentioned prayer. . . .

How delighted they were in Berlin (not all of them, but those of a certain circle, particularly those with whom I had once been associated) when they heard this new twist: "Ten Steps Back to the Source." I knew beforehand what they would do with it. It didn't bother me. I was concerned only with clarification.

Their newspapers—I received copies in the days following— made fun of me. One journal reported: "We witnessed a total surrender to mysticism, dangerous enough when a person like the author of *Berlin Alexanderplatz* wishes to dissociate himself from party, organization, State, and socialism concerned with class struggle and take ten steps back to—pray!"

What I had said was: It was important to find a new position from which to deal appropriately with the structures of State, organization, and party.

Another paper reported: "We have already heard often enough

what Alfred Döblin said to us in Charlottenburg, or things to the same effect, and it didn't help a bit that it came from a famous writer and infrequent guest."

My answer to that is: You've never heard it. And if you heard it with your ears you didn't comprehend it, and you'll never comprehend it because you don't want to.

A "flight from reality" is how other articles described it. "Alfred Döblin, once one of the sharpest, most relentless intellects among German writers, and a representative of a scientifically streamlined prose, has returned from emigration a devout Christian. His conversion has caused a sensation."

Later, at a reception, I encountered a number of writers living in Berlin, some of whom I knew. There was no real communication between us. Moreover, I responded to my welcome in a way that displeased many of them. They're always writing and talking about reality and the present, but I told them that I did not see that they really lived in the present, they needed to figure out which year it was their present dated from, the present they lived and thought in.

Later, of course, came the attacks on my religious book. One critic wrote, "The book documents the path taken by a member of the avant-garde, a member of the antireligious, radical left, on his way to Christ on the cross."

I can reply only that I have never been antireligious in my life. They wrote that I, as an intellectual, had capitulated to mysticism. I see nothing of capitulation in the acknowledgement of what is enigmatic and mysterious in the world. "He fled from the world of real things." To the contrary—I abandoned illusions and faced reality. "If Alfred von Bollstädt, the teacher of Thomas Aquinas, considered rational, scientific thought to be the highest achievement, the seventy-year-old Döblin has turned in the last years of his life toward the metaphysical, the irrational, and mystical." I'm as rational as anyone. But how do these men react to the reality lying beyond rationality? They turn their backs to it. But it does exist and, in being ignored, forfeits neither its existence nor its significance. If they are of the opinion, as it appears, that this is the only world, the absolute world, that this is our place and we must limit our thinking, our actions, and our attitudes to what our senses provide us with, then I do not agree. They isolate themselves in this and restrict themselves unnaturally to a small part of what the human being is capable of.

They don't even assign thought its right place, they don't even correctly understand what reason is. They have their theories and they use them to block the view of reality. They fight a good fight against the tyranny of State dictatorship, against social injustice. But they are not satisfied with the good fight. They believe their authority derives from some self-made theory. Theory ruins the thing. They are idealists.

A schism between religion and science occurred during the Renaissance. Recently discovered as well as suppressed knowledge emerged in a surprising way. It caused anxiety among the religious community and its emissaries. They rejected science, became inflexible, and the new sciences, neither understood nor accepted, threw themselves totally on the side that was antagonistic to religion. The religious side clung too tightly, too fearfully, too needlessly to the written word, which reveals God, it is true, but which was filtered through the human spirit and formed by the human language. Christ had written nothing at the time he died. The writing commenced only later, and there are four Gospels on his life and teachings. When Christ departed this world he continued to worry, in the weeks that followed until Pentecost, about whether or not his disciples would tend his flock. He knew why it was necessary to send the Holy Spirit to them—the spirit, to be sure, but Holy.

It is something more than resolution when a grown man, an old man, falls to his knees and becomes lost in thought, when he laments and repents much, and thinks and feels nothing but: "Lord, forgive us our trespasses," and "Your will be done on earth as it is in heaven."

It is not a loss of power, nor a feeling of incapacitation, of servile surrender. Say I lived in Italy near Vesuvius. Would it emasculate me, would I become passive and renounce all activity if, when building my house and planting my fields and vineyards, I were to take into consideration the natural world around me—including the character and capriciousness of a volcano? Would it be unreasonable of me to avoid certain areas altogether?

This world, however, is more mysterious, less easy to understand, more powerful and frightening than any volcano. I would do well to know how to deal with it. It is a blessing that we need not learn mathematics and physiology in order to be able to eat, to swallow, to digest. We "know" how to do that, as we say, we "learn" that from birth, at home. I can say: "Like this." But I cannot say how. It comes to us naturally, it is built into our nature. I expand on this view, hold it fast in my thoughts, and work and deal with it. And as a result I know the terrain better and am more "rational" than those who merely use their five senses rationally, that is to say irrationally, half-blind and half-deaf.

There is activity that is blind and activity that has vision. Activity is strengthened by true vision, is made more effective by it.

They attack the Church with quotes from the Bible, from the Gospels—a cheap and long-since tiresome tactic—and point to the ornate cathedrals, the processions, the overly elaborate Masses: these are the opinions of onlookers, of sightseers.

Compare with them the riches of the liturgy, the wonderful simplicity and truth of the Mass, the truth and profundity of the teachings.

They bring up certain popes, injustices, degeneracy, power struggles.

Compare to that the quiet, almost supernatural existence of the Church. The flood of belief that continually issues forth from millions of people throughout the millennia.

# 29

# 1948

*A*nd so 1948 has ended and I have turned seventy. During my disturbing and strange trip through France in the summer of 1940, I often had the feeling that I had been robbed, laid bare. It seemed to me as if everything had been taken out of my hands. Then I comprehended that I was perceiving only what already existed; it was being demonstrated to me. Now, in 1948, I am having a similar experience. Age and increasing infirmity unsettle the body, wear it out. It's as if something were being torn from me. Actually, something new is evolving. Bricks are being removed from my house piece by piece, its beams are being sawed in two. My house—but that was not I, that was not I.

The house was part of me but I was never told how I learned that "I am the house."

My body—I have known this for some time—has many layers. It is constructed of a number of elements that are scattered about in the world, they are gathered together from all over the world, and are innocuously called "chemical elements." But they are not simple structures, they are complicated ones. However, I do not know what they are nor how they contribute to this concerto called "I."

They say that cells are the body's most elementary basic form, they combine, die, are very diverse, make up flora and fauna.

And when I feel, wish, perceive, desire—from which layer do these things come? What is dominant? What is representative? I say

[ *316* ]

that I "perceive." But what does all that entail, how many worlds is my *I* made up of? Am I a unity?

If I now am beginning to lose my body, if the structure is beginning to decay, I know only that there is something here whose role is finished, but it seems to me that it was never something with which I truly identified myself.

I have certainly not stormed through life: "Great and mighty at first, now wise and prudent."

I passed most of my existence like any other citizen, in the same country I left sixteen years ago. I did what I had to do, spent time observing nature and other things, did all kinds of thinking and fantasizing, some of which I wrote about. In the end—oh, what a divided, chaotic time, what a divided, chaotic country I live in now.

When I first visited Berlin (I have mentioned this before), and we were walking from Friedrichstrasse along Lindenstrasse, a desolate street empty of people, a young and energetic Russian soldier approached us from the other side of the street with his bride. He was walking arm in arm with her across the deserted street, with the statue of Friedrich II standing walled off in the background. I found this to be a prophetic sight. My companion added to my observation in his own way; he said the East was on the move, and noted astutely that it wasn't going to stop here, "Unter den Linden." We should meet again in ten years to discuss it, he said. I now hear and read much the same thing. What kind of future are they depicting in a time that is already so anxiety-ridden and dispirited? But even if these cities lie in ruins, we are in another plane of creation, we exist in another plane where there is no destruction. This, here, is the negative side of the world.

At this point in history people are obliged to organize themselves into nations, and join other nations like themselves. But at the very moment that this need is being realized, and that the demarcation line between a third nation is drawn, this need is mixed with the tendency to measure oneself against the third and fourth nation and to dominate them—though one knows, or should know, how little we are masters of our own fate. And once again in the sea of history there comes a wave, but it merely crashes against the mainland to be tossed back, surging, into the sea.

## 30

# The End of the
# Report and Its Conclusion

With this ends not destiny's journey, but what I have to report of it. Age and infirmity have crossed my threshold. They reside under my roof and are preparing me for a new and great change to come.

For a while the body and its energy was a source of natural pleasure, and this became the true justification of existence. Existence in its physical form was like a constantly flowing stream that one could drink from when, and for as long as, one wished. Now the water table is sinking. Will I be able to see the riverbed?

### The Passing of the Trees

I know you, standing there like me in your physical form—I know you, trees. I watch you every day. You stand in front of my window. It is winter now. You are standing there, black and wooden. You're getting ready for a little outing. You feel a new spring. You will begin to change. Your roots are beginning to form new strands, sucking and pumping under the earth. Your machine works are slowly starting to move. There is a jolt, a nudge, a departure signal; you vaguely anticipate it, you don't pay any attention, it overpowers you and you permit it. Then your center self breaks through to the light. Outside, the sun has become stronger and warmer. Your branches are covered with tender spots; they will become buds. They grow, they swell and unfold, are first brown then green, they are leaves, they will soon be leaves. Yes, this is destined to be. It has happened before, last year, three years ago, ten, thirty, fifty years ago, perhaps further back. You feel it. You stand there, transformed overnight, green on green, leafy, one tree next to the other. It is April. You feel that it will soon be May and then June. It seems to you as if your blossoms will soon begin to form; that is the way of the world, just as May and June follow April. And then it will be summer and your blossoms will open and the bees will circle them and suck out the honey which they will carry to their honeycombs where they will build cells of wax, hundreds of bees living together, they are industrious workers. Ants will crawl up your trunks.

So you will stand there for a while, strong and sturdy, in summer and fall. You are part of each moment of time. And then it is in the nature of time—a time that is not unfamiliar—that your blossoms will fade. Your leaves will spread for a while yet, lifted and dropped pleasantly by the wind, their lovely dance with the wind. And then they will begin to get heavier and more tired and to turn yellow and brown. Their stems will dry out and decay. Your leaves will fall. They will leave you to mix with the earth, with the soil from which you grew and on which you stand, and which gives you sustenance. And then the wind will rush through you— not to play but to rend and shake you and to twist off your leaves. I see already how they will dance across the earth, mixed with dust, and perhaps this dust itself is foliage fallen long ago. And so from year to year, each generation of the same tree greets the next, and the latest generation is always called the "young." And again you stand there, black and bare in the fall mist. You feel winter coming on, it is time to go home, to stay at home and shut the doors, for outside a terrible monster is raging, shaking your trunks and trying to tear you apart: the cold, the cold. That's how it is with you. You never really go home, you always are at home. But we humans . . .

## The Passing of Humans

We don't form rings of age. We don't experience that kind of recapitulation, that simple addition. Unlike us, you attain a certain number of years before nature fells you, unless the ax gets to you first. We are also felled by exhaustion—but with us there is a price.

Any person who attains a certain age witnesses new generations grow up around him. They don't know anything, they enter the game fresh. And then, at any given time, there are the millions of invisible or hidden people who are sick and ailing, and who continue to be so. And both the well and the sick are surrounded by cemeteries where earlier generations rest. Only a fraction, a minimal fraction of humanity, is alive. The vast number of people who populated the past millennia are dead. The human being, Adam, is the sum total of human beings moving through time and unfolding within it. Larger in number and in significance are the dead, or those we call dead because our reason and our senses cannot comprehend them. Their lives, in some part reflected in and attached to our physical existence, flow through us and beyond us.

To those of us who are isolated, this world is interconnected in a mysterious, mighty, and terrible way. But it was created by love, and it is love that forms its essence, that does not allow it to come to a rest, nor to fall. What Isaiah said is true for all of creation: " 'For as the rain and the snow come down from heaven, and return not thither but water the earth, making it bring forth and sprout, giving seed to the sower and bread to the eater, so shall my word be that goes forth from my mouth; it shall not return to me empty, but it shall accomplish that which I purpose and prosper in the thing for which I sent it,' says the Lord God the Almighty."

Schopenhauer thought that blind will constituted the core of reality. Buddha was of much the same opinion. They also posited a specific end of the journey for those who were enlightened, who had comprehended the world's illusion. Original will would gradually weaken and then dissolve, and in the end man would achieve nothingness.

But it was not vacuous will, not a meaningless or irrational will that formed the world and from which the world expanded. For us, therefore, there is no mere accumulation of time and then a dying, but rather history and fate. The infinite creative power, the power of love, is what spirit is, and what "the essence of existence" means. The world emerged from a primal mystery that man can name, but that he can neither comprehend nor determine. For this reason nothingness will not devour this world, created and sustained the way it is. I escaped the insatiable Moloch called anonymity, I know that God said: "I am, that I am."

God is person—that was the first thing revealed to me on my journey.

The second thing was that infinite creative power, the power of love, is the first cause.

## The Will of Time

I sit in the streetcar on my way into the city. The hills outside are shrouded in fog. The trees arc leafless and black. The bare branches droop sadly. But the fruits, the seeds, the sprouts are already in the earth, and are waiting. The trees can decline in peace.

And what rushes through time is the longing for eternity, not merely a memory of it. They emulate eternity in time. They chase after it in dying, in dying a death that is not a true death. They try to reproduce themselves. Hence this touching cry, this plea of fertility.

Standing before them, among them, is man. Nature is his, after all. The Trinity, a single God in three persons: an ample, spiritual, abundant bounty; the Father-Creator from whom the Son emerged in days gone by, the Word, the loving understanding that pours forth.

The most basic law is not that of the struggle for existence.

We are uplifted in our temporality by God the Trinity, and carried to original love, the true reality, through the sacrament.

Glad tidings have been delivered unto us. Now, when I look to the Gospels, where is the darkness, the gloom and suffering that frightened me so before? He came into the world to bring love. Do not become cold. Warm yourself with God.

"In the midst of life we are surrounded by death," goes the old refrain. But there's more. The rest goes: "In the midst of life we are illuminated by paradise's glow." What are joy, happiness, beauty, love, and tenderness, rare and weak and unstable as they appear to be, other than a residue—but more than a mere memory—of our previous, truly human existence.

No one should belittle this joy, this happiness, beauty, and love. St. Thomas Aquinas himself witnessed them and pronounced them good.

"In the midst of life we are surrounded by death." That is true. But add to that a sentence from the Gospel according to John: "He came to his own home." It reads: "He was in the world, and the world was made through him, yet the world knew him not. He came to his own home and his own people received him not."

When, at the beginning of my own journey of destiny, I attended a Christian service in France—as an outsider, then—I was surprised by its somber and sad nature. Christianity, after all, bears glad tidings. I saw that sadness was not really the message. Those who are believers, absentminded and playful as they are—like children, really—must be led to the true reality, to seriousness, to great and then greater things. Solemnity, respect, and humility are required. I was almost a cipher in the face of the inscrutable prime mover that I was led to out of my everyday existence in order to become one of God's creatures, a child. In the face of our not very appropriate, not very innocent existence, we need a dose of sadness, of dejection and remorse, they need even to dominate. And when that best of all possible examples of true and pure existence, the Passion, occurred and we experienced how we received that original love, and when a terrible light illuminated our pitiful life—then basically there was room only for a grievous, bitter, if not totally despairing solemnity.

But it remains true that this world is his home.

And if they did not recognize him then he recognized them and did not turn away, no matter how they treated him. Nor, so that there be no doubt about him, did he call for the appearance of some "Messiah" under impossible conditions, even for the distant future. Original love needed no go-between. It came to its own home in its own way: unnoticed, simply. Though we have among us only a small amount of love, goodness, happiness, peace, and beauty that we can draw sustenance from, the direct source of it was there with him, a concentrated light that emitted the magnificent radiance we so long for.

We believe that things only needed to be put right in order for happiness, beauty, peace, and love to have taken their correct places. But man remained free, master of his fate. Man and his ally nature now pretend to autonomy: they even claim the small amount of love, happiness, and peace they find in their existence to be products of their own making, as goods wrested from nature. And heavenly paradise, creation with love at its core, was (and is) ignored, truth is stood on its head and deception has reached its peak: God and all of original creation have become illusions and phantoms, and desolation and meaninglessness and blind coincidence have become truth and the measure of all things.

And because we turn our backs to the real truth and to the potential we have been given, we croak like frogs and call it philosophy.

## Happiness, Beauty, and Love in This Life

As surely as this era is permeated by war and discord among its peoples, as surely as people fight among themselves even though they know what a blessing peace and goodwill are—so surely, too, is it that man will succumb to illness, become crippled, deaf, blind, be sought out by an old age that makes him helpless and sickly, so surely is it that we all, no matter how we have led our lives, will be taken by death. So sure as all of this is, it is also certain that everyone fights this, doesn't desire it, attempts to escape the public and private battles, sickness, old age and death as well. Buddha, moved as he was by sickness and old age and death, saw this and yet didn't fully comprehend it. The fact that people see these things at all, that they find them horrifying and recoil from them and are affected by them shows that they are aware of something else in addition. They are incapable of acknowledging the fate that has befallen them, they do not accept it. They remove themselves from the bitter and bad things which contradict not only what man wants, but even what seems fair to him and suited to his nature. And he also sees them as contradicting the greatness, the splendor and beauty of creation. He cannot do otherwise, he sees these things as flaws, as outside disturbances that have penetrated his grand structure. But the beauty, greatness, and order of this world exist side by side with discord, hate, and evil, and sickness, old age, and death as well.

The ancient Greeks combined the words for "strife" and "love" to form the word "eros." Love, however, is sweet harmony, the desire to merge to the point of relinquishing the self. Eros, strife, is the battle for self-assertion, and the wish to annihilate the other. If it is the case that death and love often meet in literature and in life as well, then that only reveals the extent of natural degeneration and the total obfuscation of truth.

It is in peace, in happiness, and in love that we feel ourselves truly represented and alive. It is from here, and not the other way around, that hate, wars, sickness, old age, and death should be viewed. Happiness, beauty, peace, and love seem to be man's normal condition. That is the "paradise" of the Bible, and it is a recognition, an ancient piece of knowledge, a deeply grounded memory, and not a fable.

No one can deny that this era is marked by original sin. Each death, each illness and conflict, is a reminder of this atrocious original sin that brought misery into the world. It induced a break in the connection to the first cause, and brought on a steady decline. Hence man's urge to return, to turn back, without realizing that he is still falling. The first cause must announce itself as love and demonstrate what love is. Jesus' path on this earth is one long revelation and lesson in that respect. He is able and wants to heal the individual. The world in its present state cannot be remade, even by him. But he can heal individuals completely, for he is the original, creative word.

With the Annunciation and Mary's total acceptance of it, this creation emerged from original love and original love still forms the center of the world. Mary is still, or again, the sole human example of the original connection to the innocence of paradise, and to salvation.

## Toward a New and Greater Enlightenment

Anyone who depends solely on his senses and his reason is beyond help. He adapts a philosophy, or he doesn't—his life goes by, it passes somehow. He knows that he was born and he accepts that. He notes what is set before him by his family, by society or the State. He accepts it, or he doesn't. He marries and has children, or he doesn't

Alfred Döblin

marry and has no children. He gets sick or he stays healthy. He gets old, or dies young 'or unexpectedly.

There is neither sense nor momentum to such a life. What calls itself life is really death. And there are times when he understands this, when his flight allows him to rest, his flight into the activities of daily life, into a profession or politics or love or art or sport or success—or if he fails in his flight.

He who sees in himself more than his five senses and the potential of his reason can be helped, or has been helped already. He values his five senses and the wonderful impressions they convey, he uses his reason. But he feels that both his senses and his reason emanate from his essence, from his human essence, and at the same time he feels that they will not deplete him. Like his senses and his reason, his life has come to him as a gift from an elemental force. How can he do other than accept this gift in trust and be happy with it for as long as he is allowed?

He doesn't understand why his senses and his reason should be exalted. If he receives messages, tidings, revelations from great and cryptic depths, from ancient times, he embraces them and they confirm and strengthen his own basic feelings. They augment and protect him.

Transcendental force is received by him as grace. It brings faith with it. And that is feasible, for it has a central source and, because it is a meeting of equals, there is no need for proof.

Reality is not only as threatening and confused as we all feel it to be. It is also marked by innocence and bliss, a fact that we often overlook. Countless people live happily in ignorance from day to day like young animals. They live as if there were no guilt or knowledge. They wander through their existence. They are asleep. Should they be awakened? Let us assume that they will allow themselves to be awakened—what for? So that they can do what others do? No. But the world would only profit if they became informed, enlightened, awakened, if they were brought to knowledge and to the light. There has already been one Enlightenment. A new and greater one must follow.

Everything already has been said, been thought, revealed, and taught. We have the Holy Scriptures, the explanations and interpretations with clarifications and elucidations, insofar as the mystery can be elucidated.

The meal is ready. We don't need to seek any other sustenance. What we need is people to lead us to the table and to serve us. The time of blossoming, of early growth, is over for religion. The trunk has developed its branches. The crown is full with leaves. The tree has already weathered heavy storms. It is still standing. The time to flourish and mature is approaching.

And so an era announces itself that is no longer concerned with nations and their struggles, with their mighty efforts at unification. But it is not solely our era with its catastrophes that we exist in. We do not just execute its laws blindly and automatically. We belong to its creators, we are called upon to prevail. We know this. People try, they look at their general situation, their present historical situation, and they analyze it but they get caught up in external signs that are not causes but results; and the social world belongs to this, as well as the attempt to bring about change through it because it is the basis for everything. But it is not the basis. It is merely a symptom.

To achieve introspection, to cultivate "piety"—but do we know what that is?—to allow piety to become more pure, more intense, more sacred. Only in this way can we approach action and make decisions, and get control of the wheel that is throwing the ship off course.

What must develop out of momentum, out of inclination and insight and knowledge, out of exertion and perseverance is a truer, more profound transmutation of our attitude toward "piety." This is the place where virtue, tranquillity, justice, true wisdom, stability, and tolerance abound. Two things are decisive here: the introduction of truth and its reintegration—and manifestation.

The individual is caught up in events and there begins a transformation that is actually a liberation and restoration. For the individual came from a sphere of creation different from the one he now belongs to, from a higher sphere closer to the first cause than that of natural creatures, from the angels. Transformation is the detachment from nature made possible by an act of divine salvation, and with it comes an end to confusion, to entanglement, constraint, to human helplessness and inner fear that vent themselves in the thrusts

[ *326* ]

Alfred Döblin

and eruptions in nature and history—it is the end of perversion, of the era of sin and punishment.

In approaching the first cause, the individual is granted virtue and grace, which have an effect on people and on society. And that brings about something new, something different from what man alone is capable of, and from what he and his society can achieve within the framework of "history."

He passes through the gates of suffering and want, through the gates of sickness and age and death. That is his lot and—his reward.

For when he passes through these gates is he not accompanied by belief and hope, is he not guided by joy and conviction?

Peace and joy flow into him. His heavy crust loosens, as if it is being washed away. The old, painful scars soften.

A heavy mask falls away. He sees that a thick mask of clay had been pressed onto him and was presenting itself as his *I*.

# DEPARTURE
# AND RETURN

# When I Departed . . .

At nine one morning I heard on the radio that the Reichstag had been set afire. The fire was put out, the arsonist was apprehended; it had been done by Communists—it was a monstrous crime against the German people, etc. I turned off the radio. Words failed me. I was accustomed to the influence radio exerted at that time, but this was the limit. The Reichstag apparently really had been set afire—but by the Communists? They dared to try to trick us with something like this? *Cui bono*? I asked myself, who stands to gain? The answer was obvious.

I was not worried for myself—if at the same time I was deeply disturbed and angry—until someone called and asked me what I was going to do. I was surprised. Do? Well— the arrests; I should make plans. Ridiculous, I thought. But I couldn't get the conversation out of my mind. Then several people approached me; their drift was always the same: I should disappear, at least for a while; I was in danger, there were lists of names. . . . It didn't make sense to me. I wasn't capable of making the leap from a constitutional state of government to a dictatorship, a pirate state. By evening I became capable.

My wife agreed. We would take a trip, let the storm pass. Then a worker I knew called: I should leave right away, he said, he was well informed, it need only be for a short time, three or four months at the most, then this thing with the Nazis would be over.

Friends came to say goodbye to us, tears were shed. I laughed and was calm, I left alone with one small suitcase.

Downstairs I encountered a surprise. A Nazi wearing a civilian overcoat over his uniform was standing in front of the shingle for my practice. He fixed me with a stare—and followed me to the subway. He waited to see which train I would take and then entered the same compartment. I got out to change trains and he got out too. At least I immediately caught on to *this* situation. He followed me. We came to a crowd getting off an arriving train, I ran down the steps to another platform and traveled first in one, then in another direction to my destination, the Möcken Bridge at Potsdamer Platz. I wanted to reach the Anhalter station. A train was leaving from there for Stuttgart around ten o'clock. I booked a sleeping berth; I carried that ticket in my wallet for the entire twelve years of emigration; I have taken it out now, it's with my other papers. As the train departed, I stood at the window in the corridor. It was dark. I had traveled this stretch many times. I loved the lights of the city. It was always the same when I arrived back in Berlin and saw them: I would take a deep breath, I felt good, I was at home. So I set off, I lay down to sleep. A strange situation that had nothing to do with me, really.

A few hours in Stuttgart; it's peaceful, the Nazis are calling assembly meetings—a comedy, why am I leaving? Ridiculous; I'll be embarrassed by this later. We come to Überlingen, I spend the night there, then cross the lake to Kreuzlingen. I cross the border by car; everything goes smoothly.

In Kreuzlingen I visited a sanatorium physician whom my wife and I had visited the year before (what a happy time that had been). Now I show up as a refugee, a role that seems absurd, meaningless to me. But who was it who was fleeing? And from what? Everything looked so peaceful, so normal, totally normal. I saw myself as ridiculous. I was ashamed to tell him the story. But he thought foresight preferable to hindsight.

So there I was, as if on an unexpected vacation. I wrote letters home. Until one day I was summoned outside the sanatorium; someone was asking for me. It was (I am superstitious about numbers, but not overly so) the third day of the third month, March of 1933. I had noted the date that morning as I was reading the newspaper. What does it signify, what will it bring?

Outside stood my entire family, with the exception of one son.

Alfred Döblin

And then it became a different situation entirely. My wife was in tears; she described the awful things that were occurring in Berlin, the things she had heard in the train. The whole family was in danger, she said; they couldn't have remained there.

So here they were. It frightened me, this day of March 3, 1933. But I got over it; I had other worries: where we were to live, for instance, or going for walks, or conversations and plans. Had I left the country for good or was I merely waiting to return? I didn't know. And I wasn't much concerned.

My wife recognized the reality of the situation, she knew that she had left her home and that our children had been uprooted from everything they knew, she saw the mountain of worries, the clouds of uncertainty—she wept a great deal; I in comparison (being who I was) was elated. Yes, elated. . . .

During those months I kept remembering words from Schiller's *The Diver*: "But all was for his best, he was carried on high!"

But what was "best"? Everything in Germany had become unbearable, not only politically but spiritually. It was as though the political chaos and the stagnation had taken hold of spiritual life and paralyzed it. I fought it in my own way. Finally, at the end of 1932, a vision appeared to me that I could not rid myself of: an ancient and obsolete god approaching his own demise leaves his domicile in heaven and descends to the people of earth to rejuvenate himself and to do penance for his past sins. Once a god and ruler, he is now a human being like everyone else (*Babylonian Journey*). It was my foreboding and anticipation of exile.

Exile: the separation and isolation, the escape from the dead end—this descent appeared to be for my "best." Something in me sang, "It carried me on high. . . ." I couldn't help it. I was in an exalted state (it also affected the book that I worked on for a year).

And so I went into exile. That's the way it was when I took my leave.

# When I Returned . . .

*A*nd when I returned—I didn't return. There is a wonderful novel by Thomas Wolfe called *You Can't Go Home Again*. Why can't you? Because you are no longer the person you were when you went away, you no longer find the home you left. You don't know that when you go away, but you feel it on the way back, you experience it as you approach, as you enter the house. Then you know everything, and behold: not yet everything.

At the beginning of October 1945, a huge ocean liner refurbished as a transport ship took us, this family melted down to three, from America back to Europe, from the New World back to the Old. We had been six when we left Nazi Germany in 1933. One son was now an American and had remained there, one could not come with us when we left for America in 1940, and was now in Nice, he had married young, and another could not follow us. We thought of him all the time and did not know where he was and why he didn't write: he had been lying in a soldier's grave in the Vosges Mountains since June 21, 1940, slain by the enemy, the Nazis, our Wolfgang, a gifted mathematician, his mother's favorite, her heart's joy.

When we left Europe in October 1940 (my Babylonian journey—had it carried me on high? It has been a long time since I have felt optimistic, I know much more now than I did when I crossed the Swiss border), the lights of Lisbon were the last thing we saw of

Europe. We left at night and we returned at night. The huge black ship docked at the man-made pier at Le Havre (the old pier had been destroyed). And the first thing I saw of Europe from the ship's deck was this: down below in the darkness moved a car affixed with a bright spotlight that threw its blinding light onto the lower part of our ship. A wide ladder was set against the open door of the cargo hold. And then in the light men all dressed alike ascended the rungs. From above they looked like gnomes. They disappeared into the belly of the ship, reappeared dragging crates and cartons, clambered down the ladder two by two, set down their load, and retraced their steps. They moved mechanically, as if on a stage; from above we heard not one sound. These were Germans, prisoners of war. That was my first sight of Germans again. The sight fascinated me. When we got off the ship a group of them were standing together. They observed us wanderers from the other side of the ocean silently, without expression. People walked by them as if they did not exist. That was my first encounter, horrible and depressing.

This eerie impression (of the vanquished, the condemned, the war) did not leave me the whole time I was in Paris. I saw poor Paris suffering as well, it could not defend itself against the darkness of evening and was glad to hide its pain under cover of night. Then I left for the north, for Germany.

I went alone, alone once again as I had been on my carefree departure in 1933. My wife and youngest son did not come with me; they preferred to remain behind in Paris, in cold rooms that were not their own.

What did I think, what did I feel as I rode all night and approached the border? I was awake most of the time, and asked myself questions.

No, it was not the same feeling I once had at seeing the lights of Berlin upon returning there, when I had taken a deep breath, felt good, was home. I remembered my first trip to France twenty years before; I had taken a manuscript with me then, I wanted to do some writing under way. But I had to put the manuscript away, and only when we returned to Cologne at the end of the vacation could I go back to it again and write as though I had stopped only the day before. Now I search and question myself. But the original feeling is gone. I have all kinds of feelings, but not the one from before. I am no longer who I was when I left.

I left my home easily and gladly, it's true. It was like being saved from suffocation. Fate threw that my way. And I rejoiced: "It was for my best, and carried me on high!" The dethroned god of *Babylonian Journey* laughs, revels in the change in him that had been planned as punishment, he goes his way unbroken, all cheerfulness and joy.

I was not this god. I found this out slowly, gradually, in fits and starts.

Didn't I read in an article by a writer who remained in Germany during the war about the "armchairs and easy chairs" of emigration? There are a lot of things being printed, there is much more to come, ignorance knows no bounds. To flee from country to country—to lose everything you know, everything that has nourished you, always to be fleeing and to live for years as a beggar when you are still strong, but you live in exile—that's what my "arm chair," my "easy chair" looked like, as did that of many who left.

Within our own four walls we wrote and worked as never before and were sentenced not only to total silence, we not only lost our rights, but in addition we were humiliated, treated worse than illiterates, who at least could communicate with their neighbors.

There were those who did very well in exile, it is true: they managed to accomplish something abroad in countries they were not really at home in. But how many of them were there? Most of us were happy to get past the first or fifteenth of each month. Merchants, painters, and musicians had it easier (though with a loss in status); women unencumbered by responsibilities occasionally did well. But those of us who were devoted body and soul to language, what became of us? Those of us who didn't want to abandon our language, who couldn't do so because we knew that language wasn't just "speech," it was thinking and feeling and much else besides. Abandon that? That is more than to change your skin, it is to disembowel yourself, to commit suicide. So we stayed as we were, and though we endured and ate and drank and laughed, we were living corpses. And now I am returning . . . geographically. At the train station in Strasbourg I see the ruins that I will later see in Germany, the symbol of the times.

There is the Rhine. I had worshiped it, it was a word suffused with meaning for me. I seek its meaning now. What I think of is "war" and "strategic border," bitter things. The crushed train bridge lies in the water like a felled elephant. I think of Niagara Falls with its

Alfred Döblin

roiling mass of water that I saw at the end of my stay in that immense, vast country of America that is behind me now. I cross the river in the train, quiet and alone . . .

. . . and am in Germany. I pick up the newspaper lying next to me: When am I entering this country that I left on that fateful day of March 3, 1933? What is the date? I lower the paper in shock, and then look again: it is the 9th of November. It is the date of the 1918 Revolution, the date of its failure, of a failed revolution—at that time I was also on my way from France to Germany, the date wouldn't let me be: I wrote four novels on that November, 1918, in my last years of exile. What does this date mean to me? Will everything be as bad this time as it was then, shouldn't, mustn't there be a new start this time, a true one?

The bell of "November 9" has tolled, I am venturing into the land that I spent my life in and that I left, left its suffocating air and fled with the feeling: it is for the best. And this is the country I left, and it seems to me as though I am gazing into my past. Germany has suffered what I was able to escape. Now it is clear: a moloch sprung up here, he made his presence known, he straddled this land arrogantly, raging, destructively—and see what he has left behind. They had to beat him to death with clubs.

There are neatly planted fields here, Germany is an orderly country. The people are industrious, they always were. They have cleared the fields and smoothed the paths. The German forest, so often honored in song! The trees are bare, though some still have their autumnal foliage (take a look at this, you Californians, these are the beech and chestnut trees you dreamed of under your wonderful palms by the ocean. How are you doing? There they stand.)

Now I see piles of rubble, holes in the ground, craters created by shells and bombs, the skeletons of houses behind them. Then again (in bright rows) bare fruit trees, staked up. An undamaged sawmill, the houses near it destroyed.

Children stand in the field and wave to the train. The sky is overcast. We pass clusters of crushed and burned cars, their bodies twisted and demolished. In the distance a dark line appears, it is mountains, the Black Forest, we are traveling at a distance along the base of them.

There are neat piles of bluish bulbs, turnips that have been dug up. We are in Achern. There are factories with many chimneys, they

[ *337* ]

are undamaged, but none is smoking. It all makes a sad, lifeless impression. Something happened here once, but now it is over.

There are pretty little houses with red-shingled roofs. The steam of the locomotive gathers in white clumps outside my window and dissolves in tufts. We pass through Ottersweier, a tin sign says KAISER'S COUGH CARAMELS, a sign from peaceful times when one did something for one's cough. Then come bigger houses, the first group of people, a troop of soldiers waving the French tricolor. I read the town signs: STEINBACH, BADEN, SINZHEIM, BADEN-OOS. That station is terribly crowded; many people are changing trains there. Baden-Baden. I have arrived.

I have arrived; but where? I wander with my suitcase through German streets. (Nightmares during exile: I have been spirited away to this place, I see Nazis, they are coming toward me to interrogate me.)

I shiver: someone beside me is speaking German. Someone is speaking German on the street! I don't look at the streets and the people as I did before. There is a cloud over everything that happened, and also over what I carry within me: twelve dismal years of pain. One escape after another. Sometimes I shudder, sometimes I have to look away in my bitterness.

And then I see their pain and see that they have not yet experienced what it is they have experienced. It is intolerable. I want to help.

pg 19. ?
Jun letter.

pg 46 - To christianity ?

Desc of
Kurfurstendamm Shasse
p301

276 -
p278 - a City's Instruction

269. Return

pg. Desc of
Berlin
1947

pg 85 - What
Propaganda did
to the people.